中外文学作品
精读与鉴赏

INTENSIVE READING AND APPRECIATION

主编 单俊 张锦红 张曼
参编 余嘉 王慧

重庆大学出版社

图书在版编目（CIP）数据

中外文学作品精读与鉴赏：英文／单俊，张锦红，张曼主编. --
重庆：重庆大学出版社，2022.1（2024.6重印）
ISBN 978-7-5689-2776-5

Ⅰ.①中… Ⅱ.①单… ②张… ③张… Ⅲ.①英语–语言读物②世界
文学–文学欣赏 Ⅳ.①H319.4：I

中国版本图书馆 CIP 数据核字（2021）第 230481 号

中外文学作品精读与鉴赏
ZHONGWAI WENXUE ZUOPIN JINGDU YU JIANSHANG

主编 单俊 张锦红 张曼
责任编辑:张春花 版式设计:张春花
责任校对:王倩 责任印制:赵晟
*
重庆大学出版社出版发行
出版人:陈晓阳
社址:重庆市沙坪坝区大学城西路21号
邮编:401331
电话:(023) 88617190 88617185(中小学)
传真:(023) 88617186 88617166
网址:http://www.cqup.com.cn
邮箱:fxk@ cqup.com.cn (营销中心)
全国新华书店经销
POD:重庆新生代彩印技术有限公司
*
开本:787 mm×1092 mm 1/16 印张:11.25 字数:367 千
2022 年 1 月第 1 版 2024 年 6 月第 3 次印刷
ISBN 978-7-5689-2776-5 定价:39.00 元

序　言

　　2020年，教育部印发的《高等学校课程思政建设指导纲要》指出，要在所有高校、所有学科专业全面推进课程思政建设，发挥每门课程的思政作用，提升高校人才培养质量。在这一背景下，各地高校都开展了课程思政教学改革，大家充分认识到课程思政是时代育人的要求。在新时代下，高等教育应该发挥好育人功能，培养新时代社会主义建设者和接班人，中国特色社会主义的建设者，培养时代的开拓者和创新者。

　　外语人才以跨语言跨文化思想交流（信息交互）和语言转换（翻译）为基本形式，在中华民族伟大复兴的战略全局和世界百年未有之大变局中起着沟通中国与世界的桥梁作用，不可或缺。外语人才承担着积极推动中华文化走出去，有效开展国际舆论引导，提升我国的国际话语权和影响力的重要使命。面对国际环境的不断变化，外语专业需全力培育新时代下的国际传播专门人才队伍，这个重大的责任和使命要求外语类专业人才坚定"四个自信"，熟悉党和国家方针政策，了解我国国情；具有家国情怀、中华优秀文化素养和社会主义道德修养；具有全球视野，通晓国际规则，熟练运用外语，精通中外谈判和沟通；以对中国共产党领导的社会主义祖国和中国人民浓厚的感情，用敏锐的世界眼光洞悉两个大局，开展跨语言、跨文化的思想交流和语言转换。

　　人才的培养决定着接班人的问题，未来的外语专业人才需要着力提升国际传播的影响力，中华文化的感召力，中国形象的亲和力，中国话语的说服力，国际舆论的引导力。培养立足中国实际、讲好中国故事、传播中国声音的优秀外语人才的目标可以分成四步去实现：第一步，让学生具备扎实的外语功底，过硬的听说读写译的语言基本技能；第二步，让学生了解我国的历史文化、经典文学作品、当代国情、中国共产党的执政理念等，使学生具有中国情怀、中国优秀文化素养，以及基本政治素养；第三步，让学生了解语言对象国的历史、文化、文学、国情；第四步，让学生通过中外对比，换位思考，以客观包容的心态审视中外文学、文化、思想上的差异和共性，熟悉中外在书写模式和表述范式上的不同，从而可以采用对方文化喜闻乐见的形式"讲好中国故事"。

　　本书的编写正是围绕以上四个方面进行的，利用阅读经典名篇、完成挑战性的任务来提升学生的语言基本功；通过赏析鲁迅、沈复等中国作家的经典篇章，引导学生了解中国博大精深的历史、文化、国情；通过赏析欧·亨利、杰克·伦敦等外国作家的经典作品，引导学生了解他国广博丰富的历史、文化、国情；最后通过中外对比，启发学生领会"人类命运共同体"的概念，引导学生思辨性地理解、认识问题，并用外语表达观点。

　　本书力求将思政元素有机融入课程教学中，从个人、文化、国家、国际等角度增加课程的知识性、人文性，提升时代性、创新性。本书按照主题划分章节，每个单元通过设计主题语境将课程的整体思政目标进行拆分和细化，单元主题如"人与家庭""人与自然"

"人与国家"等,从个人、家庭、国家多个角度由小及大地将公民义务与责任、社会发展与环境、国家意识等诸多内容融入外语课程,使知识传授与思政教育系统性地结合。例如,书中收入了方志敏的《清贫》、沈复的《浮生六记》等语篇,旨在通过对这些语篇的赏析来引导学生加强对党史、中国传统文化等方面知识的学习和理解。书中同时强调对中外文学作品的对比学习,并结合热点话题,设置有挑战度的产出任务,引导学生进入"自觉的文化批判和价值重构",使其文化自信上升到"文明互鉴"的高度。

本书注重价值引领,紧紧围绕一条主线和五个重点选择篇章,即坚定学生的理想和信念这条主线,以及习近平新时代中国特色社会主义思想、社会主义核心价值观、中华优秀传统文化、宪法法治、职业理想和职业道德五个重点。本书同时也注重语言能力的提高和知识素养的提升,外国篇章都为名家作品,中国作品选用的是名家翻译版本,能很好地提升学生的阅读水平、艺术鉴赏力,并引导学生积累有用的文学、文化知识,同时在教学过程中重视学生运用语言的能力,通过设计一些开放性、复杂性和真实性的任务,引导学生阐述不同观点,促进学生进行意义协商、知识构建和身份形成。单元的产出任务将价值观塑造、知识传授和能力培养融为一体,如话题作文:"人与自然和谐共生,建设美丽中国",TED 演讲:中华民族的"根"与"魂"等。

外语专业的课程思政建设在国家、社会、个人等层面都有着重要的意义。外语课程思政是教育理念和教育方法的结合,一方面要倡导立德树人的教育理念,另一方面要结合时代需求改革教学内容、教学方法和手段等,以润物细无声的方式达到教书育人的目的。

本书编写中,单俊负责选篇 2、10、12、13、14 的撰写工作;张锦红负责选篇 3、4、5、7、9 的撰写工作;张曼负责选篇 1、6、8、11、15 的撰写工作。本书的出版是在课程改革方面所做的探索和尝试,书中难免有不当和疏漏之处,敬请广大使用者批评指正。

单俊
2021 年冬于成都

Contents

The New Year's Sacrifice

Chapter One   Women's Fate

One is not born, but, rather becomes a woman.

Simone de Beauvoir
The Second Sex

女人不是天生的,而是逐渐形成的。

——(法)西蒙娜·德·波伏娃《第二性》

1

The New Year's Sacrifice

Lu Xun

【作品简介】

《祝福》（*The New Year's Sacrifice*）是中国著名文学家鲁迅创作的短篇小说,讲述了"我"四叔鲁四老爷家的女仆祥林嫂的故事。小说的标题"祝福"指的是我国某些地区在除夕时祭祀天地、祈求赐福的一种旧俗。祥林嫂原本是个童养媳,在丈夫死后,她被婆婆卖到山里给贺老六当老婆。不幸的是,贺老六感染风寒死去,她唯一的儿子阿毛也被狼叼走,祥林嫂只得重新回到四叔家做工。然而,鲁四老爷认为其败坏了风俗,在年末新年祝福时,不让她沾手祭祀相关的东西。受到丧夫和丧子双重打击的祥林嫂越发精神萎靡,做事心不在焉,因而被赶了出去,成了乞丐。最终,在家家户户准备年终大典"祝福"时,她死在了漫天飞舞的大雪之中。本文选自外文出版社于1960年出版的杨宪益和戴乃迭翻译的《鲁迅小说选》,注释中出现的中文原文出自人民文学出版社于2015年出版的《鲁迅小说全集:丁聪插图本》。

【作者简介】

鲁迅(1881—1936),原名周树人,浙江绍兴人,中国著名文学家、翻译家、思想家和革命家。他是中国现代文学的奠基人之一,也是新文化运动的主将,被毛泽东称为"中国文化革命的主将""文化战线上的民族英雄"。"鲁迅"是他在1918年发表《狂人日记》时所用的笔名,也是他影响最为广泛的笔名。他所开创的杂文文体富有批判性和战斗性,是后世作家最常使用的"批判武器"。其代表作品有小说集《呐喊》《彷徨》和《野草》,散文集《朝花夕拾》,杂文集《而已集》《华盖集》《二心集》《南腔北调集》等。此外,鲁迅还翻译了大量外国作品,译作代表有《死魂灵》《毁灭》等。

【译者简介】

杨宪益(1915—2009),中国著名翻译家,出生于中国天津。

戴乃迭(Gladys Yang,1919—1999),国际上享有崇高声誉的翻译家,生于北京一个英国传教士家庭。

杨宪益和夫人戴乃迭于1937年相识于牛津大学,1940年在重庆举办婚礼。夫妻二人被誉为翻译界的"神雕侠侣",曾携手将大量中国文学作品翻译成英文,代表译作有《红楼梦》《儒林外史》《诗经》《楚辞》《史记》《鲁迅选集》等。

（1）New Year's Eve of <u>the old calendar</u>[1] seems after all more like the real New Year's Eve; for, to say nothing of the villages and towns, even in the air there is a feeling that New Year is coming. From the pale, lowering evening clouds <u>issue</u>[2] frequent flashes of lightning, followed by a <u>rumbling</u>[3] sound of firecrackers celebrating the departure of the <u>Hearth God</u>[4]; while, nearer by, the firecrackers explode even more violently, and before the <u>deafening</u>[5] report dies away the air is filled with a faint smell of powder. <u>It was on such a night that I returned to Luchen, my native place.</u>[6] Although I call it my native place, I had had no home there for some time, so I had to <u>put up</u>[7] temporarily with a certain Mr. Lu, the fourth son of his family. He is a member of our <u>clan</u>[8], and belongs to the generation before mine, so I ought to call him "Fourth Uncle." <u>An old student of the imperial college</u>[9] who went in for <u>Neo-Confucianism</u>[10], I found him very little changed in any way, simply slightly older, but without any moustache as yet. When we met, after exchanging a few polite remarks he said I was fatter, and after saying that immediately started a violent attack on the revolutionaries. I knew this was not meant personally, because the object of the attack was still <u>Kang Yu-wei</u>[11]. Nevertheless, conversation proved difficult, so that in a short time I found myself alone in the study.

（2）The next day I got up very late, and after lunch went out to see some relatives and friends. The day after I did the same. None of them was greatly changed, simply slightly older; but every family was busy preparing for "the sacrifice." This is the great end-of-year ceremony in Luchen, when people <u>reverently</u>[12] welcome <u>the God of Fortune</u>[13] and <u>solicit</u>[14] good fortune for the coming year. They kill chickens and geese and buy pork, <u>scouring</u>[15] and <u>scrubbing</u>[16] until all the women's arms turn red in the water. Some of them still wear twisted silver <u>bracelets</u>[17]. After the meat is cooked some chopsticks are thrust into it at random, and this is called the "<u>offering</u>[18]." It is set out at dawn when <u>incense</u>[19] and candles are lit, and they

---

[1] the old calendar: 旧历，即"农历"，中国传统历法。

[2] issue /ˈɪʃuː/ v. 发出

[3] rumble /ˈrʌmbl/ v. 发出隆隆声

[4] Hearth God: 灶神，俗称灶王爷。

[5] deafening /ˈdefnɪŋ/ adj. 震耳欲聋的

[6] 强调句型，将时间状语"on such a night"提前，强调我是在这样一个夜晚回到故乡鲁镇的。

[7] put up: 留宿

[8] clan /klæn/ n. 氏族；家族

[9] an old student of the imperial college: 一个老监生。监生，明清两代取得入国子监（中国古代最高学府和教育管理机构）读书资格的人。

[10] Neo-Confucianism: 理学；新儒家思想

[11] Kang Yu-wei: 康有为，中国晚清时期重要的政治家，资产阶级改良派的代表人物。

[12] reverent /ˈrevərənt/ adj. 非常尊敬的

[13] the God of Fortune: 财神

[14] solicit /səˈlɪsɪt/ v. 索求；请求给予

[15] scour /ˈskaʊə(r)/ v.（用粗糙的物体）擦净；擦亮

[16] scrub /skrʌb/ v. 擦洗；刷洗

[17] bracelet /ˈbreɪslət/ n. 手镯

[18] offering /ˈɒfərɪŋ/ n. 祭品；供品

[19] incense /ˈɪnsens/ n.（常用于宗教

reverently invite the God of Fortune to come and partake[20] of the offering. Only men can be worshippers, and after the sacrifice they naturally continue to let off firecrackers as before. This happens every year, in every family, provided they can afford to buy the offering and firecrackers; and this year they naturally followed the old custom.

（3）The day grew overcast[21]. In the afternoon it actually started to snow, the biggest snow-flakes as large as plum blossom petals fluttered about the sky[22]; and this, combined with the smoke and air of activity, made Luchen appear in a ferment[23]. When I returned to my uncle's study the roof of the house was already white with snow. The room also appeared brighter, the great red rubbing[24] hanging on the wall showing up very clearly the character for Longevity[25] written by the Taoist saint Chen Tuan[26]. One of a pair of scrolls[27] had fallen down and was lying loosely rolled up on the long table, but the other was still hanging there, bearing the words: "By understanding reason we achieve tranquillity of mind."[28] Idly, I went to turn over the books on the table beneath the window, but all I could find was a pile of what looked like an incomplete set of *Kang Hsi's Dictionary*[29], a volume of Chiang Yung's *Notes to Chu Hsi's Philosophical Writings*[30] and a volume of *Commentaries on the Four Books*[31]. At all events, I made up my mind to leave the next day.

（4）Besides, the very thought of my meeting with Hsiang Lin's Wife the day before made me uncomfortable. It happened in the afternoon. I had been visiting a friend in the eastern part of the town. As I came out I met her by the river, and seeing the way she fastened[32] her eyes on me I knew very well she meant to speak to me. Of all the people I had seen this time at Luchen none had changed as much as she: her hair, which had been streaked[33] with white five years before, was now completely white, quite unlike someone in her forties. Her face was fearfully thin and dark in its sallowness[34],

仪式的）香

[20] partake /pɑːˈteɪk/ v. 吃；喝；享用

[21] overcast /ˌəʊvəˈkɑːst/ adj. 多云的；阴暗的

[22] 明喻（simile）。梅花大的雪花漫天飞舞。（flutter /ˈflʌtə(r)/ v. 飘动）

[23] ferment /ˈfɜː(r)ment/ n. 动乱；骚动

[24] rubbing /ˈrʌbɪŋ/ n. 拓本

[25] longevity /lɒnˈdʒevəti/ n. 长寿；长命（这里指挂在墙上的"寿"字）

[26] 陈抟老祖，一位宋代的道学家。

[27] scroll /skrəʊl/ n. 长卷纸；对联

[28] 此句原文为"事理通达心平气和"。

[29] *Kang Hsi's Dictionary*:《康熙字典》，清朝三十多位著名学者奉康熙圣旨编撰的一部具有深远影响的汉字辞书。

[30] *Notes to Chu Hsi's Philosophical Writings*:《近思录集注》，由清朝江永所著。

[31] *Commentaries on the Four Books*:《四书衬》，清朝吴兴骆、培坦轩解说"四书"的一本书（南宋朱熹将《礼记》中的《大学》《中庸》《论语》和《孟子》合在一起进行注解，称之为"四书"）。

[32] fasten /ˈfɑːsn/ v. 使固定

[33] streak /striːk/ v. 使布满条纹或条痕

[34] sallow /ˈsæləʊ/ adj. 灰黄色的

and had moreover lost its former expression of sadness, looking as if carved[35] out of wood. Only an occasional flicker[36] of her eyes showed she was still a living creature. In one hand she carried a wicker[37] basket, in which was a broken bowl, empty; in the other she held a bamboo pole longer than herself, split at the bottom：it was clear she had become a beggar.

（5）I stood still, waiting for her to come and ask for money.

（6）"You have come back?" she asked me first.

（7）"Yes."

（8）"That is very good. You are a scholar, and have travelled too and seen a lot. I just want to ask you something." Her lustreless[38] eyes suddenly gleamed[39].

（9）I never guessed she would talk to me like this. I stood there taken by surprise.

（10）"It is this." She drew two paces nearer, and whispered very confidentially[40]："After a person dies, does he turn into a ghost or not?"

（11）As she fixed her eyes on me I was seized with foreboding[41]. A shiver[42] ran down my spine and I felt more nervous than during an unexpected examination at school, when unfortunately the teacher stands by one's side. Personally, I had never given the least thought to the question of the existence of spirits. In this emergency how should I answer her? Hesitating for a moment, I reflected[43]："It is the tradition here to believe in spirits, yet she seems to be sceptical[44]—perhaps it would be better to say she hopes：hopes that there is immortality[45] and yet hopes that there is not. Why increase the sufferings of the wretched? To give her something to look forward to, it would be better to say there is."

（12）"There may be, I think," I told her hesitantly[46].

（13）"Then, there must also be a Hell?"

（14）"What, Hell?" Greatly startled[47], I could only try to evade[48] the question. "Hell? According to reason there should be one too—but not necessarily. Who cares about it anyway? …"

[35] carve /kɑː(r)v/ v. 雕刻；刻

[36] flicker /ˈflɪkə(r)/ n. 闪烁；闪现

[37] wicker /ˈwɪkə(r)/ n. (编制筐篮、家具等用的)柳条；枝条

[38] lustreless /ˈlʌstə(r)ləs/ adj. 无光泽的

[39] gleam /gliːm/ v. 隐约闪光；闪烁

[40] confidentially /ˌkɒnfɪˈdenʃəli/ adv. 私下地；悄悄地

[41] foreboding /fɔːˈbəʊdɪŋ/ n. (对不祥或危险事情的)强烈预感

[42] shiver /ˈʃɪvə(r)/ n. (因寒冷、恐惧等)颤抖；哆嗦

[43] reflect /rɪˈflekt/ v. 沉思；深思

[44] sceptical /ˈskeptɪkl/ adj. 怀疑的

[45] immortality /ˌɪmɔːˈtæləti/ n. 永生；不朽

[46] hesitantly /ˈhezɪtəntli/ adv. 迟疑地；踌躇地

[47] startle /ˈstɑːtl/ v. 使惊吓

[48] evade /ɪˈveɪd/ v. 躲避；逃避

（15）"Then will all the people of one family who have died see each other again?"

（16）"Well, as to whether they will see each other again or not. ..." I realized now that I was a complete fool; for all my hesitation and reflection I had been unable to answer her three questions. Immediately I lost confidence and wanted to say the exact opposite of what I had previously said. "In this case ... as a matter of fact, I am not sure. ... Actually, regarding the question of ghosts, I am not sure either."

（17）In order to avoid further importunate[49] questions, I walked off, and beat a hasty[50] retreat[51] to my uncle's house, feeling exceedingly[52] uncomfortable. I thought to myself: "I am afraid my answer will prove dangerous to her. Probably it is just that when other people are celebrating she feels lonely by herself, but could there be another reason? Could she have had some premonition[53]? If there is another reason, and as a result something happens, then, through my answer, I shall be held responsible to a certain extent." Finally, however, I ended by laughing at myself, thinking that such a chance meeting could have no great significance, and yet I was taking it so to heart; no wonder certain educationalists called me a neurotic[54]. Moreover I had distinctly[55] said, "I am not sure," contradicting[56] my previous answer; so that even if anything did happen, it would have nothing at all to do with me.

（18）"I am not sure" is a most useful phrase.

（19）Inexperienced and rash[57] young men often take it upon themselves to solve people's problems for them or choose doctors for them, and if by any chance things turn out badly, they are probably held to blame; but by simply concluding with this phrase "I am not sure," one can free oneself of all responsibility. At this time I felt even more strongly the necessity for such a phrase, since even in speaking with a beggar woman there was no dispensing with it[58].

（20）However, I continued to feel uncomfortable,

[49] importunate /ɪmˈpɔːtʃənət/ adj. 再三要求的；纠缠不休的

[50] hasty /ˈheɪsti/ adj. 匆忙的；草率的

[51] retreat /rɪˈtriːt/ n. 逃避；躲避

[52] exceedingly /ɪkˈsiːdɪŋli/ adv. 极其；非常

[53] premonition /ˌpreməˈnɪʃn/ n.（尤指不祥的）预感

[54] neurotic /njʊəˈrɒtɪk/ n. 神经过敏者

[55] distinctly /dɪsˈtɪŋktli/ adv. 无疑地；确实地

[56] contradict /ˌkɒntrəˈdɪkt/ v. 反驳

[57] rash /ræʃ/ adj. 轻率的；鲁莽的

[58] 即使和讨饭的女人说话，也是万不可省的(摘自中文原文，后均简称原文)。(dispense with sth.：摒弃；省却；不用)

and even after a night's rest my mind kept running on this, as if I had a premonition of some untoward[59] development. In that oppressive[60] snowy weather, in the gloomy study, this discomfort increased. It would be better to leave: I should go back to town the next day. The boiled shark's fins[61] in the Fu Hsing Restaurant used to cost a dollar for a large portion, and I wondered if this cheap and delicious dish had increased in price or not. Although the friends who had accompanied me in the old days had scattered, even if I was alone the shark's fins still had to be tasted. At all events[62], I made up my mind to leave the next day.

(21) After experiencing many times that things which I hoped would not happen and felt should not happen invariably did happen, I was desperately afraid this would prove another such case.[63] And, indeed, strange things did begin to happen. Towards evening I heard talking—it sounded like a discussion—in the inner room; but soon the conversation ended, and all I heard was my uncle saying loudly as he walked out: "Not earlier nor later, but just at this time—sure sign of a bad character!"

(22) At first I felt astonished, then very uncomfortable, thinking these words must refer to me. I looked outside the door, but no one was there. I contained[64] myself with difficulty till their servant came in before dinner to brew[65] a pot of tea, when at last I had a chance to make some enquiries[66].

(23) "With whom was Mr. Lu angry just now?" I asked.

(24) "Why, still with Hsiang Lin's Wife," he replied briefly.

(25) "Hsiang Lin's Wife? How was that?" I asked again.

(26) "She's dead."

(27) "Dead?" My heart suddenly missed a beat.[67] I started, and probably changed colour too. But since he did not raise his head, he was probably quite unaware of

[59] untoward /ˌʌntəˈwɔːd/ adj. 异常的；意外的

[60] oppressive /əˈpresɪv/ adj. 让人感到压抑的；使人苦恼的

[61] shark's fins: 鱼翅

[62] at all events: 无论如何

[63] 我因为常见些但愿不如所料，以为未必竟如所料的事，却每每恰如所料的起来，所以很恐怕这事也一律（原文）。(invariably /ɪnˈveəriəbli/ adv. 总是)

[64] contain /kənˈteɪn/ v. 控制；抑制

[65] brew /bruː/ v. 冲泡；沏

[66] enquiry /ɪnˈkwaɪəri/ n. 询问；打听

[67] beat /biːt/ n. (心脏等的)跳动

how I felt. Then I controlled myself, and asked:

（28）"When did she die?"

（29）"When? Last night, or else today, I'm not sure."

（30）"How did she die?"

（31）"How did she die? Why, of poverty of course." He answered placidly[68] and, still without having raised his head to look at me, went out.

（32）However, my agitation[69] was only short-lived, for now that something I had felt imminent[70] had already taken place, I no longer had to take refuge in[71] my "I'm not sure," or the servant's expression "dying of poverty" for comfort. My heart already felt lighter. Only from time to time something still seemed to weigh on[72] it. Dinner was served, and my uncle solemnly[73] accompanied me. I wanted to ask about Hsiang Lin's Wife, but knew that although he had read, "Ghosts and spirits are properties of Nature[74]," he had retained[75] many superstitions, and on the eve of this sacrifice it was out of the question to mention anything like death or illness. In case of necessity one could use veiled allusions[76], but unfortunately I did not know how to, so although questions kept rising to the tip of my tongue, I had to bite them back. From his solemn expression I suddenly suspected that he looked on me as choosing not earlier nor later but just this time to come and trouble him, and that I was also a bad character; therefore to set his mind at rest I told him at once that I intended to leave Luchen the next day and go back to the city. He did not press me greatly to stay. So we quietly finished the meal.

（33）In winter the days are short and, now that it was snowing, darkness already enveloped[77] the whole town. Everybody was busy beneath the lamplight, but outside the windows it was very quiet. Snow-flakes fell on the thickly piled snow, as if they were whispering[78], making me feel even more lonely. I sat by myself under the yellow gleam of the vegetable oil lamp and thought, "This poor woman, abandoned by people in the dust as a

68 placidly /ˈplæsɪdli/ adv. 平静地

69 agitation /ˌædʒɪˈteɪʃn/ n. 焦虑不安
70 imminent /ˈɪmɪnənt/ adj. 即将发生的
71 take refuge in: 求助于；用……搪塞过去
72 weigh on: （使）某人焦虑
73 solemnly /ˈsɒləmli/ adv. 一本正经地；沉着脸

74 Ghosts and spirits are properties of Nature: 鬼神者二气之良能也（原文），意即：人们所谓的鬼神其实是阴阳二气自然变化而成的。鲁迅在这里其实是对鬼神论作了一种无神论的解释。
75 retain /rɪˈteɪn/ v. 保持；保留
76 allusion /əˈluːʒn/ n. 间接提到；暗指

77 envelop /ɪnˈveləp/ v. 裹住；盖住

78 拟人（personification）。雪花纷纷落下，发出簌簌声，仿佛是在窃窃私语。

tiresome[79] and worn-out toy, once left her own imprint[80] in the dust, and those who enjoy life must have wondered[81] at her for wishing to prolong[82] her existence; but now at least she has been swept clear by eternity. Whether spirits exist or not I do not know; but in the present world when a meaningless existence ends, so that someone whom others are tired of seeing is no longer seen, it is just as well, both for the individual concerned and for others.[83]" I listened quietly to see if I could hear the snow falling outside the window, still pursuing this train of thought[84], until gradually I felt less ill at ease[85].

(34) Fragments of her life, seen or heard before, now combined to form one whole.

(35) She did not belong to Luchen. One year at the beginning of winter, when my uncle's family wanted to change their maidservant, Old Mrs. Wei brought her in and introduced her. Her hair was tied with white bands, she wore a black skirt, blue jacket and pale green bodice[86], and was about twenty-six, with a pale skin but rosy cheeks. Old Mrs. Wei called her Hsiang Lin's Wife, and said that she was a neighbour of her mother's family, and because her husband was dead she wanted to go out to work. My uncle knitted[87] his brows and my aunt immediately understood that he disapproved of her because she was a widow. She looked very suitable, though, with big strong feet and hands, and a meek[88] expression; and she had said nothing but showed every sign of being tractable[89] and hard-working. So my aunt paid no attention to my uncle's frown, but kept her. During the period of probation[90] she worked from morning till night, as if she found resting dull, and she was so strong that she could do a man's work; accordingly[91] on the third day it was settled, and each month she was to be paid five hundred cash.

(36) Everybody called her Hsiang Lin's Wife. They did not ask her her own name; but since she was introduced by someone from Wei Village who said she was a neighbour, presumably[92] her name was also Wei. She

[79] tiresome /ˈtaɪəsəm/ adj. 令人厌烦的

[80] imprint /ˈɪmprɪnt/ n. 印记；痕迹

[81] wonder /ˈwʌndə(r)/ v. 感到诧异

[82] prolong /prəˈlɒŋ/ v. 延长

[83] 魂灵的有无，我不知道；然而在现世，则无聊生者不生，即使厌见者不见，为人为己，也还都不错（原文）。

[84] train of thought：思绪；思路

[85] ill at ease：不自在；心神不宁

[86] bodice /ˈbɒdɪs/ n. 女紧身马甲

[87] knit /nɪt/ v. 皱（眉）

[88] meek /miːk/ adj. 温顺的；顺从的

[89] tractable /ˈtræktəbl/ adj. 温顺的

[90] probation /prəˈbeɪʃn/ n. 试用期；考察期

[91] accordingly /əˈkɔːdɪŋli/ adv. 因此；所以

[92] presumably /prɪˈzjuːməbli/ adv. 大

was not very talkative, only answering when other people spoke to her, and her answers were brief. It was not until a dozen days or so had passed that they learned little by little that she still had a severe mother-in-law at home and a younger brother-in-law more than ten years old, who could cut wood. [93] Her husband, who had been a woodcutter too, had died in the spring. He had been ten years younger than she. [94] This little was all that people learned from her.

（37）The days passed quickly. She worked as hard as ever; she would eat anything, and did not spare herself [95]. Everybody agreed that the Lu family had found a very good maidservant, who really got through more work than a hard-working man. At the end of the year she swept, mopped, killed chickens and geese and sat up to boil the sacrificial meat, single-handed [96], so the family did not have to hire extra help. Nevertheless she, on her side, was satisfied; gradually the trace [97] of a smile appeared at the corner of her mouth. She became plumper [98] and her skin whiter.

（38）New Year was scarcely over when she came back from washing rice by the river looking pale, and said that in the distance she had just seen a man wandering [99] on the opposite bank who looked very like her husband's cousin, and probably he had come to look for her. My aunt, much alarmed, made detailed enquiries, but failed to get any further information. As soon as my uncle learned of it he frowned and said, "This is bad. She must have run away from her husband's family."

（39）Before long this inference [100] that she had run away was confirmed [101].

（40）About a fortnight [102] later, just as everybody was beginning to forget what had happened, Old Mrs. Wei suddenly called, bringing with her a woman in her thirties who, she said, was the maidservant's mother-in-law. Although the woman looked like a villager, she behaved with great self-possession [103] and had a ready tongue [104] in her head. After the usual polite remarks she

概；想必是

[93] 强调句型，It was not until… that…。直到十几天之后，大家才陆续得知她家里还有个严厉的婆婆和一个小叔子，小叔子十多岁，能打柴了。

[94] 丈夫比她小十岁，可见祥林嫂是个童养媳。

[95] spare oneself：怕吃苦，偷懒

[96] single-handed /ˌsɪŋglˈhændɪd/ adv. 独自；单枪匹马地

[97] trace /treɪs/ n. 痕迹；踪迹

[98] plumper /ˈplʌmpə/ adj. 丰腴的；微胖的

[99] wander /ˈwɒndə(r)/ v. 游荡；闲逛

[100] inference /ˈɪnfərəns/ n. 推理；推论

[101] confirm /kənˈfɜːm/ v. 证实；证明

[102] fortnight /ˈfɔːtnaɪt/ n. 两星期

[103] self-possession /ˌself pəˈzeʃn/ n. 沉着；镇静

[104] have a ready tongue：伶牙俐齿；巧

apologized for coming to take her daughter-in-law home, saying there was a great deal to be done at the beginning of spring, and since there were only old people and children at home they were short-handed.

（41）"Since it is her mother-in-law who wants her to go back, what is there to be said?" was my uncle's comment.

（42）Thereupon[105] her wages were reckoned up[106]. They amounted to[107] one thousand seven hundred and fifty cash, all of which she had left with her mistress without using a single coin. My aunt gave the entire amount to her mother-in-law. The latter also took her clothes, thanked Mr. and Mrs. Lu and went out. By this time it was already noon.

（43）"Oh, the rice! Didn't Hsiang Lin's Wife go to wash the rice?" my aunt exclaimed[108] some time later. Probably she was rather hungry, so that she remembered lunch.

（44）Thereupon everybody set about[109] looking for the rice basket. My aunt went first to the kitchen, then to the hall, then to the bedroom; but not a trace of it was to be seen anywhere. My uncle went outside, but could not find it either; only when he went right down to the riverside did he see it, set down fair and square[110] on the bank, with a bundle[111] of vegetables beside it.

（45）Some people there told him that a boat with a white awning[112] had moored[113] there in the morning, but since the awning covered the boat completely they did not know who was inside, and before this incident no one had paid any attention to it. But when Hsiang Lin's Wife came to wash rice, two men looking like country people jumped off the boat just as she was kneeling down and seizing hold of her carried her on board. After several shouts and cries, Hsiang Lin's Wife became silent: they had probably stopped her mouth. Then two women walked up, one of them a stranger and the other Old Mrs. Wei. When the people who told this story tried to peep[114] into the boat they could not see very clearly, but

舌如簧

105 thereupon /ˌðeərəˈpɒn/ adv. 立即；随即

106 reckon up：计算；合计

107 amount to：等同；接近；总计

108 exclaim /ɪkˈskleɪm/ v. 惊叫；呼喊

109 set about：开始；着手

110 fair and square：公正地；正中目标

111 bundle /ˈbʌndl/ n. （一）捆，包

112 awning /ˈɔːnɪŋ/ n. 遮阳篷，雨篷

113 moor /mɔː(r)/ v. 停泊

114 peep /piːp/ v. 窥视；偷看

Hsiang Lin's Wife seemed to be lying bound on the floor of the boat.

（46）"Disgraceful[115]! Still …" said my uncle.

（47）That day my aunt cooked the midday meal herself, and my cousin Ah Niu lit the fire.

（48）After lunch Old Mrs. Wei came again.

（49）"Disgraceful!" said my uncle.

（50）"What is the meaning of this? How dare you come here again!" My aunt, who was washing dishes, started scolding[116] as soon as she saw her. "You recommended[117] her yourself, and then plotted to have her carried off, causing all this stir. What will people think? Are you trying to make a laughing-stock[118] of our family?"

（51）"Aiya, I was really taken in[119]! Now I have come specially to clear up[120] this business. When she asked me to find her work, how was I to know that she had left home without her mother-in-law's consent? I am very sorry, Mr. Lu, Mrs. Lu. Because I am so old and foolish and careless, I have offended my patrons[121]. However, it is lucky for me that your family is always so generous and kind, and unwilling to be hard on your inferiors[122]. This time I promise to find you someone good to make up for my mistake."

（52）"Still …" said my uncle.

（53）Thereupon the business of Hsiang Lin's Wife was concluded, and before long it was also forgotten.

（54）Only my aunt, because the maidservants taken on afterwards were all lazy or fond of stealing food, or else both lazy and fond of stealing food, with not a good one in the lot[123], still often spoke of Hsiang Lin's Wife. On such occasions she would always say to herself, "I wonder what has become of her now?" meaning that she would like to have her back. But by the following New Year she too gave up hope.

（55）The New Year's holiday was nearly over when Old Mrs. Wei, already half tipsy[124], came to pay her respects[125], and said it was because she had been back to Wei Village to visit her mother's family and stayed a few

[115] disgraceful /dɪsˈɡreɪsfl/ adj. 可耻的

[116] scold /skəʊld/ v. 训斥；责骂

[117] recommend /ˌrekəˈmend/ v. 推荐；举荐

[118] laughing-stock /ˈlɑːfɪŋ stɒk/ n. 笑柄

[119] take in: 欺骗；使上当

[120] clear up: 消除（误会）

[121] patron /ˈpeɪtrən/ n. 老主顾；顾客

[122] inferior /ɪnˈfɪəriə(r)/ n. 不如别人的人；级别（或地位）低的人

[123] lot /lɒt/ n. （一）组，群

[124] tipsy /ˈtɪpsi/ adj. 微醉的

[125] pay her respects: 拜年

days that she had come late. During the course of conversation they naturally came to speak of Hsiang Lin's Wife.

(56) "She?" said Mrs. Wei cheerfully. "She is in luck now. When her mother-in-law dragged her home, she had already promised her to the sixth son of the Ho family in Ho Village. Not long after she reached home they put her in the bridal chair[126] and sent her off."

(57) "Aiya! What a mother-in-law!" exclaimed my aunt in amazement.

(58) "Ah, madam, you really talk like a great lady! We country folk, poor women, think nothing of that. She still had a younger brother-in-law who had to be married. And if they hadn't found her a husband, where would they have found the money for his wedding? But her mother-in-law is a clever and capable woman, who knows how to drive a good bargain[127], so she married her off into the mountains. If she had married her to someone in the same village, she wouldn't have got so much money; but since very few women are willing to marry someone living deep in the mountains, she got eighty thousand cash. Now the second son is married, the presents only cost her fifty thousand, and after paying the wedding expenses she still has over ten thousand left. Just think, doesn't this show she knows how to drive a good bargain? ..."

(59) "But was Hsiang Lin's Wife willing?"

(60) "It wasn't a question of being willing or not. Of course anyone would have protested. They just tied her up with a rope, stuffed her into the bridal chair, carried her to the man's house, put on the bridal headdress[128], performed the ceremony in the hall and locked them in their room; and that was that. But Hsiang Lin's Wife is quite a character[129]. I heard she really put up[130] a great struggle, and everybody said she was different from other people because she had worked in a scholar's family. We go-betweens[131], madam, see a great deal. When widows remarry, some cry and shout, some

126 bridal chair: 花轿

127 drive a good bargain: 做成一笔好生意

128 headdress /ˈheddres/ n. 头巾；头饰

129 quite a character: 很有个性；出格

130 put up: 进行(抵抗)

131 go-between /ˈgəu bɪtwiːn/ n. 中间人；媒人

threaten to commit suicide[132], some when they have been carried to the men's house won't go through the ceremony, and some even smash[133] the wedding candlesticks[134]. But Hsiang Lin's Wife was different from the rest. They said she shouted and cursed all the way, so that by the time they had carried her to Ho Village she was completely hoarse[135]. When they dragged her out of the chair, although the two chairbearers[136] and her young brother-in-law used all their strength, they couldn't force her to go through the ceremony. The moment they were careless enough to loosen their grip[137]—gracious Buddha[138]!—she threw herself against a corner of the table and knocked a big hole in her head. The blood poured out; and although they used two handfuls of incense ashes and bandaged[139] her with two pieces of red cloth, they still couldn't stop the bleeding. Finally it took all of them together to get her shut up with her husband in the bridal chamber[140], where she went on cursing. Oh, it was really dreadful!" She shook her head, cast down her eyes and said no more.

(61) "And after that what happened?" asked my aunt.

(62) "They said the next day she still didn't get up," said Old Mrs. Wei, raising her eyes.

(63) "And after?"

(64) "After? She got up. At the end of the year she had a baby, a boy, who was two this New Year. These few days when I was at home some people went to Ho Village, and when they came back they said they had seen her and her son, and that both mother and baby are fat. There is no mother-in-law over her, the man is a strong fellow who can earn a living, and the house is their own. Well, well, she is really in luck."

(65) After this even my aunt gave up talking of Hsiang Lin's Wife.

(66) But one autumn, two New Years after they heard how lucky Hsiang Lin's Wife had been, she actually reappeared on the threshold[141] of my uncle's

[132] commit suicide：自杀

[133] smash /smæʃ/ v. （哗啦一声）打碎，打破

[134] candlestick /ˈkændlstɪk/ n. 蜡烛台

[135] hoarse /hɔː(r)s/ adj. （嗓音）嘶哑的

[136] chairbearer：指轿夫

[137] grip /grɪp/ n. 紧握；紧抓

[138] gracious Buddha：阿弥陀佛

[139] bandage /ˈbændɪdʒ/ v. 用绷带包扎

[140] the bridal chamber：新娘的房间；新房；洞房

[141] threshold /ˈθreʃhəʊld/ n. 门槛；门口

house. On the table she placed a round <u>bulb-shaped</u>¹⁴² basket, and under the <u>eaves</u>¹⁴³ a small roll of bedding. Her hair was still wrapped in white bands, and she wore a black skirt, blue jacket and pale green bodice. But her skin was sallow and her cheeks had lost their colour; she kept her eyes <u>downcast</u>¹⁴⁴, and her eyes, with their <u>tear-stained</u>¹⁴⁵ <u>rims</u>¹⁴⁶, were no longer bright. Just as before, it was Old Mrs. Wei, looking very benevolent, who brought her in, and who explained at length to my aunt.

(67) "It was really <u>a bolt from the blue</u>¹⁴⁷. Her husband was so strong, nobody could have guessed that a young fellow like that would die of <u>typhoid</u>¹⁴⁸ fever. First he seemed better, but then he ate a bowl of cold rice and the sickness came back. Luckily she had the boy, and she can work, whether it is <u>chopping wood</u>¹⁴⁹, picking tea-leaves or raising <u>silkworms</u>¹⁵⁰; so at first she was able to carry on. Then who could believe that the child, too, would be carried off by a wolf? Although it was nearly the end of spring, still wolves came to the village — how could anyone have guessed that? Now she is all on her own. Her brother-in-law came to take the house, and <u>turned her out</u>¹⁵¹; so she has really no way open to her but to come and ask help from her former mistress. Luckily this time there is nobody to stop her, and you happen to be wanting a new servant, so I have brought her here. I think someone who is used to your ways is much better than a new hand. ...."

(68) "I was really stupid, really ..." Hsiang Lin's Wife raised her listless eyes to say. "I only knew that when it snows the wild beasts in the <u>glen</u>¹⁵² have nothing to eat and may come to the villages; I didn't know that in spring they came too. I got up at dawn and opened the door, filled a small basket with beans and called our Ah Mao to go and sit on the threshold and <u>shell</u>¹⁵³ the beans. He was very <u>obedient</u>¹⁵⁴ and always did as I told him: he went out. Then I chopped wood at the back of the house and washed the rice, and when the rice was in the pan and I wanted to boil the beans I called Ah Mao, but there

¹⁴² bulb-shaped: 球状的
¹⁴³ eaves /iːvz/ n. (plural) 屋檐
¹⁴⁴ downcast /ˈdaʊnkɑːst/ adj. 低垂的
¹⁴⁵ tear-stained /ˈtɪə steɪnd/ adj. 布满泪痕的
¹⁴⁶ rim /rɪm/ n. 边沿；边缘
¹⁴⁷ a bolt from the blue: 晴天霹雳
¹⁴⁸ typhoid /ˈtaɪfɔɪd/ n. 伤寒
¹⁴⁹ chop wood: 砍柴
¹⁵⁰ silkworm /ˈsɪlkwɜː(r)m/ n. 蚕
¹⁵¹ turn out: 撵走；赶出
¹⁵² glen /glen/ n. 峡谷；山坳
¹⁵³ shell /ʃel/ v. 给……去壳
¹⁵⁴ obedient /əˈbiːdiənt/ adj. 顺从的

was no answer; and when I went out to look, all I could see was beans scattered on the ground, but no Ah Mao. He never went to other families to play; and in fact at each place where I went to ask, there was no sign of him. I became desperate, and begged people to go to look for him. Only in the afternoon, after looking everywhere else, did they go to look in the glen and see one of his little shoes caught on a bramble[155]. 'That's bad,' they said, 'he must have met a wolf.' And sure enough when they went further in there he was, lying in the wolf's lair[156], with all his entrails[157] eaten away, his hand still tightly clutching that little basket. …" At this point she started crying, and was unable to complete the sentence.

（69）My aunt had been undecided at first, but by the end of this story the rims of her eyes were rather red. After thinking for a moment she told her to take the round basket and bedding into the servants' quarters. Old Mrs. Wei heaved[158] a long sigh as if relieved of a great burden. Hsiang Lin's Wife looked a little more at ease[159] than when she first came and, without having to be told the way, quietly took away her bedding. From this time on she worked again as a maidservant in Luchen.

（70）Everybody still called her Hsiang Lin's Wife.

（71）However, she had changed a great deal. She had not been there more than three days before her master and mistress realized that she was not as quick as before. Since her memory was much worse, and her impassive[160] face never showed the least trace of a smile, my aunt already expressed herself very far from satisfied. When the woman first arrived, although my uncle frowned as before, because they invariably had such difficulty in finding servants he did not object very strongly, only secretly warned my aunt that while such people may seem very pitiful they exert[161] a bad moral influence. Thus although it would be all right for her to do ordinary work she must not join in the preparations for sacrifice; they would have to prepare all the dishes themselves, for otherwise they would be unclean and the ancestors would

[155] bramble /ˈbræmbl/ n. 荆棘

[156] lair /leə(r)/ n. 兽穴；兽窝
[157] entrails /ˈentreɪlz/ n. (pl.) 内脏；(尤指)肠

[158] heave /hiːv/ v. 缓慢发出(声音)
[159] at ease：安逸；自在

[160] impassive /ɪmˈpæsɪv/ adj. 无表情的

[161] exert /ɪgˈzɜː(r)t/ v. 施加(影响等)

not accept them.

（72） The most important event in my uncle's household was the ancestral sacrifice[162] , and formerly this had been the busiest time for Hsiang Lin's Wife; but now she had very little to do. When the table was placed in the centre of the hall and the curtain fastened, she still remembered how to set out the winecups and chopsticks in the old way.

（73）"Hsiang Lin's Wife, put those down!" said my aunt hastily[163] .

（74） She sheepishly[164] withdrew her hand and went to get the candlesticks.

（75）"Hsiang Lin's Wife, put those down!" cried my aunt hastily again. "I'll fetch them."

（76） After walking round several times without finding anything to do, Hsiang Lin's Wife could only go hesitantly away. All she did that day was to sit by the stove and feed the fire.

（77） The people in the town still called her Hsiang Lin's Wife, but in a different tone from before; and although they talked to her still, their manner was colder. She did not mind this in the least, only, looking straight in front of her, she would tell everybody her story, which night or day was never out of her mind.

（78） "I was really stupid, really,"[165] she would say. "I only knew that when it snows the wild beasts in the glen have nothing to eat and may come to the villages; I didn't know that in spring they came too. I got up at dawn and opened the door, filled a small basket with beans and called our Ah Mao to go and sit on the threshold and shell them. He was very obedient and always did as I told him: he went out. Then I chopped wood at the back of the house and washed the rice, and when the rice was in the pan and I wanted to boil the beans I called Ah Mao, but there was no answer; and when I went out to look, all I could see was beans scattered on the ground, but no Ah Mao. He never went to other families to play; and in fact at each place where I

[162] the ancestral sacrifice: 祭祖

[163] hastily /ˈheɪstɪli/ adv. 匆忙地
[164] sheepish /ˈʃiːpɪʃ/ adj. 窘迫的；难为情的

[165] "我真傻，真的，"这句话成了祥林嫂的口头禅，她逢人便说起阿毛被狼叼走的经过。

went to ask, there was no sign of him. I became desperate, and begged people to go to look for him. Only in the afternoon, after looking everywhere else, did they go to look in the glen and see one of his little shoes caught on a bramble. 'That's bad,' they said, 'he must have met a wolf.' And sure enough when they went further in there he was, lying in the wolf's lair, with all his entrails eaten away, his hand still tightly clutching that small basket. ..." At this point she would start crying and her voice would <u>trail away</u>[166].

（79）This story was rather effective, and when men heard it they often stopped smiling and walked away <u>disconcerted</u>[167], while the women not only seemed to forgive her but their faces immediately lost their <u>contemptuous</u>[168] look and they added their tears to hers. There were some old women who had not heard her speaking in the street, who went specially to look for her, to hear her sad tale. When her voice trailed away and she started to cry, they joined in, shedding the tears which had gathered in their eyes. <u>Then they sighed, and went away satisfied, exchanging comments.</u> [169]

（80）She asked nothing better than to tell her sad story over and over again, often gathering three or four hearers. But <u>before long</u>[170] everybody knew it by heart, until even in the eyes of the most kindly, Buddha fearing old ladies not a trace of tears could be seen. In the end, almost everyone in the town could recite her tale, and it bored and <u>exasperated</u>[171] them to hear it.

（81）"I was really stupid, really ..." she would begin.

（82）"Yes, you only knew that in snowy weather the wild beasts in the mountains had nothing to eat and might come down to the villages." <u>Promptly</u>[172] cutting short her <u>recital</u>[173], they walked away.

（83）She would stand there open-mouthed, looking at them with a <u>dazed</u>[174] expression, and then go away too, as if she also felt disconcerted. But she still <u>brooded over</u>[175] it, hoping from other topics such as small baskets,

[166] trail away：(声音)逐渐减弱，越来越小

[167] disconcert /ˌdɪskən'sɜː(r)t/ v. 使不安；使尴尬

[168] contemptuous /kən'temptʃuəs/ adj. 蔑视的；鄙视的

[169] 听完故事便满足地离去，这些老太太们，又有谁是真心同情祥林嫂呢？

[170] before long：不久；很快

[171] exasperate /ɪg'zæspəreɪt/ v. 使恼怒

[172] promptly /'prɒmptli/ adv. 立即

[173] recital /rɪ'saɪtl/ n. 逐一列举；赘述

[174] dazed /deɪzd/ adj. 茫然的

[175] brood over：郁闷地沉思

beans and other people's children, to lead up to the story of her Ah Mao. If she saw a child of two or three, she would say, "Oh dear, if my Ah Mao were still alive, he would be just as big. ..."

（84）Children seeing the look in her eyes would take fright[176] and, clutching[177] the hems[178] of their mothers' clothes, try to tug[179] them away. Thereupon she would be left by herself again, and finally walk away disconcerted. Later everybody knew what she was like, and it only needed a child present for them to ask her with an artificial smile, "Hsiang Lin's Wife, if your Ah Mao were alive, wouldn't he be just as big as that?"

（85）She probably did not realize that her story, after having been turned over and tasted by people for so many days, had long since become stale[180], only exciting[181] disgust[182] and contempt[183]; but from the way people smiled she seemed to know that they were cold and sarcastic, and that there was no need for her to say any more. She would simply look at them, not answering a word.

（86）In Luchen people celebrate New Year in a big way: preparations start from the twentieth day of the twelfth month onwards[184]. That year my uncle's household found it necessary to hire a temporary manservant, but since there was still a great deal to do they also called in another maidservant, Liu Ma, to help. Chickens and geese had to be killed; but Liu Ma was a devout[185] woman who abstained[186] from meat, did not kill living things, and would only wash the sacrificial dishes. Hsiang Lin's Wife had nothing to do but feed the fire. She sat there, resting, watching Liu Ma as she washed the sacrificial dishes. A light snow began to fall.

（87）"Dear me, I was really stupid," began Hsiang Lin's Wife, as if to herself, looking at the sky and sighing.

（88）"Hsiang Lin's Wife, there you go[187] again," said Liu Ma, looking at her impatiently. "I ask you: that wound on your forehead, wasn't it then you got it?"

---

[176] take fright：受到惊吓

[177] clutch /klʌtʃ/ v. 紧握；抓紧

[178] hem /hem/ n.（衣服等的）褶边，卷边

[179] tug /tʌg/ v. 拉；拖；拽

[180] stale /steɪl/ adj. 陈腐的；没有新意的；老掉牙的

[181] excite /ɪkˈsaɪt/ v. 引发；引起

[182] disgust /dɪsˈgʌst/ n. 厌恶；反感

[183] contempt /kənˈtempt/ n. 轻蔑；鄙视

[184] onwards /ˈɒnwədz/ adv. 从（某时）起一直

[185] devout /dɪˈvaʊt/ adj. 虔诚的

[186] abstain /əbˈsteɪn/ v. 戒；戒除

[187] there you go：你又来这一套

（89）"Uh, huh," she answered vaguely[188].

（90）"Let me ask you: what made you willing after all?"

（91）"Me?"

（92）"Yes. What I think is, you must have been willing; otherwise. ..."

（93）"Oh dear, you don't know how strong he was."

（94）"I don't believe it. I don't believe he was so strong that you really couldn't keep him off. You must have been willing, only you put the blame on[189] his being so strong."

（95）"Oh dear, you ... you try for yourself and see." She smiled.

（96）Liu Ma's lined face broke into a smile too, making it wrinkled like a walnut[190]; her small beady[191] eyes swept Hsiang Lin's Wife's forehead and fastened on her eyes. As if rather embarrassed, Hsiang Lin's Wife immediately stopped smiling, averted[192] her eyes and looked at the snow-flakes.

（97）"Hsiang Lin's Wife, that was really a bad bargain," continued Liu Ma mysteriously. "If you had held out longer or knocked yourself to death, it would have been better. As it is, after living with your second husband for less than two years, you are guilty of a great crime. Just think: when you go down to the lower world[193] in future, these two men's ghosts will fight over you. To which will you go? The King of Hell[194] will have no choice but to cut you in two and divide you between them. I think, really. ..."

（98）Then terror showed in her face. This was something she had never heard in the mountains.

（99）"I think you had better take precautions[195] beforehand. Go to the Tutelary God's Temple[196] and buy a threshold[197] to be your substitute, so that thousands of people can walk over it and trample[198] on it, in order to atone[199] for your sins in this life and avoid torment after death."

188 vaguely /ˈveɪɡli/ adv. 含糊地

189 put the blame on: 把责任推到……身上

190 明喻（simile）。柳妈皱起的脸像个核桃。

191 beady /ˈbiːdi/ adj. 小圆珠般的

192 avert /əˈvɜː(r)t/ v. 转移（目光）

193 the lower world: 地狱

194 The King of Hell: 阎王

195 precaution /prɪˈkɔːʃn/ n. 预防；防备

196 the Tutelary God's Temple: 土地庙，中国民间供奉土地神的庙宇。

197 buy a threshold: 捐门槛。封建迷信认为，门槛代表自己或者自己所

（100）At the time Hsiang Lin's Wife said nothing, but she must have taken this to heart, for the next morning when she got up there were dark circles beneath her eyes. After breakfast she went to the Tutelary God's Temple at the west end of the village, and asked to buy a threshold. The temple priests would not agree at first, and only when she shed tears did they give a grudging[200] consent. The price was twelve thousand cash.

（101）She had long since given up talking to people, because Ah Mao's story was received with such contempt; but news of her conversation with Liu Ma that day spread, and many people took a fresh interest in her and came again to tease her into talking. As for the subject, that had naturally changed to deal with the wound on her forehead.

（102）"Hsiang Lin's Wife, I ask you: what made you willing after all that time?" one would cry.

（103）"Oh, what a pity, to have had this knock for nothing," another looking at her scar would agree.

（104）Probably she knew from their smiles and tone of voice that they were making fun of her, for she always looked steadily at them without saying a word, and finally did not even turn her head. All day long she kept her lips tightly closed, bearing on her head the scar which everyone considered a mark of shame, silently shopping, sweeping the floor, washing vegetables, preparing rice. Only after nearly a year did she take from my aunt her wages which had accumulated. She changed them for twelve silver dollars, and asking for leave went to the west end of the town. In less time than it takes for a meal she was back again, looking much comforted, and with an unaccustomed[201] light in her eyes. She told my aunt happily that she had bought a threshold in the Tutelary God's Temple.

（105）When the time came for the ancestral sacrifice at the winter equinox[202], she worked harder than ever, and seeing my aunt take out the sacrificial utensils[203] and with Ah Niu carry the table into the middle

犯下的罪行，自知有罪过的人便花钱到庙里让人做个门槛，以代替自己，让千人踩，万人蹋，来赎清自己这一世的罪过。

[198] trample /ˈtræmpl/ v. 踩踏；践踏

[199] atone /əˈtəʊn/ v.（赎）罪

[200] grudging /ˈɡrʌdʒɪŋ/ adj. 勉强的；不情愿的

[201] unaccustomed /ˌʌnəˈkʌstəmd/ adj. 不寻常的；奇怪的

[202] the winter equinox：冬至，多译作 the winter solstice。

[203] utensil /juːˈtensl/ n. 用具；器皿

of the hall, she went confidently to fetch the winecups and chopsticks.

(106) "Put those down, Hsiang Lin's Wife!" my aunt called out hastily.

(107) She withdrew her hand as if scorched, her face turned ashen-grey, and instead of fetching the candlesticks she just stood there dazed. Only when my uncle came to burn incense and told her to go, did she walk away.[204] This time the change in her was very great, for the next day not only were her eyes sunken, but even her spirit seemed broken.[205] Moreover she became very timid, not only afraid of the dark and shadows, but also of the sight of anyone. Even her own master or mistress made her look as frightened as a little mouse that has come out of its hole in the daytime[206]. For the rest, she would sit stupidly, like a wooden statue.[207] In less than half a year her hair began to turn grey, and her memory became much worse, reaching a point when she was constantly forgetting to go and prepare the rice.

(108) "What has come over[208] Hsiang Lin's Wife? It would really have been better not to have kept her that time." My aunt would sometimes speak like this in front of her, as if to warn her.

(109) However, she remained this way, so that it was impossible to see any hope of her improving. They finally decided to get rid of her and tell her to go back to Old Mrs. Wei. While I was at Luchen they were still only talking of this; but judging by what happened later, it is evident that this was what they must have done. Whether after leaving my uncle's household she became a beggar, or whether she went first to Old Mrs. Wei's house and later became a beggar, I do not know.

(110) I was woken up by firecrackers exploding noisily close at hand[209], saw the glow of the yellow oil lamp as large as a bean[210], and heard the splutter[211] of fireworks as my uncle's household celebrated the sacrifice. I knew that it was nearly dawn. I felt bewildered[212], hearing as in a dream the confused

[204] 直到四叔来上香的时候，叫她走开，她才走开。此句为强调句型，将时间状语提前到了句首。

[205] 祥林嫂在捐了门槛之后，原本以为已经赎了这一世的罪，却不曾想四婶仍然不让她碰祭祀用品，她受到致命的打击，彻底失去了希望，精神也垮了。

[206] 明喻（simile）。害怕得像一只白天出洞的小老鼠。

[207] 其他时候，祥林嫂则像个木雕似的傻坐着。like a wooden statue 用了明喻（simile）。

[208] come over：支配；影响

[209] close at hand：在附近；在近旁

[210] 明喻（simile）。看见油灯发出像豆子一样大的光。（oil lamp：油灯）

[211] splutter /ˈsplʌtə(r)/ n. 噼啪声

[212] bewildered /bɪˈwɪldə(r)d/ adj. 困

continuous sound of distant crackers which seemed to form one dense cloud of noise in the sky, joining the whirling[213] snow-flakes to envelop the whole town. Wrapped in this medley[214] of sound, relaxed and at ease, the doubt which had preyed[215] on me from dawn to early night was swept clean away by the atmosphere of celebration, and I felt only that the saints of heaven and earth had accepted the sacrifice and incense and were all reeling[216] with intoxication[217] in the sky, preparing to give the people of Luchen boundless good fortune.

February 7, 1924

惑不解的

213 whirl /wɜː(r)l/ *v.* 旋转；回旋

214 medley /ˈmedli/ *n.* 混成曲

215 prey /preɪ/ *v.* 不断困扰；折磨

216 reel /riːl/ *v.* 摇摇晃晃地挪动；蹒跚

217 intoxication /ɪnˌtɒksɪˈkeɪʃn/ *n.* 喝醉；醉酒

◤ 精华赏析 ◥

祥林嫂在漫天飞雪中死去了,她的悲剧让作为男性的"我"困惑犹豫了片刻,但是镇上燃放的爆竹声让"我"不由自主地沉浸在节日的喜庆氛围之中,很快便将这件小事抛诸脑后。在那个封建父权制社会,女性的地位低下,一个无家可归的女乞丐之死更不会激起任何水花。鲁迅先生似乎只是平平淡淡地讲述了这个故事,却能让祥林嫂的形象牢牢地印在读者的脑海中,进而让读者忍不住思考一些问题:祥林嫂并非一个好吃懒做的人,她也没有犯过什么大的罪过,那到底是什么原因,使得祥林嫂无路可走,流落街头,直至死亡呢? 她也想过要自食其力,但是为什么就遇到了重重阻碍呢? 难道仅仅因为她改嫁了,就不为世人所容吗? 那为何男性妻妾成群就合情合理,无人抨击呢? 女性和男性,真的太不平等了!

这世上有很多人意识到男女不平等这一现象,并试图找到解决之道。女性主义(Feminism)便是为促进男女性别平等而创立和发起的社会理论与政治运动,这个阵营十分庞大,流派繁多,常见的就有自由女性主义、社会主义女性主义、激进女性主义、后现代女性主义等,各流派的观点不尽相同,但是他们都有着一个共同的目标,那就是"在全人类实现男女平等",且有着一个基本的前提,那就是"女性在全世界范围内是一个受迫害、受歧视的等级,即女性主义思想泰斗波伏娃(Simone de Beauvoir)所说的'第二性'"(李银河,2018:2)。这也是女性不能获得与男性平等的地位和权利的原因,因为女性不是作为主体而存在的,她们是被排除在男性以外的"他者",被认为是男性的附属品,因此必须依赖于男性而存在。祥林嫂就是这样一个"他者"形象,在这篇小说中,作者通过展示祥林嫂的悲剧,揭示了女性悲剧与时代背景之间的关系以及封建社会中的女性意识普遍缺乏这一事实。

一、祥林嫂的"他者"形象

作为小说的女主角,祥林嫂就是一个依赖于男性而存在的"他者"形象。她没有自己的姓名,至于她姓甚名谁,没人知道,也没人在乎,自始至终,人们只根据她已经去世的第一任丈夫来称呼她。在那个时代,女性没有自己的姓名,这就表明她们只能是附属于男性存在的"他者"。鲁迅通过"祥林嫂"这个名字,揭露了封建社会下的女性对男性的绝对依附性(杨烈祥,邹巅,2004)。

祥林嫂的悲剧,从本质上来说,是封建社会下荒谬的封建伦理制度造成的。中国封建社会惯用"三从四德"来约束女性的行为与道德,要求女性未嫁从父,出嫁从夫,夫死从子。因此,女性永无自由可言,她们的命运始终掌握在别人的手中。没结婚时,她们要听从父母的安排;而结了婚的女性,则必须听从于那些手握"夫权"的人们——丈夫和婆家人。作为"他者"的祥林嫂,自然是没有婚姻自主权的。年轻的时候她被卖作童养媳,成为婆家的"物品";丈夫去世后,家里的婆婆和小叔子便替死去的丈夫行使"夫权",她仍然无法决定自己的前途和命运。她从婆婆家偷偷逃出来,到鲁四老爷家做工养活自己,但婆婆为给小叔子筹集聘礼,便强行把她卖给山里的贺老六当老婆。这种事情在当今社会是不合法的,但当时的人们则默认这种行为是合理的。比如封建礼制的卫道夫鲁四老爷,在听到祥林嫂的婆婆要她回去时,认为这是无可厚非的,他丝毫没想过要不要咨询祥林嫂的意见,在祥林嫂不在场的情况下,便将工资付给了她的婆婆。而当四婶向卫婆子发出祥林嫂怎么会接受改嫁的疑问时,得到的回复是:"这有什么依不依。——闹是谁也总要闹一闹的;只要用绳子一捆,塞在花轿里,抬到男家,捺上花冠,拜堂,关上房门,就完事了"(鲁迅,2015:152)。卫婆子的这段话道出了那个时代女性的悲哀,无论如何,作为"他者"的女性只能听从男性的安排,她们在婚姻上只能被动服从,不能主动选择。

但祥林嫂是不接受改嫁的,她拼死反抗,在婚礼当天撞破了头。悲剧的是,即便如此,人们仍然认为改嫁是女性的错。男权制的代表鲁四老爷,在祥林嫂再次丧偶来到鲁家时,就认为她伤风败俗,告诫四婶不许祥林嫂沾手祭祀用品。更让人难以理解的是,当时大多数女性也肯定且坚决帮助男性去维护女性的"他者"地位。镇子上的女性们丝毫不同情祥林嫂,她们全都站在了祥林嫂的对立面,为了维护男权下的道德准则,蔑视她,指责她,似乎丈夫和儿子的死全是她的错。比如说介绍祥林嫂到鲁家的卫婆子,助纣为虐,伙同其婆婆,偷偷将祥林嫂绑了回去,以便能够把她卖到山里;村里那些老太太,在祥林嫂丧偶回来之后,眼神里都是鄙视;与祥林嫂同样阶层的柳妈,在跟祥林嫂聊天时也表现出对女性的歧视,在祥林嫂的伤口上撒盐,故意提及阎罗王,认为祥林嫂改嫁了,就犯了不可饶恕的大罪,死后会被阎罗王砍成两半,要去寺庙捐门槛来减轻罪恶。由此可见,在男权制度的压迫下,女性已经丧失了要求独立的意识,她们已经接受了自己是男性的附属这个事实,将这种男性伦理制度下的压迫当成了必然,心甘情愿成为封建礼教的帮凶,维持那些有反抗意识的女性的"他者"形象。

二、祥林嫂的女性意识的缺乏

那作为下层女性的祥林嫂是不是也有着一些女性意识呢?在第一任丈夫去世后,为了不被婆婆卖掉,早寡的她偷偷逃出婆家,挣脱了牢笼,来到鲁四老爷家做工,通过自己的努力,自食其力,获得了经济上的独立。表面看起来,祥林嫂似乎有着追求自由和经济独立的愿望,也在一定程度上付诸实践了。但可惜的是,她缺乏女性意识,没能看到封建礼制的残酷性,没能未雨绸缪,最后被婆婆抓了回去。在被卖给贺老六当老婆后,祥林嫂虽然也曾以死抗争,在婚礼上撞破脑门,可是这也并不代表祥林嫂有女性意识,因为她没有质疑封建家长对自己的摆布,没能意识到封建礼教是导致自己悲剧的根源,因此她的撞香案只是出于对"再嫁"的恐惧,对不能"守节"的恐惧,是悔不能维护封建礼教(姬玉,2008)。

对于封建伦理制度,实际上祥林嫂本人也是接受并认同的,因此在丧夫丧子后,面对镇上人们的奚落与揶揄,她也只是一味忍受;在柳妈指责她未能从一而终,改嫁给贺老六就是犯了罪,所以死后会受到阎罗王惩罚时,她非但不质疑,反而坚定不移地相信了这一说法;她坚信自己就是有罪,便将自己挣得的工钱全部拿去寺庙捐门槛,以赎清这一世的罪过。由此可见,祥林嫂的思想仍然受到了封建礼教的禁锢,她没有女性意识,也没有进行有意识的反抗,而她"最大的悲哀并不是她经历的坎坷不幸,而是她对这种不幸的屈从和认同,她先是成为封建伦理秩序下的牺牲品,然后又不自觉地成为了这种伦理道德的屈从和捍卫者,最后又被这套秩序所放逐,在饥寒中带着追问离世"(黄晓娟,2002)。从根本上而言,她自己也是封建伦理制度的维护者与践行者,她的悲剧结局跟自己的封建意识也是分不开的,假如她能够看清封建伦理制度的不合理性,跟自己和解,那她的悲剧结局也许能被改写。

那祥林嫂的悲剧是由什么造成的呢?首先,祥林嫂的悲剧是时代的产物,封建社会的伦理制度巩固了女性的"他者"地位,无论是男性还是女性,都肯定了男性的绝对地位,要求女性绝对服从,整个社会都与女性为敌,让女性困在其中,无处可逃。其次,祥林嫂自身也缺乏独立和自主的意识,她也认同压迫自己的男权制度。因此,只有铲除封建礼教,从根本上构建女性思想与意识的独立性,才能改变女性的命运,让祥林嫂的悲剧故事不再重演(金雅,2001)。

参考文献

[1] 黄晓娟. 女性的飞翔与自我意识[J]. 广西教育学院学报,2002(4):99-103.
[2] 姬玉. 失败的抗争——《离婚》和《祝福》中劳动妇女的悲剧[J]. 安徽文学,2008(8):25-26.
[3] 金雅. 女性命运的文学风向标——二十世纪中国文学与女性解放[N]. 文艺报,2001-12-15.
[4] 李银河. 女性主义[M]. 上海:上海文化出版社,2018.
[5] 鲁迅. 鲁迅小说全集[M]. 北京:人民文学出版社,2015.
[6] 杨烈祥,邹巅. 解读《祝福》的女性意识[J]. 湘南学院学报,2004(6):62-65.

阅读思考

1. 如果你是祥林嫂,在她所处的时代背景下,会不会选择以死抗婚呢?
2. 对于祥林嫂的悲剧,生活在新时代的你有何感想?

❷

Hills Like White Elephants

Ernest Hemingway

【作品简介】

《白象似的群山》(*Hills Like White Elephants*)写于 1927 年,收在海明威的短篇小说集《没有女人的男人们》(*Men without Women*)中。故事发生在西班牙北部一个火车站上,一对年轻的情侣正在等待去马德里的火车,火车还有 40 分钟才到,于是这对情侣到车站的酒吧里等待火车到来。他们在酒吧里展开了一段对话,在交谈中反复提到要不要做一个手术。不过直到故事结尾,作者都没有告诉读者这是个什么手术,这让不少读者在初读这篇小说时不免一头雾水。

这篇小说很能体现海明威的文体特点,全文使用的词语大多是英语当中的小词、常用词,使用的句式多为比较简单的陈述句。在讲故事的过程中,海明威采用的方式是将故事发生的场面直接展现在读者眼前,期间叙述者不做任何评论,故事背后的事情需要读者根据展示出来的细节去想象和猜测。这就是海明威的"冰山理论",他说:"如果一位散文作家对于他想写的东西心里很有数,那么他可以省略他所知道的东西,读者呢,只要作者写得真实,会强烈地感觉到他所省略的部分,好像作者已经写出来似的。冰山在海里移动很是威严壮观,这是因为它只有八分之一露出水面。"(董衡巽,1986)

【作者简介】

厄内斯特·海明威(Ernest Hemingway)是美国现代文学史上最重要的作家之一,是"迷惘的一代"的代表作家之一。1953 年,他因《老人与海》(*The Old Man and the Sea*)一书获得普利策奖;1954 年,他又因《老人与海》获得诺贝尔文学奖。他是第五个获得诺贝尔文学奖的美国作家。2001 年,他的《太阳照样升起》(*The Sun Also Rises*)与《永别了,武器》(*A Farewell to Arms*)两部作品被美国现代图书馆列入"20 世纪中的 100 部最佳英文小说"中。有的评论家认为海明威是继马克·吐温之后对美国文学语言影响最大的作家,他独特的文体风格影响了不止一代人。

海明威于 1899 年生于芝加哥(Chicago)一个富裕的医生家庭。童年时期的海明威聪明,学习成绩好,又擅长足球、拳击等各类运动。暑假期间,他父亲常常带他到密歇根州(Michigan)北部林中去钓鱼、打猎。少年时期的这些经历不仅影响了他日后的生活方式,也构成了他作品的重要内容。

海明威 18 岁中学毕业后到《堪萨斯州明星报》(*The Kansas City Star*)当见习记者,主要采访的是医院和警察局,在工作中常常接触到流血和暴力事件。这段记者生涯一方面培养了海明威使用简洁文字的能力,另一方面也为他日后的写作积累了丰富的原始素材。

1918 年,海明威本想加入美国陆军,但是因为眼睛视力不达标而未能如愿。于是他加入了美国红十字会的救护车队,当了一名司机。后来他在意大利受了重伤,住进了米兰的一家医院,在做了多次手术后才取出了体内大部分榴霰弹碎片。此时他结识并爱上了一名护士,即《永别了,武器》(*A Farewell to Arms*)中女主人公的原型。海明威自己说在第一次世界大战中他的身心都受到了重创,他的亲属回忆说海明威在这次战争后变成了一个他们不熟悉的人。

1920 年,海明威当了《多伦多明星报》(*Toronto Star*)的国外通讯记者。1922 年,海明威到了巴黎,通过舍伍德·安德森写的一封介绍信进入了美国作家斯泰因的文艺沙龙。斯泰因的文艺沙龙是当时一些知名作家如庞德、菲茨杰拉德、乔伊斯等人经常聚会的地方。海明威在此期间得到了斯泰因和庞德等人的不少帮助。

1926 年,海明威发表了《太阳照样升起》(*The Sun Also Rises*)。这部小说使海明威成了"迷惘的一代"的代言人。在小说正文前面,海明威引用了斯泰因的话:"你们这些在战争中服役的年轻人。你们都是迷惘的一代。"("All of you young people who served in the war. You are a lost generation.")

使海明威获得巨大成功的是在 1929 年出版的《永别了,武器》(*A Farewell to Arms*),这本小说直接描写了战争。发表于 1927 年的《没有女人的男人》(*Men without Women*)和发表于 1933 年的《胜者无所得》(*Winner Take Nothing*)两部短篇小说集确立了海明威作为短篇小说大师的地位。1937 年,海明威以记者身份参加了西班牙内战,他对这一反法西斯战争的态度与对第一次世界大战的态度截然不同。海明威把维护西班牙的自由和维护世界自由紧密联系起来,在 1940 年发表了反映西班牙内战的小说《丧钟为谁而鸣》(*For Whom the Bell Tolls*)。

1950 年,海明威发表了让众人失望的《过河入林》(*Across the River and into the Trees*)。当时的评论家普遍认为海明威的创作才能已经耗尽,不会再有建树。但是他于 1952 年发表的《老人与海》(*The Old Man and the Sea*)一书获得了普利策奖,后来又"因其精通现代叙事艺术"而获得诺贝尔文学奖。

此后几年,海明威的健康每况愈下,情绪也日益低落,最使他苦恼的是失去了创作的能力。1961 年 7 月他在爱达荷州(Idaho)的家中用父亲留给他的猎枪,以和父亲同样的方式自杀了。

（1）The hills across the valley of the Ebro were long and white. On this side there was no shade and no trees[1] and the station was between two lines of rails in the sun. Close against the side of the station there was the warm shadow of the building and a curtain, made of strings[2] of bamboo beads, hung across the open door into the bar, to

[1] "没有树木也没有树荫",这里的景色描写和后文形成对比。

[2] string /strɪŋ/ *n.* 一串;线;细绳

keep out flies. The American and the girl with him sat at a table in the shade, outside the building. It was very hot and the express from Barcelona[3] would come in forty minutes. It stopped at this junction for two minutes and went on to Madrid[4].

（2）"What should we drink?" the girl asked. She had taken off her hat and put it on the table.

（3）"It's pretty hot," the man said.

（4）"Let's drink beer."

（5）"*Dos cervezas*," the man said into the curtain.

（6）"Big ones?" a woman asked from the doorway.

（7）"Yes. Two big ones."

（8）The woman brought two glasses of beer and two felt pads[5]. She put the felt pads and the beer glasses on the table and looked at the man and the girl. The girl was looking off at the line of hills. They were white in the sun and the country was brown and dry.

（9）"They look like white elephants[6]," she said.

（10）"I've never seen one," the man drank his beer.

（11）"No, you wouldn't have."

（12）"I might have," the man said. "Just because you say I wouldn't have doesn't prove anything."

（13）The girl looked at the bead curtain. "They've painted something on it," she said. "What does it say?"[7]

（14）"Anis del Toro[8]. It's a drink."

（15）"Could we try it?"

（16）The man called "Listen" through the curtain. The woman came out from the bar.

（17）"Four reales."

（18）"We want two Anis del Toro."

（19）"With water?"

（20）"Do you want it with water?"

（21）"I don't know," the girl said. "It is good with water?"

（22）"It's all right."

（23）"You want them with water?" asked the

[3] Barcelona 巴塞罗那,位于伊比利亚半岛东北部,濒临地中海,是西班牙第二大城市,也是加泰罗尼亚自治区的首府,以及巴塞罗那省(隶属于加泰罗尼亚自治区)的省会,加泰罗尼亚自治区的议会、行政机构、高等法院均设立于此。
[4] Madrid 马德里,西班牙首都,也是马德里自治区的首府,位于西班牙国土中部,曼萨纳雷斯河贯穿市区。
[5] pad /pæd/ n. 软垫
[6] 白象是古印度最高贵的动物,被当作神物供奉,然而普通人家无力供养一头大象,所以它成了最珍贵又最没有使用价值、甚至会带来麻烦的礼物。
[7] 说明女孩不懂西班牙语。
[8] 一种烈性酒

woman.

（24）"Yes, with water."

（25）"It takes like licorice⁹," the girl said and put the glass down.

⁹ licorice /ˈlɪkərɪʃ/ n. 甘草精

（26）"That's the way with everything."

（27）"Yes," said the girl. "Everything tastes of licorice. Especially all the things you've waited so long for, like absinthe¹⁰."

¹⁰ absinthe /ˈæbsɪnθ/ n. 苦艾酒
这里女孩说所有等待很久的东西都像是苦艾酒，是有所寓意的，所以男人才会打断女孩的话。

（28）"Oh, cut it out."

（29）"You started it," the girl said. "I was being amused. I was having a fine time."

（30）"Well, let's try and have a fine time."

（31）"All right. I was trying. I said the mountains looked like white elephants. Wasn't that bright?"

（32）"That was bright."

（33）"I wanted to try this new drink: That's all we do, isn't it — look at things and try new drinks?"

（34）"I guess so."

（35）The girl looked across at the hills.

（36）"They're lovely hills," she said. "They don't really look like white elephants. I just meant the coloring of their skin through the trees."

（37）"Should we have another drink?"

（38）"All right."

（39）The warm wind blew the bead curtain against the table.

（40）"The beer's nice and cool," the man said.

（41）"It's lovely," the girl said.

（42） "It's really an awfully simple operation, Jig¹¹," the man said. "It's not really an operation at all."

¹¹ 女孩的名字叫 Jig，她是小说中唯一有名字的人物，而这名字绝非一个简单的符号而已，Jig 是种快步舞，符合女主人公年轻、四处漂泊的形象。

（43）The girl looked at the ground the table legs rested on.

（44）"I know you wouldn't mind it, Jig. It's really not anything. It's just to let the air in.¹²"

（45）The girl did not say anything.

（46）"I'll go with you and I'll stay with you all the time. They just let the air in and then it's all perfectly

¹² 他们提到了一个手术，男人说这个手术算不上什么，就是进去些空气。后文男人会继续说服女孩相信这是一个十分简单的手术。

natural."

(47) "Then what will we do afterward?"

(48) "We'll be fine afterward. Just like we were before.¹³"

(49) "What makes you think so?"

(50) "That's the only thing that bothers us. It's the only thing that's made us unhappy."

(51) The girl looked at the bead curtain, put her hand out and took hold of two of the strings of beads.

(52) "And you think then we'll be all right and be happy."

(53) "I know we will. You don't have to be afraid. I've known lots of people that have done it."

(54) "So have I," said the girl. "And afterward they were all so happy."

(55) "Well," the man said, "if you don't want to you don't have to. I wouldn't have you do it if you didn't want to. But I know it's perfectly simple.¹⁴"

(56) "And you really want to?"

(57) "I think it's the best thing to do. But I don't want you to do it if you don't really want to."

(58) "And if I do it you'll be happy and things will be like they were and you'll love me?"

(59) "I love you now. You know I love you."

(60) "I know. But if I do it, then it will be nice again if I say things are like white elephants, and you'll like it?"

(61) "I'll love it. I love it now but I just can't think about it. You know how I get when I worry."

(62) "If I do it you won't ever worry?"

(63) "I won't worry about that because it's perfectly simple."

(64) "Then I'll do it. Because I don't care about me."¹⁵

(65) "What do you mean?"

(66) "I don't care about me."

(67) "Well, I care about you."

(68) "Oh, yes. But I don't care about me. And I'll

¹³ 男人说只要做了这个手术我们就和以前一样好了。全文都没有告诉读者这个手术是什么手术，这是海明威"冰山理论"的体现，省略了作者知道的一些信息，留给读者去想象和猜测。

¹⁴ 这里男人告诉女孩要是你不想做这个手术就别做，我不会让你做你不情愿的事情，但是这真是一个特别简单的手术。男人一边反复劝说女孩做手术，一边又称自己不会强迫女孩，前后矛盾。

¹⁵ 女孩说自己同意做手术，是因为她不在乎自己。此时女孩的内心感受需要读者自己去揣摩。

do it and then everything will be fine. "

（69） "I don't want you to do it if you feel that way. "

（70） The girl stood up and walked to the end of the station. <u>Across, on the other side, were fields of grain and trees along the banks of the Ebro.</u>^{16} Far away, beyond the river, were mountains. The shadow of a cloud moved across the field of grain and she saw the river through the trees.

（71） "And we could have all <u>this</u>^{17} ," she said. "And we could have everything and every day we make it more impossible. "

（72） "What did you say?"

（73） "I said we could have everything. "

（74） "We can have everything. "

（75） "No, we can't. "

（76） "We can have the whole world. "

（77） "No, we can't. "

（78） "We can go everywhere. "

（79） "No, we can't. It isn't ours any more. "

（80） "It's ours. "

（81） "No, it isn't. And once they take <u>it</u>^{18} away, you never get it back. "

（82） "But they haven't taken it away. "

（83） "We'll wait and see. "

（84） "Come on back in the shade," he said. "You mustn't feel that way. "

（85） "I don't feel any way," the girl said. "I just know things. "

（86） "I don't want you to do anything that you don't want to do — "

（87） "Nor that isn't good for me," she said. "I know. Could we have another beer?"

（88） "All right. But you've got to realize — "

（89） "I realize," the girl said. "Can't we maybe stop talking?"

（90） They sat down at the table and the girl looked across at the hills on the <u>dry side</u>^{19} of the valley and the

^{16} 这里的景色描写和前文的描写形成对比，现在女孩看到的景象是河岸两边的农田和树木，不再是之前的没有树木也没有树荫，乡野是灰褐色和干巴巴的一片。不同的景色描写既折射出了女孩的心态，又具有象征意义。

^{17} this 指代的是什么，不是很明确。海明威使用了不少模糊的表达，留给读者去补充缺失的信息。

^{18} 从79段开始到82段多次出现 it 这个词，it 指代的是什么仍然需要读者自己去思考。

^{19} 女孩看到的景色又变成了干巴巴

man looked at her and at the table.

（91）"You've got to realize," he said, "that I don't want you to do it if you don't want to. I'm perfectly willing to go through with it if it means anything to you."

（92）"Doesn't it mean anything to you? We could get along."

（93）"Of course it does. But I don't want anybody but you. I don't want any one else. And I know it's perfectly simple.²⁰"

（94）"Yes, you know it's perfectly simple."

（95）"It's all right for you to say that, but I do know it."

（96）"Would you do something for me now?"

（97）"I'd do anything for you."

（98）"Would you please please please please please please please stop talking?"

（99）He did not say anything but looked at the bags against the wall of the station. There were labels on them from all the hotels where they had spent nights.²¹

（100）"But I don't want you to," he said "I don't care anything about it."

（101）"I'll scream," the girl said.

（102）The woman came out through the curtains with two glasses of beer and put them down on the damp felt pads. "The train comes in five minutes," she said.

（103）"What did she say?"²² asked the girl.

（104）"That the train is coming in five minutes."

（105）The girl smiled brightly at the woman, to thank her.

（106）"I'd better take the bags over to the other side of the station," the man said. She smiled at him.

（107）"All right. Then come back and we'll finish the beer."

（108）He picked up the two heavy bags and carried them around the station to the other tracks. He looked up the tracks but could not see the train. Coming back, he walked through the barroom, where people waiting for the train were drinking. He drank an Anis at the bar and

---

的一片。

²⁰ 男人再次强调手术十分简单。

²¹ 这里说明他们去过很多地方，读者可以猜测二人的生活状态。

²² 女孩不懂西班牙语，需要男人帮忙翻译。

²³ 海明威的文字十分简洁，他自己说他是站着写初稿，以免写得冗长，但是坐着改，这样可以仔细斟酌。贝茨说："海明威所孜孜以求的，是眼睛和对象之间、对象和读者之间直接相通，产生光鲜如画的感受。为了达到这个目的，他斩伐了整座

looked at the people. They were all waiting reasonably for the train. He went out through the bead curtain. She was sitting at the table and smiled at him.

(109) "Do you feel better?" he asked.

(110) "I feel fine," she said. "There's nothing wrong with me. I feel fine."[23]

森林的冗言赘词，还原了基本枝干的清爽面目。他删去了解释、探讨、甚至议论；砍掉了一切花花绿绿的比喻；清除了古老神圣、毫无生气的文章俗套；直到最后，通过疏疏落落、经受了锤炼的文字，眼前才豁然开朗，能有所见。"

□ 精华赏析 □

　　语用学是研究在特定情景中的话语，即说话人（或作者）与听话人（或读者）使用语言进行交际时所传达的意义，所以有人认为语用学研究的是说话人的意义（speaker's meaning）、话语意义（utterance meaning）或者语境意义（contextual meaning）（刘世生，2006）。

　　语用学研究语言在使用中的意义，因此其中一些理论很容易被应用到文体学中来解释文学作品中语用的突出。本文拟用语用文体学对 Ernest Hemingway 的 *Hills Like White Elephants* 进行分析，从合作原则以及话论转换两个方面探讨这篇小说中语言使用展现出来的文体效果。

一、合作原则理论（Cooperative Principle）的运用

　　格莱斯（Grice）于 1976 年提出了自己的一套理论——合作原则（Cooperative Principle）。这一原则认为双方在交谈时必须遵守一些基本的原则。这些基本原则为：量的原则（Quantity Maxim），质的原则（Quality Maxim），关联原则（Relation Maxim）和方式原则（Manner Maxim）。所谓量的原则是指所说的话要包含当时交谈的必要信息，不要涉及不必要的信息；质的原则是指不说虚假的话，不说缺乏足够证据的话；关联原则是指整个话语要有关联；方式原则要求避免晦涩、歧义、啰嗦，并且要有条理。

　　但在实际的交谈中，尤其是在文学作品中，会话的合作原则常常被打破。打破的方式有违背（violate）和违反（flout）。违背是指为了隐瞒他人而对准则进行暗中破坏；违反是指说话人明显不遵守合作原则，这种违反往往是说话人含有其他的意思，需要听话人推导出来。

　　小说中的主人公为一对男女，他们在车站酒吧里展开了一段对话。海明威的"冰山理论"在这里显露无遗，通篇叙述者对男女主人公的情况、背景、心理活动没有给出任何讨论和评价，看起来就像是拍电报一样，语言简洁，真实记录了当时的场景，不加渲染，不做解释。初看此文，人们常常会觉得有些迷茫。

　　但是，如果我们仔细阅读，就会发现，在小说中合作原则被不断打破，这就成为我们理解作者写作意图和分析人物性格的一个重要突破口。让我们来看看"男人—女孩（Jig）"间的谈话。

　　例如：

"With water?"

"Do you want with water?"

"I don't know," the girl said. "It is good with water?"

"It's all right."

"You want them with water?" asked the women.

"Yes, with water."

"It takes like licorice," the girl said and put the glass down.

"That's the way with everything."

当女孩问男人"在酒里加水好吗?"男人没有向女孩做清晰、具体的解释,比如加水后会是什么味道,口感好不好等,他只随意地回答道"都还行吧",用这样的字眼敷衍女孩。男人此时违反了量的原则。

再如下面这段对话:

The girl looked across at the hills.

"They're lovely hills," she said. "They don't really look like white elephants. I just meant the coloring of their skin through the trees."

"Should we have another drink?"

"All right."

女孩儿对屋外的山很感兴趣,男人却打断了她的话,他问女孩:"我们再来点别的什么喝的吧?"男人在这里又违反了关联原则。

接下来,男人把话题引向了重点,我们再来看下面这段对话:

"It's really an awfully simple operation, Jig," the man said, "It's not really an operation at all."

The girl looked at the ground the table legs rested on.

"I know you wouldn't mind it, Jig. It's really not anything. It's just to let the air in."

The girl did not say anything.

"I'll go with you and I'll stay with you all the time. They just let the air in and then it's all perfectly natural."

男人在这里,提到了"operation",通过后文,我们可以猜测出这里的"operation"指的是堕胎。对于这样的手术,究竟是怎么回事,简单或是复杂,自然还是痛苦,男人并不清楚。但他却对自己根本不可能了解或体会的事情妄下定论。他在这里所说的话缺乏足够证据,违反了质的原则。

紧接着又是这样一段话:

"Well," the man said, "if you don't want to you don't have to. I wouldn't have you do it if you didn't want to. But I know it's perfectly simple."

"And you really want to?"

"I think it's the best thing to do. But I don't want you to do it if you don't really want to."

我们继续往下看,男人继续说道:

"I don't want you to do anything that you don't want to do."

"You've got to realize," he said, "that I don't want you to do it if you don't want to. I'm perfectly willing to go through with it if it means anything to you."

我们清楚地看到,一句"我不会强迫你做自己不想做的事情。"被男人前前后后重复了四遍,不符合方式原则中"简练,避免啰嗦"的要求。

在这篇不算长的小说中,主人公之一,这位连姓名都没出现的男人,几乎打破了合作原则中的所有准则。这是为什么呢?他在话语中暗示了些什么呢?

接下来,我们对上文所举的例子一一加以说明。

当男人打破量的原则时,我们可以看出他对女孩的谈话并没有太关注,或许他根本没有认真听她在说什么,所以给出了模棱两可的答案。我们可以这样猜测,男人可能根本不在乎、不关心身边这位女孩,对一个无关紧要的人提出的问题,也就可以理所当然地置之不理。但是从后文中我们发现,这对男女并不是酒吧里无意碰上的陌生人,他们是情侣。所以我们可以做出第二种猜测,可能男人心里正在想着另外一件事儿,才没注意女孩的问题,他可能正在思量自己接下来该说些什么。那么,让男人心猿意马的事情究竟是什么呢?我们带着这个问题继续读下去。

在接下来的例子中,男人打破了关联原则。女孩似乎对远处的山很感兴趣,但男人打断了她的话,他大概不想继续这个他认为不重要的话题,急于把谈话拉回正题。随着二人之间的对话继续,我们知道了男人急于谈论的是关于"手术"的话题。于是,这篇使人倍感困惑的小说此时终于让读者看到了一丝曙光。究竟是什么手术让男人着急、困惑、不知所措呢?

在第三个例子中,男人说手术很简单、很自然。真是这样吗?男人和女孩是情侣关系,又知道这个手术是影响他们之间感情的关键所在,聪明的读者已经猜出来了,"operation"就是堕胎手术。那么男人对手术的描述自然也就违反了质的原则。读者在这里也许会思考几个问题:(1)男人许诺只要打掉孩子他们的生活就会像以前一样幸福,是真的吗?(2)男人难道不知道堕胎会给女孩带来身体上和心理上的伤害吗?(3)男人真的爱女孩吗?

在第四个例子中,男人大概是找不出更好的理由说服女孩和自己,只得一遍一遍重复着"我不会勉强你做自己不愿意做的事情。"并且又不断重申,"不过,这个手术真的很简单。"

在男人不断打破合作原则的过程中,我们可以看到他虚伪、不负责任的一面。他没有真正去关心自己的爱人,"她想不想要这个孩子","堕胎手术会对她带来什么伤害"等,男人所想的、所做的只是在为自己考虑和打算,他不想承担责任,不想打破现有的生活,所以反复劝说女人堕胎,好让生活回归"正轨"。故事发生的地点在此时看来似乎也有些深意,车站的酒吧,提着行李的男人,暗示男人可能只是女孩生命中的一个匆匆过客。

二、权利和话轮转换(Power and Turn-taking)

权利包括身体权利、机构权利、社会权利、个人权利,和人物之间的话轮转换的关系十分密切,话轮能体现权利关系。话轮是由哈维·赛克斯(Harvey Sacks)、伊曼纽尔·谢高夫(Emanuel Schegolff)和盖尔·杰佛逊(Gail Jefferson)提出的。一般认为,话轮转换是指发话者与受话者不断交换所扮演的角色而形成的,即"发话者变为受话者,受话者变为发话者"。话轮分析框架可以大体由五个方面构成:(1)话题的提出和控制(initiation and control of topics);(2)话轮长度(turn length);(3)话轮类型(turn-type);(4)话语打断(interruption);(5)话轮控制策略(turn-control strategies)(刘世生,2006)。

这篇小说几乎全部由对话构成,下面我们按照以上五个方面分析一下男人—女孩之间体现出来的权利关系。

(一)话题的提出和控制

话题的提出和控制指的是话题由谁提出,又如何发展和改变,谁在控制话题等方面。

全文男人—女孩之间的话轮总数为 93 次,其中 54 次都是在谈论堕胎手术。而这个谈论最多的话题是由男人提出的,他成功控制了话题。女孩曾经三次提出关于山的话题,都没能继续下去。

(二)话轮的长度

话轮长度关心的是谁的话轮最长,话轮数目最多。

人 物	词 数	话轮数	平 均
男人	505	48	50.5
女孩(Jig)	425	45	42.5

男人的话轮最短的是 2 个单词,最长的 35 个。女孩的话轮最短的是 2 个单词,最长的 26 个。男人的话轮长于女孩的,再次证明男人是对话的主导方。

(三)话轮类型

话轮类型包括发话和反应。女孩刚到酒馆时,问男人墙上的字是什么意思,又问给酒里加水好喝吗,还几次追问对面的山像白象吗。男人的反应是要么敷衍了事,要么直接打断,他在小说的前一部分,常常显得急不可耐地要使自己成为发话方。可女孩却截然相反,她的几次发话都没成功,但在自己的话题被打断时,依然对男人的话题作出积极反应,给予答复。

我们可以清楚看出,不管男人怎么重申自己会尊重对方的决定,都不再可信。因为他作为两者之间的控制方,自然会成为事件的终极裁决者。他和女孩之间的地位是不平等的。另一方面,我们也发现,他在争夺发话权的过程中,也表现出对女孩的不够尊重,更谈不上关心了,明知女孩不懂西班牙语,也不打算帮她解释墙上的广告。在这个陌生的城市里,如果女孩都得不到自己爱人的体贴和关心,就显得更加孤立无援了。

(四)话语打断

话语打断指的是话轮的转换发生在话轮不应该终止的地方。

人 物	打断次数
男人	2
女孩(Jig)	3

男人打断女孩的话轮是在小说的前半部分,当女孩说:"Everything tastes of licorice. Especially all the things you've waited so long for, like absinthe." 显然这句话是有所指的,这里期待已久的东西大概就是那未出生的孩子。于是男人不悦地打断女孩"Oh, cut it out." 第二次打断女孩的话轮,原因是男人急于谈论自己想说的话题,于是他没有对女孩的山像白象的

话题给出回应,而是转换话题,道:"Should we have another drink?"

女孩打断男人的话轮全部出现在接近文章结尾的地方。一次是:

"All right. But you've got to realize —"

"I realize," the girl said. "Can't we maybe stop talking?"

第二次:

"Would you do something for me now?"

"I'd do anything for you."

"Would you please please please please please please stop talking?"

第三次,女孩喊道:"I'll scream."

第一次女孩还尽量客气地要求男人停下来、别说了。但到后面女孩连用了 7 个 "please",我们可以想象她已经对男人无可奈何了,此时她的忍受已经到了极限,威胁男人道:"你要是再不停止,我可要尖叫了。"

我们从女孩三次打断男人的话轮的方式,可以分析出她情绪的变化。在文章开始,她总是很合作地给男人以相应的回应,到结尾处,她连续三次打断男人的话轮,可见她对男人已经完全失去了信心。起初,她可能还奢望只要打掉孩子他们就可以回到从前,所以不断追问"你是爱我的吧","我们以后还是会幸福的吧"。可能女孩本打算为自己的爱人做出牺牲,只要他依然爱自己。最后,她终于幡然醒悟,认识到自己爱的人虚伪、不愿意承担责任、虚情假意,于是她想要尖叫,想要爆发,想要宣泄自己的感情。

(五)话轮控制策略

话轮控制策略即话轮分配规则,可大致分为两类:一类是当前说话人选择下一个谈话人或让出话题控制权的策略;另一类是说话人抢夺话题控制权并延续自己话轮的策略。一般情况下,会话者总是希望谈论自己想要谈论的话题,以达到自己的交际目的。为了谈论自己关心的话题,男人抢过话题,并成功延续了自己的话题。

三、结语

以上从合作原则以及话轮转换两方面探讨了《白象似的群山》中语言使用展现出来的文体效果。通过对文章的文体分析,我们可以洞悉到男人不仅主宰着男女之间的爱情,更控制着一个生命的存亡。而女孩在放弃做母亲的权利的同时,也不得不挥手告别自己的爱情。

参考文献

[1] 董衡巽,等编著. 美国文学简史[M]. 北京:人民文学出版社,1980.
[2] 胡壮麟. 语言学教程第三版[M]. 北京:北京大学出版社,2006.
[3] 刘世生. 文体学概论[M]. 北京:北京大学出版社,2006.
[4] 秦秀白. 英语语体和文体要略[M]. 上海:上海外语教育出版社,2001.
[5] 张汉熙. 高级英语教师用书[M]. 北京:外语教学与研究出版社,1995.

◪ 阅读思考 ◪

1. 小说中的女孩名叫 Jig，为什么没有出现男人的名字？

2. 请根据小说中的细节分析男人和女孩的性格特征。

3. 小说中的很多事物都具有象征意义，比如群山、白象、车展、火车、酒吧、行李箱等，你能分析下这些事物的象征意义分别是什么吗？

4. 有的评论家认为海明威是继马克·吐温之后对美国文学语言影响最大的作家，你同意这个说法吗？请结合两位作家的作品分析一下他们的语言特色。

3

Life of Ma Parker

Katherine Mansfield

【作品简介】

Life of Ma Parker(《帕克大妈的人生》)选自凯瑟琳·曼斯菲尔德(Katherine Mansfield)的短篇小说集《园会》(*The Garden Party*),是作者诸多女性主题小说中最具悲剧色彩的一篇。故事通过主人公绝望的内心世界描述了一位身处社会底层的老妇人的悲惨一生:七个孩子早逝,丈夫早年患肺病去世,女婿死于溃疡,小外孙因肺结核夭折,子女们个个都离她而去……处于社会边缘地位的帕克大妈在经济上无依无靠,精神上孤独绝望,人格被肆意践踏,她没有任何权利,没有任何社会地位,甚至连容她痛哭一场的地方都没有。

【作者简介】

凯瑟琳·曼斯菲尔德(1888—1923),生于新西兰,后移居英国,是英国短篇小说史上最重要的作家之一。在她短暂的一生中,著有短篇小说集《在一个德国公寓里》(*In a German Pension*)、《幸福》(*Bliss*)、《园会》(*The Garden Party*)、《鸽巢》(*The Dove's Nest*)等。曼斯菲尔德在短篇小说领域中突破传统小说的叙事风格,不断探索新的表现手法,广泛使用象征主义、意识流、情节淡化等多种写作技巧,具有典型的现代主义文学特征,为英国短篇小说和现代主义文学的发展做出了重要贡献。曼斯菲尔德塑造了众多的女性形象,尤其擅长通过女性细腻的内心活动刻画人物鲜明的个性,真实反映她们在生活重压下孤独的挣扎和精神的幻灭,具有浓郁的悲剧色彩。1923 年 1 月 9 日,常年罹患肺结核的曼斯菲尔德在法国枫丹白露逝世,年仅 35 岁。在她去世的半年前,中国诗人徐志摩曾和她见过一面,她去世后,徐志摩写下了那首有名的诗歌《哀曼殊斐儿》表达哀思。

(1) When the literary gentleman[1], whose flat old Ma Parker cleaned every Tuesday, opened the door to her that morning, he asked after[2] her grandson. Ma Parker stood on the doormat inside the dark little hall, and she stretched out her hand to help her gentleman shut the door before she replied. "We buried 'im yesterday, sir," she said quietly.

[1] literary gentleman:作家先生

[2] ask after:问候

（2）"Oh! dear me! I'm sorry to hear that," said the literary gentleman in a shocked tone. He was in the middle of his breakfast. He wore a very shabby dressing-gown and carried a <u>crumpled</u>³ newspaper in one hand. But he felt awkward. He could hardly go back to the warm sitting-room without saying something—something more. Then because these people <u>set such store by</u>⁴ funerals he said kindly, "I hope the funeral went off all right."

（3）"Beg <u>parding</u>⁵, sir?" said old Ma Parker huskily.

（4）<u>Poor old bird!</u>⁶ <u>She did look dashed.</u>⁷ "I hope the funeral was a—a—success," said he. Ma Parker gave no answer. She bent her head and hobbled off to the kitchen, <u>clasping</u>⁸ the old fish bag that held her cleaning things and an apron and a pair of felt shoes. The literary gentleman raised his eyebrows and went back to his breakfast.

（5）"Overcome, I suppose," he said aloud, helping himself to the <u>marmalade</u>⁹.

（6）Ma Parker drew the two <u>jetty spears</u>¹⁰ out of her <u>toque</u>¹¹ and hung it behind the door. She <u>unhooked</u>¹² her worn jacket and hung that up too. Then she tied her apron and sat down to take off her boots. To take off her boots or to put them on was an agony to her, but it had been an agony for years. <u>In fact, she was so accustomed to the pain that her face was drawn and screwed up ready for the twinge before she'd so much as untied the laces.</u>¹³ That over, she sat back with a sigh and softly rubbed her knees. …

（7）"<u>Gran</u>¹⁴! Gran!" Her little grandson stood on her lap in his button boots. He'd just come in from playing in the street.

（8）"Look what a state you've made your gran's skirt into—you wicked boy!"

（9）But he put his arms round her neck and rubbed his cheek against hers.

（10）"Gran, gi' us a penny!" he <u>coaxed</u>¹⁵.

（11）"<u>Be off with you: Gran ain't got no pennies.</u>¹⁶"

³ crumple /ˈkrʌmpl/ v. 使变皱；压皱

⁴ set... store by：重视；珍视

⁵ 应为 pardon。

⁶ 可怜的老太婆！（old bird：老家伙，带贬义）

⁷ 她看起来的确很消沉。

⁸ clasp /klɑːsp/ v. 握紧；抱紧

⁹ marmalade /ˈmɑːməleɪd/ n. 橘子酱

¹⁰ jetty spears：（插在帽子上的）帽针

¹¹ toque /təʊk/ n. 无边女帽

¹² unhook /ʌnˈhʊk/ v. 解开（衣服的）钩子

¹³ 实际上，她早就习惯了这种痛苦。在解鞋带时，她的脸就缩起来准备好承受阵阵疼痛了。（screw up：扭曲面部；twinge /twɪndʒ/ n. 阵痛；刺痛）

¹⁴ 即 grandma。从此处开始到第 17 段结束是 Ma Parker 的回忆。

¹⁵ coax /kəʊks/ v. 哄；劝

¹⁶ 奶奶可没有钱。

(12) "Yes, you 'ave. "

(13) "No, I ain't. "

(14) "Yes, you 'ave. Gi' us one!"

(15) Already she was feeling for the old, squashed[17], black leather purse.

(16) "Well, what'll you give your gran?"

(17) He gave a shy little laugh and pressed closer. She felt his eyelid quivering against her cheek. "I ain't got nothing," he murmured. …[18]

(18) The old woman sprang up, seized the iron kettle off the gas stove and took it over to the sink[19]. The noise of the water drumming in the kettle deadened her pain, it seemed.[20] She filled the pail[21], too, and the washing-up bowl[22].

(19) It would take a whole book to describe the state of that kitchen. During the week the literary gentleman "did"[23] for himself. That is to say, he emptied the tea-leaves now and again into a jam jar set aside for that purpose, and if he ran out of clean forks he wiped over one or two on the roller towel[24]. Otherwise, as he explained to his friends, his "system"[25] was quite simple, and he couldn't understand why people made all this fuss about[26] housekeeping.

(20) "You simply dirty everything you've got, get a hag in[27] once a week to clean up, and the thing's done."

(21) The result looked like a gigantic dustbin. Even the floor was littered[28] with toast crusts, envelopes, cigarette ends. But Ma Parker bore him no grudge[29]. She pitied the poor young gentleman for having no one to look after him. Out of the smudgy[30] little window you could see an immense expanse of sad-looking sky, and whenever there were clouds they looked very worn, old clouds, frayed at the edges, with holes in them, or dark stains like tea[31].

(22) While the water was heating, Ma Parker began sweeping the floor. "Yes," she thought, as the broom knocked, "what with one thing and another I've had my share.[32] I've had a hard life."

[17] squash /skwɔʃ/ v. 压扁

[18] 本故事穿插了几段 Ma Parker 的回忆，均以"…"符号标出。

[19] sink /sɪŋk/ n. 水槽

[20] 水流进水壶里发出咚咚声，似乎减缓了她的痛苦。

[21] pail /peɪl/ n. 桶

[22] washing-up bowl: 洗碗碟的盆

[23] 指"做家务"。

[24] 如果干净的餐叉用完了，他就拿一两个用过的在毛巾上擦擦接着用。

[25] 他的那一套（收拾家务的）做法。

[26] make a fuss about: 为……小题大做

[27] get a hag in: 雇一个老太婆（hag /hæg/ n. 老女人）

[28] litter /ˈlɪtə (r)/ v. 乱扔；使乱七八糟

[29] grudge /ɡrʌdʒ/ n. 怨恨

[30] smudgy /ˈsmʌdʒɪ/ adj. 有污迹的

[31] 这里使用了 metaphor 的修辞手法，把云比作破旧的布。（fray /freɪ/ v. 磨损）

[32] 倒霉事一件接一件，让我吃尽了苦头。

（23）Even the neighbours said that of her. Many a time, hobbling home with her fish bag, she heard them, waiting at the corner, or leaning over the area railings[33], say among themselves, "She's had a hard life, has Ma Parker." And it was so true she wasn't in the least proud of it. It was just as if you were to say she lived in the basement-back[34] at Number 27. A hard life! …

（24）At sixteen she'd left Stratford[35] and come up to London as kitchen-maid. Yes, she was born in Stratford-on-Avon. Shakespeare, sir? No, people were always arsking[36] her about him. But she'd never heard his name until she saw it on the theatres.

（25）Nothing remained of Stratford[37] except that "sitting in the fireplace of an evening you could see the stars through the chimley[38]," and "Mother always 'ad 'er side of bacon 'anging from the ceiling."[39] And there was something—a bush, there was—at the front door, that smelt ever so nice. But the bush was very vague.[40] She'd only remembered it once or twice in the hospital, when she'd been taken bad[41].

（26）That was a dreadful place—her first place[42]. She was never allowed out. She never went upstairs except for prayers morning and evening. It was a fair cellar.[43] And the cook was a cruel woman. She used to snatch[44] away her letters from home before she'd read them, and throw them in the range because they made her dreamy. … And the beedles[45]! Would you believe it? —until she came to London she'd never seen a black beedle. Here Ma always gave a little laugh, as though—not to have seen a black beedle! Well! It was as if to say you'd never seen your own feet.

（27）When that family was sold up she went as "help" to a doctor's house, and after two years there, on the run[46] from morning till night, she married her husband. He was a baker.

（28）"A baker, Mrs. Parker!" the literary gentleman would say. For occasionally he laid aside his tomes[47] and lent an ear[48], at least, to this product called

[33] 房屋地下室前面空地周围的栅栏。

[34] 地下室的后间。由于阴暗潮湿且光线不足，没人会愿意住地下室后间。

[35] 即 Stratford-on-Avon，位于英格兰中部沃里克郡的小镇斯特拉福，莎士比亚的故乡。

[36] 应为 asking（后文中 arsk、arsking 的拼写亦如此）

[37] 在斯特拉福的日子没有留下任何记忆。

[38] 应为 chimney。

[39] 妈妈总是把熏猪肉挂在天花板上。

[40] 关于灌木丛的印象也很模糊了。

[41] take bad：take ill

[42] 指她第一次帮佣的地方。

[43] 这地方比地窖强点罢了。

[44] snatch /snætʃ/ v. 一把夺过

[45] 应为 beetles。

[46] on the run：忙碌，奔波

[47] tome /təum/ n. 大部头书；巨著

[48] lend an ear：倾听（别人诉说）

life. "It must be rather nice to be married to a baker!"

(29) Mrs. Parker didn't look so sure.

(30) "Such a clean trade," said the gentleman.

(31) Mrs. Parker didn't look convinced.

(32) "And didn't you like handing the new loaves[49] to the customers?"

(33) "Well, sir," said Mrs. Parker, "I wasn't in the shop above a great deal. We had thirteen little ones and buried seven of them. If it wasn't the 'ospital[50] it was the infirmary[51], you might say!"

(34) "You might, indeed, Mrs. Parker!" said the gentleman, shuddering[52], and taking up his pen again.

(35) Yes, seven had gone, and while the six were still small her husband was taken ill with consumption[53]. It was flour on the lungs[54] the doctor told her at the time.… Her husband sat up in bed with his shirt pulled over his head, and the doctor's finger drew a circle on his back.

(36) "Now, if we were to cut him open here, Mrs. Parker," said the doctor, "you'd find his lungs chock-a-block[55] with white powder. Breathe, my good fellow!" And Mrs. Parker never knew for certain whether she saw or whether she fancied she saw a great fan of white dust come out of her poor dear husband's lips.[56]…

(37) But the struggle she'd had to bring up those six little children and keep herself to herself[57]. Terrible it had been! Then, just when they were old enough to go to school her husband's sister came to stop with them[58] to help things along, and she hadn't been there more than two months when she fell down a flight of steps and hurt her spine. And for five years Ma Parker had another baby—and such a one for crying! —to look after. Then young Maudie went wrong and took her sister Alice with her; the two boys emigrimated[59], and young Jim went to India with the army, and Ethel, the youngest, married a good-for-nothing little waiter who died of ulcers[60] the year little Lennie was born. And now little Lennie—my grandson. …

---

[49] loaf /ləʊf/ n. 一条面包

[50] 即 hospital。

[51] infirmary /ɪnˈfɜːmərɪ/ n. 诊所；医务室

[52] shudder /ˈʃʌdə(r)/ n. 战栗；发抖

[53] 这里指肺痨。

[54] 吸入过多面粉造成的尘肺。

[55] chock-a-block: 塞满的；充满的

[56] 扇面似的一大片白色粉末从她可怜的丈夫的嘴中喷出，帕克大妈一直不确定这是她亲眼所见还是臆想中的画面。(有的版本"dear"作"dead"。)

[57] keep herself to herself: 把一切都憋在心里

[58] stop with sb.: 与……暂住在一起

[59] 应为 emigrated。

[60] ulcer /ˈʌlsə(r)/ n. 溃疡

（38）The piles of dirty cups, dirty dishes, were washed and dried. The ink-black knives were cleaned with a piece of potato and finished off with a piece of cork[61]. The table was scrubbed[62], and the dresser and the sink that had sardine[63] tails swimming in it. ...

（39）He'd never been a strong child—never from the first. He'd been one of those fair babies that everybody took for a girl. Silvery fair curls he had, blue eyes, and a little freckle like a diamond on one side of his nose. The trouble she and Ethel had had to rear that child! The things out of the newspapers they tried him with![64] Every Sunday morning Ethel would read aloud while Ma Parker did her washing.

（40）"Dear Sir,—Just a line to let you know my little Myrtil was laid out for dead ... After four bottils ... gained 8 lbs. in 9 weeks, and is still putting it on."[65]

（41）And then the egg-cup of ink would come off the dresser and the letter would be written, and Ma would buy a postal order on her way to work next morning.[66] But it was no use. Nothing made little Lennie put it on[67]. Taking him to the cemetery, even never gave him a colour[68]; a nice shake-up in the bus never improved his appetite.[69]

（42）But he was gran's boy from the first. ...

（43）"Whose boy are you?" said old Ma Parker, straightening up from the stove and going over to the smudgy window. And a little voice, so warm, so close, it half stifled[70] her—it seemed to be in her breast under her heart—laughed out, and said, "I'm gran's boy!"

（44）At that moment there was a sound of steps, and the literary gentleman appeared, dressed for walking.

（45）"Oh, Mrs. Parker, I'm going out."

（46）"Very good, sir."

（47）"And you'll find your half-crown[71] in the tray of the inkstand."

（48）"Thank you, sir."

（49）"Oh, by the way, Mrs. Parker," said the literary gentleman quickly, "you didn't throw away any

[61] cork /kɔːk/ n. 软木塞
[62] scrub /skrʌb/ v. 擦洗，刷洗
[63] sardine /ˌsɑːˈdiːn/ n. 沙丁鱼

[64] 自己和埃塞尔抚养这个孩子花费了多少工夫啊。她们甚至从报纸上找法子给他试。
[65] 这是 Ethel 读的报纸上的一封读者来信，是某药物的广告。（bottils 应为 bottles；lb：英美重量单位"磅"。）

[66] 这里是说帕克大妈根据报纸上的广告写信给外孙买药。
[67] put on：增长（体重）
[68] 也没让他脸上有点血色。
[69] 公交车上那么颠簸也没让他胃口好点。

[70] stifle /ˈstaɪfl/ v.（使）窒息

[71] half-crown：克朗为英国旧币，半克朗相当于两先令六便士

cocoa[72] last time you were here—did you?"

(50) "No, sir. "

(51) "Very strange. I could have sworn I left a teaspoonful of cocoa in the tin. " He broke off. He said softly and firmly, "You'll always tell me when you throw things away—won't you, Mrs. Parker?" And he walked off very well pleased with himself[73], convinced, in fact, he'd shown Mrs. Parker that under his apparent carelessness he was as vigilant[74] as a woman.

(52) The door banged. She took her brushes and cloths into the bedroom. But when she began to make the bed, smoothing, tucking[75], patting, the thought of little Lennie was unbearable. Why did he have to suffer so? That's what she couldn't understand. Why should a little angel child have to arsk for his breath and fight for it? There was no sense in making a child suffer like that.

(53) … From Lennie's little box of a chest there came a sound as though something was boiling. There was a great lump[76] of something bubbling in his chest that he couldn't get rid of. When he coughed, the sweat sprang out on his head; his eyes bulged, his hands waved, and the great lump bubbled as a potato knocks in a saucepan[77]. But what was more awful than all was when he didn't cough he sat against the pillow and never spoke or answered, or even made as if he heard. Only he looked offended.

(54) "It's not your poor old gran's doing it, my lovey[78], " said old Ma Parker, patting back the damp hair from his scarlet ears. But Lennie moved his head and edged away[79]. Dreadfully offended with her he looked—and solemn. He bent his head and looked at her sideways as though he couldn't have believed it of his gran.

(55) But at the last … Ma Parker threw the counterpane[80] over the bed. No, she simply couldn't think about it. It was too much—she'd had too much in her life to bear. She'd borne it up till now, she'd kept herself to herself, and never once had she been seen to cry. Never by a living soul. Not even her own children had seen Ma

[72] cocoa /ˈkəʊkəʊ/ n. 可可粉

[73] 洋洋自得地走开了

[74] vigilant /ˈvɪdʒɪlənt/ adj. 警觉的；警惕的

[75] tuck /tʌk/ v. (把床单的边缘)塞进,掖好(床单的)边角

[76] lump /lʌmp/ n. 肿块

[77] 就像土豆在炖锅里翻滚一样 (saucepan /ˈsɔːspən/ n. 炖锅,深平底锅)

[78] 应为 love。

[79] edge away: 悄悄离开,缓缓移动

[80] counterpane /ˈkaʊntəpeɪn/ n. 床单,床罩

break down[81]. She'd kept a proud face always. But now! Lennie gone—what had she? She had nothing. He was all she'd got from life, and now he was took too[82]. Why must it all have happened to me? She wondered. "What have I done?" said old Ma Parker. "What have I done?"

（56）As she said those words she suddenly let fall her brush. She found herself in the kitchen. Her misery was so terrible that she pinned on her hat, put on her jacket and walked out of the flat like a person in a dream. She did not know what she was doing. She was like a person so dazed by the horror of what has happened that he walks away—anywhere, as though by walking away he could escape.[83] ...

（57）It was cold in the street. There was a wind like ice. People went flitting[84] by, very fast; the men walked like scissors; the women trod[85] like cats. And nobody knew—nobody cared. Even if she broke down, if at last, after all these years, she were to cry, she'd find herself in the lockup[86] as like as not[87].

（58）But at the thought of crying it was as though little Lennie leapt in his gran's arms. Ah, that's what she wants to do, my dove. Gran wants to cry. If she could only cry now, cry for a long time, over everything, beginning with her first place and the cruel cook, going on to the doctor's, and then the seven little ones, death of her husband, the children's leaving her, and all the years of misery that led up to Lennie. But to have a proper cry[88] over all these things would take a long time. All the same, the time for it[89] had come. She must do it. She couldn't put it off any longer; she couldn't wait any more. ... Where could she go?

（59）"She's had a hard life, has Ma Parker." Yes, a hard life, indeed! Her chin began to tremble; there was no time to lose. But where? Where?

（60）She couldn't go home; Ethel was there. It would frighten Ethel out of her life.[90] She couldn't sit on a bench anywhere; people would come arsking her questions. She couldn't possibly go back to the

---

[81] break down：感情失控

[82] 现在他也被夺走了。（took 应为 taken）

[83] 她像是一个被经历的什么可怕的事情吓得完全不知所措的人，只想一走了之——去哪儿无所谓，好像走开了就能逃离这一切。

[84] flit /flɪt/ v. 迅速飞过；掠过

[85] tread /tred/ v. 行走；踩；踏（过去式：trod；过去分词：trodden）

[86] lockup /ˈlɒkʌp/ n. 监狱

[87] like 应为 likely。（as likely as not：很可能）

[88] have a proper cry：尽情地大哭一场

[89] 此处及本段后面的几处 it 都是指"have a proper cry"。

[90] 那样会把埃塞尔吓坏的。

gentleman's flat; she had no right to cry in strangers' houses. If she sat on some steps a policeman would speak to her.

(61) Oh, wasn't there anywhere where she could hide and keep herself to herself and stay as long as she liked, not disturbing anybody, and nobody worrying her? Wasn't there anywhere in the world where she could have her cry out—at last?

(62) Ma Parker stood, looking up and down. The icy wind blew out her apron into a balloon. And now it began to rain. There was nowhere.

精华赏析

　　19世纪后半叶,现实主义文学在西方文坛发展得如火如荼,涌现出了一大批杰出的作家,如巴尔扎克、狄更斯、托尔斯泰、马克·吐温等。与此同时,一种新的文化思潮正在酝酿、形成,这就是对整个20世纪世界文学产生巨大影响的现代主义文学。与现实主义传统倡导的忠实再现外部现实生活的主张不同,现代主义文学以非理性主义哲学为思想基础,更加注重人物的心理现实,以个体心灵活动作为文学表达的主要对象,在表现形式上追求大胆革新,有着反传统和标新立异的鲜明特征。在众多的现代主义文学流派中,以表达人的精神世界和意识活动见长的意识流小说独树一帜,在20世纪二三十年代的英、法、美等国形成了一个颇为壮观的文学派别。

　　意识流(stream of consciousness)是美国哲学家、心理学家威廉·詹姆士提出的概念,用来表示意识的流动性和不间断性。意识流小说多采用情节淡化、内心独白、自由联想、时空交替、视角转换、象征暗示等表现手法来构思篇章,塑造人物形象。凯瑟琳·曼斯菲尔德的小说创作具有明显的现代主义特征,而意识流就是她娴熟运用的具有现代主义风格的写作技巧之一。下面以《帕克大妈的人生》为例,分析意识流手法在该小说中的体现。

一、内心独白

　　内心独白是指作品中的人物对其内心活动、意识世界的独自告白,是人物的心理语言,是没有声音介质的意识层面的语言(王晓煜,2006)。意识流小说主要描写故事中人物复杂多变的内心世界和意识活动,所以作者往往使用大量的内心独白来展示人物的形象。《帕克大妈的人生》全文只有两千多词,却成功讲述了帕克大妈心酸艰难的一生。她人生中主要的经历,如童年生活,离开家乡后的第一份工作,婚姻生活,丈夫去世,子女们悲惨的现状,外孙的早夭,都是靠帕克大妈自己大量的内心独白展示的。从她轻轻揉着膝盖回忆和外孙嬉闹的温馨场景开始,读者如同倾听一位絮语不止的老人的讲述,真实地感受着她内心的压抑、孤独和绝望。

人物大量的内心独白串联在一起,内心世界和现实生活水乳交融,形成一个完整、清晰的故事结构——贫病交加的童年、悲惨绝望的中年、孤苦寂寞的老年,帕克大妈的一生如同一幅画卷徐徐展现在读者面前。人物的独白纯粹是人物自己的真实意识的流露,在这个过程中,读者很少能看到作者的行迹。作者退出小说,主观干预较少,注重表现人物的意识活动本身。这与传统心理小说中作者的身份和角色完全不同,也构成了意识流小说的一个显著特征。

二、自由联想

心理学中的联想是指由某人或某事物而想起其他相关的人或事物的心理活动,因此联想可以为一个事物和另外一个事物建立联系,并且整合在人们的意识当中。通常,联想是基于事物之间的关联性的,因此受意志支配和控制。而在意识流小说中,人物的意识活动可以在不同时间和空间中自由穿梭,不受意志的控制。这种联想稍纵即逝,任何外在的刺激都可以打断人物从前的思维过程而展开新的思绪。在《帕克大妈的人生》中,自由联想主要通过时空交替和叙述人称转换这两种技巧得以实现。

首先是故事的时空结构。在小说开始时,帕克大妈来到做工的主人家里,她走进厨房,艰难地脱掉靴子,此时仍然是现实的场景。然而下一个瞬间,或许是膝盖的疼痛产生的刺激,帕克大妈的思绪回到了过去,她回忆起了小外孙在她膝上讨要零钱的场景。当读者仍然沉浸在这温馨的场景中时,下一刻故事又回到了帕克大妈做工的厨房。她开始忙碌起来,扫帚撞击地面的声音又一次刺激着她的思绪,帕克大妈不禁感叹自己悲惨的命运:"What with one thing and another I've had my share. I've had a hard life."然后故事的场景再次变换到她的邻居,以及她的家乡斯特拉福、她第一次做工的地方、她不幸的家庭……时间和空间不停交替,现实与回忆交叠呈现,令读者目不暇接。意识流小说打破了传统小说的时空观念,消除了逻辑时间界限,将人物意识活动中的过去、现在和将来拧在一起,以心理时间构建作品。这种蒙太奇的多重时空结构为人物的自由联想提供了最大的空间,能够更真实地展现人物的内心世界和意识活动。

其次是故事的叙述人称。传统小说一般使用第一人称或者第三人称叙事,通常情况下一个作品里的叙述角度是统一的。《帕克大妈的人生》主要采用第三人称叙述,但是正如上文所述,作者的声音虽有出现,但只起到引导故事发展和解释人物内心活动的作用,作者不再是"全知全能"的叙述者。在小说的第37段,帕克大妈回忆起丈夫死后子女们的命运,"Then young Maudie went wrong and took her sister Alice with her; the two boys emigrimated, and young Jim went to India with the army, and Ethel, the youngest, married a good-for-nothing little waiter who died of ulcers the year little Lennie was born. And now little Lennie——my grandson."作者在讲述几个子女时用的第三人称,而下面提到小外孙时突然转换成了第一人称。这种叙述人称的跳转还发生在小说第58段,"But at the thought of crying it was as though little Lennie leapt in his gran's arms. Ah, that's what she wants to do, my dove."叙述视角的变化把读者的注意力从对人物现实生活的客观描述突转到人物更加复杂的内心世界,也为人物的自由联想提供了最大便利。

三、情节淡化

情节是叙事性文学作品的内容构成要素之一，完整的情节包括故事的开始、发展、高潮和最终的结局。传统小说往往具有连贯、清晰的故事情节，情节的推进通常是以物理时空为本位的线性结构模式，以狄更斯、萨克雷、乔治·艾略特、勃朗特姐妹为代表的维多利亚时期的作家都善于在作品中编织跌宕起伏的故事情节。与这种创作范式不同，曼斯菲尔德的小说大多以人物复杂多变的意识活动为主，缺乏传统小说的完整性和连贯性，其情节主要由一系列的日常细节和琐碎片段构成，并通过人物的心理活动融合、展现出来。

《帕克大妈的人生》没有惊心动魄的故事情节，小说只展示了人物一个上午几个小时的生活细节，这些琐碎片段由帕克大妈的意识活动串联起来，故事的发展不受时间和空间的限制。小说也没有明显的高潮和冲突，最后帕克大妈来到大街上，想放声痛哭又找不到哭的地方，故事戛然而止，也没有明确交代最后的结局。可见，在整个故事中，情节被淡化，而人物的主观意识得以突出，人物的形象更加饱满，读者的参与性更强。

四、象征暗示

象征、隐喻是意识流小说常用的创作技巧，用具体的形象表达抽象的概念，以细节描写传达深刻的内涵，这在曼斯菲尔德的很多小说中非常普遍。例如，帕克大妈疼痛的膝盖象征着她辛劳痛苦的一生，故事结尾处她那被风吹得圆鼓鼓的围裙象征她在别人眼里无足轻重而又无依无靠的一生，等等。此外，小说提到帕克大妈是莎士比亚的同乡，这个细节也传达了丰富的内涵。莎士比亚是西方世界妇孺皆知的伟大文学家，其作品对整个欧洲文学产生了巨大的影响，因此莎士比亚的故乡斯特拉福镇在西方人心中有着崇高的地位。帕克大妈十六岁之前就生活在这个地方，但童年在她模糊的记忆里却只有贫穷和疾病，甚至连莎士比亚的名字也是她在离开家乡之后才知道的！莎士比亚主要靠创作宫廷题材的戏剧娱乐英国王室及贵族阶层，作品中对底层贫苦阶层的生活很少关注。曼斯菲尔德以古讽今，从帕克大妈的视角嘲讽了英国上流社会文人阶层的虚无和虚伪。

《帕克大妈的人生》是曼斯菲尔德的短篇小说中比较有代表性的作品，作者娴熟地运用了多种现代主义文学的表现手法，形成了自己独特的风格。曼斯菲尔德的现代短篇小说创作充满了探索与创新，推动了英国短篇小说走向成熟。跟与她同时代的意识流作家乔伊斯和伍尔芙一样，曼斯菲尔德对英国以及整个现代主义文学的发展做出了卓越的贡献，因此在英国文学史上占有重要的地位，在世界范围内拥有众多读者。

参考文献

王晓煜. 论意识流小说的表现技法[J]. 沈阳师范大学学报(社会科学版), 2006(5):59.

阅读思考

1. 为什么说现代主义文学是反传统的文学流派?
2. 评论界对意识流小说一直褒贬不一,争议不断,你怎么看?

Chapter Two   Individual and Family

Happy families are all alike; every unhappy family is unhappy in its own way.

Leo Tolstoy

Anna Karenine

幸福的家庭都是相似的;不幸的家庭各有各的不幸。

——(俄)列夫·托尔斯泰《安娜·卡列尼娜》

4

The Sight of Father's Back

Zhu Ziqing

【作品简介】

1917 年,由于祖母去世,在北京大学读书的朱自清返乡奔丧。办完丧事后,父子同到南京,父亲亲自把儿子送上北上的火车,并为儿子选座椅,买橘子,反复叮嘱儿子,再三嘱托陪行的茶房,一幕幕细节,令人动容。朱自清的这篇回忆散文《背影》(*The Sight of Father's Back*)之所以能引起人们的普遍共鸣,就在于它真实、细腻地刻画了一个典型的"中国式父亲"。我们都有这样一位父亲,他表达爱的方式不会那么明显,却在家庭中默默付出,关心着孩子的成长,为我们撑起一片天空。

本文选自张培基译注,1999 年上海外语教育出版社出版的《英译中国现代散文选》。

【作者简介】

朱自清(1898—1948),原名自华,号实秋,字佩弦,原籍浙江绍兴,出生于江苏省东海县(今连云港市东海县平明镇),后随父定居扬州,中国现代散文家、诗人、学者、民主战士,所著《匆匆》《春》《背影》《荷塘月色》等都是中国现代文学史上脍炙人口、广为传诵的名篇。朱自清于 1916 年考入北京大学预科,次年升入北大本科哲学系,于 1919 年开始发表诗歌。1922 年,朱自清和俞平伯、叶圣陶等人共同创办了《诗》月刊,这是中国现代文学史上第一个诗刊。次年,朱自清发表散文《桨声灯影里的秦淮河》,受到文学界广泛的赞誉,从此由诗歌转向散文创作。朱自清在 1925 年任清华中文系教授,1928 年出版第一本散文集《背影》,1931 年留学英国,进修语言学和英国文学。留学期间他漫游欧洲,著有《欧游杂记》和《伦敦杂记》。朱自清于 1932 年回国,任清华大学中国文学系主任;后来又随校南迁,任西南联大教授。1946 年 10 月他返回北平,继续教书治学,并积极参加民主运动。朱自清是一位有良知、有气节的爱国主义民主斗士,为抗议美国的扶日政策,在身染重病、生活极度贫困的状况下,宁死不吃美国救济粮。1948 年 8 月 12 日,朱自清因胃穿孔病逝于北平,年仅 50 岁。

【译者简介】

张培基(1921—2021),福建福州市人,中国当代著名翻译家,1945 年毕业于上海圣约翰大学英文系;曾在远东国际军事法庭担任英文翻译,随后赴美国印第安纳大学留学;1949 年回国后,先后在中国人民解放军外国语学校(今洛阳解放军外国语学院)和对外经贸大学任教。

张培基翻译了大量 20 世纪初以来中国文学史上的散文名篇,这些译文后来被收进《英译中国现代散文选》结集出版,深受英语爱好者的欢迎;他编撰的《英汉翻译教程》也是国内英语专业翻译课程的经典教材。

（1）It is more than two years since I last saw father, and what I can never forget is the sight of his back. Misfortunes never come singly. In the winter of more than two years ago, grandma died and father lost his job. I left Beijing for Xuzhou to join father in hastening home to attend grandma's funeral. When I met father in Xuzhou, the sight of the disorderly mess in his courtyard[1] and the thought of grandma started tears trickling down my cheeks. Father said, "Now that things've come to such a pass, it's no use crying. Fortunately, Heaven always leaves one a way out."

（2）After arriving home in Yangzhou, father paid off debts by selling or pawning[2] things. He also borrowed money to meet the funeral expenses. Between grandma's funeral and father's unemployment, our family was then in reduced circumstances. After the funeral was over, father was to go to Nanjing to look for a job and I was to return to Beijing to study, so we started out together.

（3）I spent the first day in Nanjing strolling about with some friends at their invitation, and was ferrying[3] across the Yangtse River to Pukou[4] the next morning and thence taking a train for Beijing on the afternoon of the same day. Father said he was too busy to go and see me off at the railway station, but would ask a hotel waiter that he knew to accompany me there instead. He urged the waiter again and again to take good care of me, but still did not quite trust him. He hesitated for quite a while about what to do. As a matter of fact, nothing would matter at all because I was then twenty and had already travelled on the Beijing-Pukou Railway a couple of times. After some wavering[5], he finally decided that he himself would accompany me to the station. I repeatedly tried to talk him out of it, but he only said, "Never mind! It won't do to trust guys like those hotel

[1] 朱自清的父亲朱鸿钧此前在徐州任榷运局长,即"烟酒公卖局长",那是一个公认的肥差。他在扬州老家的潘姓姨太因不满他在徐州纳妾,赶去大闹了一场,朱鸿钧因此丢了差事,非常颓废。受此事影响,朱自清的祖母在老家去世。从北京回家奔丧的朱自清先到徐州与"交卸"的父亲会合,所以才有"满院狼藉"之说。

[2] pawn /pɔːn/ v. 质押;典当

[3] ferry /ˈferɪ/ v.（用船或飞机）运送（人或货物）
[4] 今南京市浦口区。

[5] waver /ˈweɪvə(r)/ v. 犹豫不决;举棋不定

boys!"

(4) We entered the railway station after crossing the River. While I was at the booking office buying a ticket, father saw to⁶ my luggage. There was quite a bit of luggage and he had to bargain with the porter over the fee. I was then such a smart aleck⁷ that I frowned upon⁸ the way father was haggling⁹ and was on the verge of¹⁰ chipping in¹¹ a few words when the bargain was finally clinched¹². Getting on the train with me, he picked me a seat close to the carriage door. I spread on the seat the brownish furlined¹³ overcoat he had got a tailor made for me. He told me to be watchful on the way and be careful not to catch cold at night. He also asked the train attendants to take good care of me. I sniggered at father for being so impractical, for it was utterly useless to entrust me to those attendants, who cared for nothing but money. Besides, it was certainly no problem for a person of my age to look after himself. Oh, when I come to think of it, I can see how smarty I was in those days!

(5) I said, "Dad, you might leave now." But he looked out of the window and said, "I'm going to buy you some tangerines¹⁴. You just stay here. Don't move around." I caught sight of several vendors¹⁵ waiting for customers outside the railings¹⁶ beyond a platform. But to reach that platform would require crossing the railway track and doing some climbing up and down. That would be a strenuous¹⁷ job for father, who was fat. I wanted to do all that myself, but he stopped me, so I could do nothing but let him go. I watched him hobble towards the railway track in his black skullcap, black cloth mandarin jacket and dark blue cotton-padded cloth long gown. He had little trouble climbing down the railway track, but it was a lot more difficult for him to climb up that platform after crossing the railway track. His hands held onto the upper part of the platform, his legs huddled up and his corpulent¹⁸ body tipped slightly towards the left, obviously making an enormous exertion¹⁹. While I was watching him from behind, tears gushed²⁰ from my eyes. I quickly wiped them away lest he or others should catch me

⁶ see to: 照料；照看

⁷ smart aleck: 自作聪明、自以为是的人

⁸ frown upon: 反对；不赞成

⁹ haggle /'hægl/ v. 争论；讲价

¹⁰ on the verge of: 濒临于；即将

¹¹ chip in: 插嘴；插话

¹² clinch /klɪntʃ/ v. 最终确定或解决

¹³ furlined: (衣物)皮毛里衬的

¹⁴ tangerine /ˌtændʒə'riːn/ n. 橘子

¹⁵ vendor /'vendə(r)/ n. 摊贩

¹⁶ railing /'reɪlɪŋz/ n. (常作复数)栏杆；栅栏

¹⁷ strenuous /'strenjuəs/ adj. 费力的；艰苦的

¹⁸ corpulent /'kɔːpjʊlənt/ adj. 发福的

¹⁹ exertion /ɪg'zɜːʃn/ n. 努力；尽力；费力

²⁰ gush /gʌʃ/ v. 喷出；涌出；冒出

crying. The next moment when I looked out of the window again, father was already on the way back, holding bright red tangerines in both hands. In crossing the railway track, he first put the tangerines on the ground, climbed down slowly and then picked them up again. When he came near the train, I hurried out to help him by the hand. After boarding the train with me, he laid all the tangerines on my overcoat, and patting the dirt off his clothes, he looked somewhat relieved and said after a while, "I must be going now. Don't forget to write me from Beijing!" I gazed after his back retreating out of the carriage. After a few steps, he looked back at me and said, "Go back to your seat. Don't leave your things alone." I, however, did not go back to my seat until his figure was lost among crowds of people hurrying to and fro and no longer visible. My eyes were again wet with tears.

(6) In recent years, both father and I have been living an unsettled life, and the circumstances of our family going from bad to worse. Father left home to seek a livelihood²¹ when young and did achieve quite a few things all on his own. To think that he should now be so downcast in old age!²² The discouraging state of affairs filled him with an uncontrollable feeling of deep sorrow, and his pent-up²³ emotion had to find a vent²⁴. That is why even mere domestic trivialities²⁵ would often make him angry, and meanwhile he became less and less nice with me. However, the separation of the last two years has made him more forgiving towards me. He keeps thinking about me and my son. After I arrived in Beijing, he wrote me a letter, in which he says, "I'm all right except for a severe pain in my arm. I even have trouble using chopsticks or writing brushes. Perhaps it won't be long now before I depart this life." Through the glistening tears which these words had brought to my eyes I again saw the back of father's corpulent form in the dark blue cotton-padded cloth long gown and the black cloth mandarin jacket. Oh, how I long to see him again!

²¹ livelihood /ˈlaɪvlɪhʊd/ n. 赚钱谋生的手段；生计
²² 朱鸿钧自徐州失业后，便仕途坎坷、生活渐拙，以至于老境颓唐，在1945年去世，终年76岁。
²³ pent-up：压抑的；积压的
²⁴ vent /vent/ n.（气体、液体的）出口
²⁵ triviality /ˌtrɪvɪˈælətɪ/ n. 琐事；小事

▣ 精华赏析 ▣

我们学习一个新的单词时，除了会读、会写，还要掌握其意义，这样才能真正把这个词用起来。词义（word meaning）是词汇学习最重要、最核心的部分，也是最难的部分。这是因为，一个单词的发音和拼写通常是唯一的，但在大多数情况下，它的意义却不止一个。以单词"heart"为例，《牛津高阶英汉双解词典》在该词条下列出来的意义有 8 条，还不包括它在相关短语、习语中的种种用法。该词的第一条意义为"hollow muscular organ that pumps blood through the body"，即人和动物的心脏器官。其他意义还包括"心形物""心灵、心肠""热心、热情""事物的中心、核心""要点、实质""菜心""心爱之人"等。但是，如果我们仔细分析这些意义之间的关系，就不难发现，后面的众多意义都是建立在该词的第一条意义之上的，是对第一条意义的发展、延伸。

语义研究上把词汇的基本意义称为词汇的外延意义（denotative meaning），而建立在基本意义之上的附加意义称为词汇的内涵意义（connotative meaning）。外延意义是词的字面意义（literal meaning），又叫概念意义（conceptual meaning），往往就是该词在字典上的第一个意义；内涵意义则是由外延意义引申而来的隐含意义（implied meaning）或者暗示意义（suggested meaning），是相对于词汇概念意义的"言外之意"。举例来说，"home"的外延意义是"人居住的地方"，但同时也有"温暖""舒适""安全"等诸多内涵意义。从语义成分的角度来看，单词"man"可以被描述为"人类""男性""成年的"（human, male, adult）。这三个义素组成了单词"man"的外延意义，不分种族、年龄、外貌、身份，甚至也不论生死，只要符合这三个特征，就可以被称为 man。但是，当你竖起大拇指，对一个男人说"You are a man！"的时候，你所传达的就不再是这个词的外延意义了，你可能是夸他敢担当，有责任心，或者威武英勇，或者坚定果断，或者刚正不阿，又或者力大无穷，这些含义附加在"man"这个词的外延意义之上，是对其外延意义的补充，反映了人们对该词的情感态度。可见，相对于词义较为单一的外延，词义的内涵更加丰富、复杂，而词义由外延到内涵的发展过程，也体现了人类认知世界的历程。

词义的内涵具有普遍性和民族性，其普遍性反映了人类认知的共性。以"stepmother"一词为例，它在东西方文化里的内涵意义几乎一样。在西方，不管是经典童话"灰姑娘""白雪公主"里的后妈，还是希腊神话里佛里克索斯的继母伊诺，都是迫害、折磨继子女的恶毒女性形象。中国有记载的最早的继母可以追溯到舜，相传他的后母联合舜的父亲瞽叟和自己的亲儿子象几次迫害舜。建安七子之一的阮瑀也在《驾出北郭门行》中描写过一个孤儿受后母虐待的悲惨故事："亲母舍我殁，后母憎孤儿。饥寒无衣食，举动鞭捶施。骨消肌肉尽，体若枯树皮。"另外，像"芦衣顺母""卧冰求鲤"等在中国民间广为流传的故事中，继母们都是搬弄是非、玩弄手段、虐待继子女的毒妇形象。词义的普遍性使语言可学、可知，是千变万化的内涵意义产生的基础。

词义的民族性是说词义体现了不同民族特有的社会文化与民族心理，也就是说，反映同一客观事物的词语，在不同的语言中受到不同的文化因素的影响，会产生不同的语义内涵。众所周知，红色在中国文化里占据着重要的地位，是当之无愧的"国色"：我们的国旗、国徽的主色调是红色,传统婚礼上到处都是红色元素,春节张贴的对联也是喜庆的"中国红"。所以,在汉语里带有"红"字的词语也多表示红火、好运、成功、繁荣、忠诚、美丽等,如"红榜""红利""大红大紫""红脸""红颜"等。然而,在西方文化里,"red"却带有"war""disaster""bleeding""fire""danger""fear""anger""wildness""pornography"等含义,英语里跟该词相关的短语如"red-headed""red-ruin""red battle""red hands""red light district""to see red"等皆包含负面、消极的语义内涵。词义的民族性对于跨文化交际尤为重要,因为词义内涵的差异是跨文化交际的主要障碍,错误的解读很容易导致误会,产生不必要的矛盾甚至冲突。

词汇的内涵意义对于文本的解读是十分有价值的。例如下面这段话,A professor of mathematics at the university was about to conduct an experiment which, as they all anticipated, was doomed to end in failure. This young man was brash enough to challenge a theory of the great Aristotle, and now he was going to turn himself into the laughing stock of Pisa. 年轻的数学教授即将实施一项实验,来挑战伟大的亚里士多德的理论,而读者是否能从文字里读懂当时的人们对于实验的态度,关键取决于读者是否真正理解了"doomed"和"brash"等词的内涵。单词"doomed"来源于基督教的"doomsday",即上帝审判世人的世界末日,而"brash"本身就有贬义的情感内涵。这两个词的使用暗示了人们对于这个科学家的实验是抱着完全看笑话似的不屑一顾的态度的。再如,小说《德伯家的苔丝》中的女主人公苔丝一出场,作者特意提到她的头发上系着一根"红色的发带"。如果读者不了解红色在西方文化里的消极内涵,就不会理解作者是从故事一开始就铺垫了女主人公的悲惨命运。

词义的内涵对于外语学习,特别是翻译练习也具有极大的指导意义。在本文中,朱自清描写父亲的背影时,两次用到了"肥胖"这个词:"他肥胖的身子向左倾斜……"(第5段),"在晶莹的泪光中,又看见那肥胖的、青布棉袍黑布马褂的背影……"(第6段)。"肥胖"这个略带贬义倾向的中性词语,在英文中对应很多单词,例如fat, obese, stout, portly, fleshy, tubby, flabby, overweight, large, 等等。但张培基的译文两处都使用了"corpulent"这个词,这是因为这个词虽有"肥胖"之意,但却带有褒义的词义内涵,专指人的发福之态,与本文的情感基调十分吻合。此外,原文第4段中作者回想起自己当初对待父亲的态度,两次提到自己是"聪明过分""太聪明了"。"聪明"一词本具褒义,但译者却分别使用了"smarty aleck"和"smarty"这两个具有贬义内涵的词语,准确传达了作者懊悔的内心情绪。在翻译过程中,译者能准确把握原文词语的内涵意义,通过恰当选词使译文做到传神达意,这反映了译者深厚的语言功底和高超的翻译技巧,也是我们作为英语学习者应该学习和努力的地方。

▢ 阅读思考 ▢

1. 怎样看待词义的普遍性和民族性?两者是什么样的关系?
2. 词汇的内涵意义是不固定的,决定词义内涵的因素是什么?

5

Loving Memories of Mother

Zhu De

【作品简介】

1944 年,朱德的母亲钟太夫人在四川老家去世。惊闻噩耗,朱德悲痛不已,写下了回忆性散文《回忆我的母亲》(*Loving Memories of Mother*)(收入《朱德选集》)。在文中,作者用朴素的语言回忆了母亲平凡而又伟大的一生,饱含真情,感人至深。在作者的回忆中,母亲勤劳简朴、善良宽厚、坚韧不屈、任劳任怨,有着旧时代中国底层劳动妇女身上的一切优秀品格。她识大体、顾大局,其言传身教引导作者走上了革命道路。作者受母亲培养、影响,心中充满对母亲无限的深情和感激。

本文选自张培基译注,1999 年上海外语教育出版社出版的《英译中国现代散文选》。

【作者简介】

朱德(1886—1976),字玉阶,四川仪陇人;1909 年考入云南陆军讲武堂,同年加入中国同盟会;1911 年在云南投身辛亥革命,参加过反对袁世凯复辟帝制的护国战争和反对北洋军阀段祺瑞的护法战争;1922 年赴德国,同年加入中国共产党;1925 年到苏联学习军事,次年回国;1927 年参加八一南昌起义,任起义军第九军副军长;1928 年参与领导湘南起义,建立工农民主政权,率起义军上井冈山,同毛泽东领导的部队会师,成立了中国工农革命军(后改称红军)第四军;抗日战争爆发后任八路军总指挥、第十八集团军总司令;解放战争时期,任中央军委副主席,中国人民解放军总司令;新中国成立后,任中央人民政府副主席、中共中央军事委员会副主席、中国人民解放军总司令、国防委员会副主席、全国人大常委会委员长等职;1955 年被授予中华人民共和国元帅军衔;1976 年 7 月 6 日在北京逝世,终年 90 岁。

（1）I was deeply grieved to learn of mother's death. I love my mother. Of her hardworking life, in particular, a great many things will forever be cherished in my memory.

（2）I come from a tenant farmer's family. My original family home was Shao Guan, Guangdong Province, into which my ancestors had moved from another province as settlers. During the mass migration of peasants from Huguang to Sichuan Province[1], my ancestors moved to Ma An Chang, Yi Long County, Sichuan. From generation to generation, they tilled land for landlords only to eke[2] out a bare subsistence. People who associated with them as friends were likewise honest impoverished peasants.

(3) Mother gave birth to thirteen children in all. But only the first eight of them survived while the next five were drowned at birth by my parents against their will because they were too poor to raise them all. How anguished, sad and helpless mother must have felt! She did manage, however, to have the eight children brought up all by herself. But she was too busily occupied with household chores and farming to look after the kids so that they were left alone crawling about in the fields.

(4) Mother was a hardworking woman. As far as I can remember, she would always get up before daybreak. In our household of more than twenty members, all women would take turns to do cooking for one year. Apart from cooking, mother did farming, planted vegetables, fed pigs, raised silkworms and spun cotton into yarn[3]. Tall and of strong build, she could carry two buckets of water or manure on a shoulder pole[4].

(5) Mother worked hard from dawn till dusk. When we kids were four or five years old, we found ourselves automatically helping her with farm work. At the age of eight or nine, I could not only carry heavy loads on a shoulder pole or on my back, but also knew how to farm the land. I remember whenever I came back from school and saw mother busy cooking in the kitchen with sweat streaming down her face, I would immediately lay down my books and sneak out[5] to carry water on a shoulder pole or graze the cattle. In some seasons, I would study in the morning and work in the fields in the afternoon. During the busy season, I would spend all day working by the side of mother. It was then that she taught me a lot about the knack[6] of farming.

[1] 湖广填四川:发生在清朝的大规模移民运动。明末清初,连年战乱,四川地区人口锐减,税款难征。清政府出台一系列措施鼓励外省移民入川垦荒,于是来自湖北、湖南、广东、广西、福建等地的移民大量涌入四川、重庆一带,史称"湖广填四川"。

[2] eke /iːk/ v. 竭力维持;勉强维持

[3] yarn /jɑːn/ n. 纱线

[4] shoulder pole：扁担

[5] sneak out：偷偷跑出去;溜走

[6] knack /næk/ n. 技能;本领

（6）The life of a tenant farmer's family was of course hard, but we somehow managed to scrape along[7] because mother was a clever and able woman. We used oil squeezed from seeds of tung trees[8] to light our lamps. We ate rice cooked with peas, vegetables, sweet potatoes or coarse grain, and all seasoned[9] with rapeseed[10] oil—food which landlords and rich people would scorn to eat. Nevertheless, mother's cooking was done so well that everybody ate with gusto[11]. Only in a good year, could we afford to have some home-made new clothes to wear. Mother would spin cotton into yarn and then asked somebody to have it woven into fabric and dyed. We called it "home spun fabric". It was as thick as a copper coin and was so durable that after the eldest brother had grown out of the home-spun garment, it could still be used by the second and third brothers in turn without being worn out.

（7）It was characteristic of an industrious household to be well-regulated and well-organized. My grandfather was a typical Chinese farmer. He went on doing farm work even when he was an octogenarian[12]. He would feel unwell without doing farm labour. He was found still working on the farm even shortly before his death. Grandmother was the organizer of the household. She was in charge of all the farm affairs, assigning tasks to each member of the household. On each New Year's Eve, she would work out all job assignments for the coming new year. Mother would be the first to get up before daybreak. Soon grandfather would be heard to rise from his bed, followed by the rest of the household. Some went about feeding pigs, some cutting firewood, and some carrying water on a shoulder pole. Mother always worked without complaint despite hardships. Amiable[13] by nature, she never beat or scolded us, let alone quarreled with anybody. Consequently, large as it was, the whole household, old and young, uncles and sisters-in-law, lived in perfect harmony. Out of her naive class consciousness, she showed sympathy for the poor.

---

[7] scrape along：勉强糊口

[8] tung tree：油桐树，其种子可以榨油。

[9] season /ˈsiːzn/ v. 加调料调味

[10] rapeseed /ˈreɪpˌsiːd/ n. 油菜；菜籽

[11] gusto /ˈɡʌstəʊ/ n. 热情；兴致

[12] octogenarian /ˌɒktədʒəˈneərɪən/ n. 八十至八十九岁的老人

[13] amiable /ˈeɪmɪəbl/ adj. 和蔼可亲的

Despite her own straitened[14] circumstances, she often went out of her way to help out[15] those relatives who were even more needy[16] than herself. She lived a very frugal[17] life. Father would occasionally smoke a long-stemmed Chinese pipe or drink some wine. To prevent us from falling into the same habit, mother kept us children under strict control. Her diligence and frugality[18], her generosity and kindheartedness—all have left a lasting impression on my mind.

(8) Chinese peasants were honest and peaceable, but disaster befell[19] them just the same. Around 1900, when Sichuan Province was hit by successive years of drought, numerous poverty-stricken peasants went hungry and had to go out in crowds to seize food from the homes of landlords. Thereupon I saw with my own eyes how a group of shabbily-dressed peasants and their families were savagely beaten up or slain[20] by government troops, the road stained with their blood for some 40 *li* and their cries rending the air[21]. In those days, my family also met with increasing difficulties. All the year round, we went without rice to eat, and simply lived on edible wild herbs and *kaoliang*. In 1904, especially, when landlords, riding rough shod over[22] tenants, pressed for higher rents on the let-out[23] pieces of land, we, unable to meet their demands, had our tenancy[24] cancelled by them and were forced to move house on New Year's Eve. On that miserable night, my family tearfully separated and thenceforth had to live in two different places. Shorthandedness and crop failure due to the natural calamity[25] brought misfortune on my family. Mother, however, did not lose heart. Adversity[26] had deepened her sympathy for the poor and needy as well as her aversion[27] to the heartless rich. The painful complaint she had uttered in one or two words and the innumerable[28] injustices I had witnessed aroused in me a spirit of revolt and a desire for a bright future. I made up my mind to seek a new life.

(9) Not long afterwards, I had to tear myself away

---

14 straitened /ˈstreɪtnd/ *adj.* 经济拮据的；穷困的

15 help out: 借钱给……；周济

16 needy /ˈniːdɪ/ *adj.* 缺乏生活必需品的；贫困的

17 frugal /ˈfruːɡl/ *adj.* 节约的；节俭的

18 frugality /fruˈɡælətɪ/ *n.* 节约；朴素

19 befall /bɪˈfɔːl/ *v.* 降临到（某人）头上；发生在（某人）身上

20 slay /sleɪ/ *v.* 杀害；残害

21 rend the air: （喊声）震天，响彻云霄

22 ride rough shod over: 对……为所欲为；粗暴对待；肆意践踏（rough shod 是指马蹄上钉有防滑钉的。因防滑钉是凸出的，以防马匹摔倒，如果骑马人不管别人死活而策马乱跑，被马踩着的人就会受伤，故有此意。）

23 let-out: 出租的；租用的

24 tenancy /ˈtenənsɪ/ *n.* （房屋、土地等的）租用期限

25 calamity /kəˈlæmətɪ/ *n.* 灾难

26 adversity /ədˈvɜːsətɪ/ *n.* 困境；逆境

27 aversion /əˈvɜːʃn/ *n.* 厌恶；憎恶

28 innumerable /ɪˈnjuːmərəbl/ *adj.* 多得数不清的

from mother when I began my schooling. As the son of a tenant, I of course could not afford to go to school. My parents, however, faced with the bullying and oppression of the local evil gentry[29], landlords and yamen bailiffs[30], decided to scrape up[31] enough money by living a very frugal life to pay for my education so that they could make a scholar of me for the family to keep up appearances[32]. At first I was sent to an old-style private school and in 1905 I took the imperial examination[33]. Later, I went farther away from home to study in Shunqing and Chengdu, both in Sichuan Province. All the tuition fees were paid with borrowed money, totalling more than 200 silver dollars. The debt was not repaid until later I became a brigade[34] commander of the Hu Guo Army[35].

(10) In 1908, I came back from Chengdu to set up a higher primary school in Yi Long County. While teaching school, I went home to see mother two or three times a year. In those days, there was a sharp conflict between old and new ideologies. Due to our leaning towards science and democracy, we met with opposition from the local conservative influential gentry in whatever we attempted for the benefit of our home town. So I decided to leave, without my mother's knowledge, for the faraway province of Yunnan, where I joined the New Army[36] and Tongmenhui[37]. On my arrival in Yunnan, I learned from my home letters that mother, instead of frowning upon my new move, gave me a lot of encouragement and comfort.

(11) From 1909 up to now, I have never paid a visit to my home town. In 1921, however, I had my parents come out to live with me. But, as confirmed[38] farm laborers, they felt unwell without land to till and subsequently had to return home. Father died on the way back, and mother continued to do farm work at home to the very last.

(12) As the Chinese revolution continued to develop, I became more and more politically aware. I joined the Chinese Communist Party as soon as I

[29] gentry /'dʒentrɪ/ n. 上流人士；贵族
[30] yamen bailiff：旧称官府中的差役（bailiff /'beɪlɪf/ n. 法警；执行官）
[31] scrape up：（艰难地）凑集；积攒；拼凑
[32] keep up appearances：装门面；撑场面
[33] 此处指科举考试。
[34] brigade /brɪ'geɪd/ n. 旅（陆军编制单位）
[35] The troops that rallied against Yuan Shikai when he attempted to restore monarchy in 1916.（译者注）
[36] Western-style army organized toward the end of the Qing Dynasty.（译者注）
[37] The United League of China (1905—1912), the antecedent of the Kuomintang.（译者注）
[38] confirmed：成习惯的

discovered the correct orientation of the Chinese revolution. When the Great Revolution of 1924—1927[39] failed in China, I completely lost contact with my family. Mother alone supported the whole family by working on the 30 *mu* of land. I did not hear from her until the outbreak of the War of Resistance to Japan. When she was informed of the great cause in which I was engaged, she eagerly looked forward to the success of China's national liberation. While living the hard life of a peasant woman at home, she was aware of the difficulties and hardships that our Party was then undergoing. During the seven years after the outbreak of the War, I managed to send her several hundred *yuan* and some photos of myself. Mother was getting old. She was always thinking of me as I was of her. Last year, a letter from my nephew says, "Grandma is 85. She's no longer as vigorous and healthy as before. She's eager to see you and chat about things that have happened since you left home…" But I never lived up to her expectations because of my dedication[40] to the cause of the War of Resistance Against Japan.

(13) The most prominent characteristic of mother was her lifelong participation in physical labour. She did cooking in the kitchen just one minute before giving birth to me. Her ardent[41] love for agricultural production remained undiminished[42] even in her old age. My nephew says in another letter to me last year, "Because of old age, grandma is no longer in good health, but she still does manual labour, and is particularly fond of spinning cotton into yarn…"

(14) I owe mother a debt of gratitude because she taught me how to cope with the numerous difficulties that I ran into at home so that later during my over 30 years of military and revolutionary life I have never bowed down[43] to any difficulty. She also bequeathed[44] me a strong constitution[45] as well as a strong inclination for labour so that I have been able to work untiringly.

(15) I owe mother a debt of gratitude because she

[39] 指1924年至1927年中国人民在中国共产党和中国国民党合作领导下进行的反帝反封建的革命斗争。

[40] dedication /ˌdedɪˈkeɪʃn/ *n.* 献身；奉献

[41] ardent /ˈɑːdnt/ *adj.* 热烈的；激情的

[42] undiminished /ˌʌndɪˈmɪnɪʃt/ *adj.* 未减少的；未减弱的

[43] bow down：向……示弱

[44] bequeath /bɪˈkwiːð/ *v.* 把……遗赠给；把……传下去

[45] constitution /ˌkɒnstɪˈtjuːʃn/ *n.* 身体素质；体格

imparted[46] to me knowledge of productive labour and a revolutionary will, thus enabling me to take to the revolutionary path. By keeping to this path, I have come to realize more and more clearly that this knowledge of productive labour and this revolutionary will are the most valuable assets[47] in the world.

[46] impart /ɪmˈpɑːt/ v. 给予；传授

[47] asset /ˈæset/ n. 有价值的人（或事物）；资产；财产

(16) Mother is gone and I shall never see her again. This is an ever-lasting sorrow. Mother is an "ordinary" person and one of the millions of labouring people who have made and are still making Chinese history. What can I do to repay her my debt of deep gratitude? I swear to remain ever loyal to our nation and the people, ever loyal to the Chinese Communist Party— the hope of our nation and the people, so that all those who share the same lot with my mother may live a happier life. That is what I can do and what I am certainly able to do.

(17) May mother rest in peace!

精华赏析

现代语言学之父索绪尔提出了 langue 和 parole 的概念，用来区分一定社会里所有成员共有的抽象的语法体系和人们在具体情景中使用的语言。可见，语言归根结底要服务于社会交际的需要，它依赖于一定的交际情景，是一个动态的过程。语言运用发生的场景不同，其语言形式也不相同。这就要求我们说话、撰文要分清场合，根据具体的情景、对象表情达意，做到语言得体，也就是俗话说的"到什么山上唱什么歌"，这是语言运用的最高准则。

不同情景中语言在发音、词汇、句式、修辞等方面的差异，形成了不同的语体风格。在西方，早在古希腊时期，人们已经注意到了语体的分类。亚里士多德在他的修辞学著作中已经明确区分了书面语体和口语语体。我国历史上最早形成比较系统的文体论是在魏晋南北朝时期，曹丕在《典论·论文》中提出了"四科八体"说的文体论："奏议宜雅，书论宜理，铭诔尚实，诗赋欲丽。"

美国语言学家马丁·裘斯(Martin Joos)在他的著作《五只钟》(The Five Clocks)一书中划分了五种不同的语体：庄严体(frozen)、正式体(formal)、商洽体(consultative)、随意体(casual)和亲密体(intimate)(秦秀白，2002)。这五种语体适用于不同的交际情景，如同酒店大堂墙上挂的五只钟，指示着世界上不同时区城市的时间。庄严体用语典雅、严谨、规范、保守、艰深，不好理解，主要用于重要的政府文件、法律条款、文献记录等；正式体语言比较严谨,语义连贯,表达清晰,无需提供语境即可被理解;商洽体发音清晰,语法完整,语义充足,主要适用于与陌生人交际的场合;随意体多用于朋友、熟人和圈内成员,较为口语化,词句常有省略,有俚语,因此并不是每个人都能解读;亲密体适用于关系非常亲昵的人之间,语言的内容往往只有交际双方才能理解,别人很难获取。

如果语体用错,在轻松随意的场合使用正式语体,就有故意卖弄斯文之嫌;相反,在庄重严肃的场合使用非正式语体也会令人觉得轻浮、无礼。语体混用轻则会闹出笑话,重则会引起误会,例如下面的故事:

A young lady home from school was explaining. "Take an egg," she said, "and make a perforation in the base and a corresponding one in the apex. Then apply the lips to the aperture, and by forcibly inhaling the breath the shell is entirely discharged of its contents." An old lady who was listening exclaimed, "It beats all how folks do things nowadays. When I was a gal they made a hole in each end and sucked."

这个故事中的女士使用了非常正式的书面文体,而这种文体被用于解释日常生活中"吸鸡蛋"这种非正式的场合,显然是不合适的,令人啼笑皆非。又例如鲁迅在《孔乙己》中塑造的穷酸迂腐的文人孔乙己,在小酒店里买酒聊天也把之乎者也挂在嘴边,这种语体的混用真实地刻画了一个受封建科举制度残害的悲惨形象,令人印象深刻。

由此可见,语体的正式程度和语言的某些特征是紧密相连的。马丁·裘斯把语体分成五种,体现了语体的渐变性,但过于细致的分类也使得相邻两种语体的语言差异表现得过于细微。因此,为了讨论的方便,在这里我们只把语体分为正式和非正式两种。刘世生、朱瑞青(2006)认为,正式语体和非正式语体在语音、语相、词汇、句法等几个方面存在差异。

一、语音

一般说来,一个语言的本族语使用者在非正式场合中的语速会稍微偏快,发音也比较模糊,经常有偏离标准发音的状况发生,语音省略(elision)、同化(assimilation)等现象非常普遍,如:

She wansta go home. ＝She wants to go home.(语音省略)

He has to (/hi hæs tu/).(同化)

正式语体要求发音非常清晰、准确,就像演播室里的播音员。当然,上面例句中的省音、同化等语音现象在正式语体中是不允许出现的。

二、语相

语相学研究"语言的视觉中介,亦即书写系统,即标点、拼写、排版、字母和段落结构"(刘世生、朱瑞青,2006)等。非正式语体往往具有以下语相特征:第一,在标点符号上,更多使用表示强烈情感的感叹号和破折号,以及网络上的视觉情感符号(emoji),多用％、￥、$等百分比和货币单位符号;第二,在数字上,大多使用阿拉伯数字,即使是十以内的数字也是如此;第三,大量使用缩写,如 What're U doing?(What are you doing?)相反,正式语体较少使用破折号和感叹号,百分比以及货币单位符号、网络情感符号也很少出现;在数字的表达上往往用单词代替阿拉伯数字(一千以下的数字);极少使用缩写形式。

三、词汇

从词汇角度来说,正式语体使用的词汇往往比较古典、华丽,甚至抽象、生僻,可以表达非常精确的概念。这些词多来自法语、希腊语或者拉丁语,给人以庄重、严谨的感觉。而非正式语体使用的词汇则主要是英国本族语,词汇的结构比较简单,词汇的意义也较模糊,指代不精准,多为动词短语,一词多义的情况比较多见,多用于世俗的日常生活场景。另外,非正式语体常常使用许多俚语、俗语、行话等不规范的词汇以及缩略词,如 ad, photo, WHO, e. g., etc.,等等。试比较下列两句话在词汇上的语体差异:

Could I just disturb you for a moment?

Got a sec?

四、句法

正式语体和非正式语体在句子结构上也存在很多区别:正式语体多用从句,因此句子长且结构复杂,非正式语体中的句子短,结构简单;正式语体多用被动结构,常用物称名词做主语,凸显名词化特征,非正式语体则多用主动句和人称主语,凸显动词;正式语体经常使用强调句、倒装句、独立主格结构等,句法结构严谨,而非正式语体中存在大量省略句,以及不符合语法规范的表达方式。试比较下列句子:

a1:You coming?(非正式语体)

a2:I am wondering if you would come tomorrow.(正式语体)

b1:The women actively participated in public life, and thus changed their role in the society.(非正式语体)

b2:The women's active participation in public life causes the change of their role in the society.(正式语体)

c1:College students should give top priority to their academic learning.(非正式语体)

c2:Top priority should be given to college students' academic learning.(正式语体)

d1:Raising pets brings about a lot of troubles, so they have never kept a pet.(非正式语体)

d2:Believing that raising pets brings about a lot of troubles, they have never kept a pet.(正式语体)

通过以上正式语体和非正式语体在语音、语相、词汇和句法等方面的对比,我们不难发现,语体上的差异直接决定文本的语言风格,而文本的语言风格也能最真实地反映文本的语体特征。这是我们研究语体这个概念的意义所在——借助纷繁复杂的语言现象,我们最终能洞察作者的所思所想、喜怒哀乐。多么神奇!

mass <u>with a practised hand</u>[34].

(17) "Give it to me quick," said Della.

(18) Oh, and the next two hours tripped by on rosy wings. Forget the <u>hashed</u>[35] metaphor. She was <u>ransacking</u>[36] the stores for Jim's present.

(19) She found it at last. It surely had been made for Jim and no one else. There was no other like it in any of the stores, and she had turned all of them inside out. <u>It was a platinum fob chain simple and chaste in design, properly proclaiming its value by substance alone and not by meretricious ornamentation—as all good things should do.</u>[37] It was even worthy of The Watch. As soon as she saw it she knew that it must be Jim's. It was like him. Quietness and value—the description applied to both. Twenty-one dollars they took from her for it, and she hurried home with the 87 cents. With that chain on his watch Jim might be properly anxious about the time in any company. Grand as the watch was, he sometimes looked at it <u>on the sly</u>[38] <u>on account of</u>[39] the old <u>leather strap</u>[40] that he used in place of a chain.

(20) When Della reached home her <u>intoxication</u>[41] gave way a little to <u>prudence</u>[42] and reason. She got out her curling irons and lighted the gas and went to work repairing the <u>ravages</u>[43] made by generosity added to love. Which is always a tremendous task, dear friends—a <u>mammoth</u>[44] task.

(21) Within forty minutes her head was covered with tiny, close-lying curls that made her look wonderfully like a <u>truant</u>[45] schoolboy. She looked at her reflection in the mirror long, carefully, and critically.

(22) "If Jim doesn't kill me," she said to herself, "before he takes a second look at me, he'll say I look like a <u>Coney Island</u>[46] chorus girl. But what could I do—oh! what could I do with a dollar and eighty-seven cents?"

(23) At 7 o'clock the coffee was made and the frying-pan was on the back of the stove hot and ready to cook the chops.

---

[34] with a practised hand: 老练地

[35] hash /hæʃ/ v. 把……弄糟；搞砸

[36] ransack /ˈrænsæk/ v. 搜遍；洗劫

[37] 一条朴素的白金表链，镂刻着花纹。正如一切优质东西那样，它只以货色论长短，不以装潢来炫耀。（张经浩 译）

[38] on the sly: 偷偷地

[39] on account of: 因为；由于

[40] leather strap: 皮革表带

[41] intoxication /ɪnˌtɒksɪˈkeɪʃn/ n. 极度兴奋；陶醉

[42] prudence /ˈpruːdns/ n. 谨慎；慎重

[43] ravage /ˈrævɪdʒ/ n. 毁坏；损坏

[44] mammoth /ˈmæməθ/ adj. 巨大的

[45] truant /ˈtruːənt/ adj. 逃学的；旷课的

[46] Coney Island：科尼岛，位于美国纽约市布鲁克林区的一个半岛，其面向大西洋的海滩是美国知名的休闲娱乐区域。

（24）Jim was never late. Della doubled the fob chain in her hand and sat on the corner of the table near the door that he always entered. Then she heard his step on the stair away down on the first flight, and she turned white for just a moment. She had a habit of saying a little silent prayer about the simplest everyday things, and now she whispered: "Please God, make him think I am still pretty."

（25）The door opened and Jim stepped in and closed it. He looked thin and very serious. Poor fellow, he was only twenty-two—and to be burdened with a family! He needed a new overcoat and he was without gloves.

（26）Jim stopped inside the door, <u>as immovable as a setter at the scent of quail</u>⁴⁷. His eyes were fixed upon Della, and there was an expression in them that she could not read, and it terrified her. It was not anger, nor surprise, nor disapproval, nor horror, nor any of the sentiments that she had been prepared for. He simply stared at her fixedly with that <u>peculiar</u>⁴⁸ expression on his face.

⁴⁷ 明喻（simile）。吉姆好像嗅到了鹌鹑气味的猎犬，一动也不动。

⁴⁸ peculiar /pɪˈkjuːliə(r)/ adj. 奇怪的；不寻常的

（27）Della <u>wriggled</u>⁴⁹ off the table and went for him.

⁴⁹ wriggle /ˈrɪgl/ v. 扭动身体

（28）"Jim, darling," she cried, "don't look at me that way. I had my hair cut off and sold because I couldn't have lived through Christmas without giving you a present. It'll grow out again—you won't mind, will you? I just had to do it. My hair grows awfully fast. Say 'Merry Christmas!' Jim, and let's be happy. You don't know what a nice—what a beautiful, nice gift I've got for you."

（29）"You've cut off your hair?" asked Jim, <u>laboriously</u>⁵⁰, as if he had not arrived at that <u>patent</u>⁵¹ fact yet even after the hardest mental labor.

⁵⁰ laboriously /ləˈbɔːriəsli/ adv. 费力地
⁵¹ patent /ˈpætnt/ adj. 明显的

（30）"Cut it off and sold it," said Della. "Don't you like me just as well, anyhow? I'm me without my hair, ain't I?"

（31）Jim looked about the room curiously.

（32）"You say your hair is gone?" he said, with an air almost of <u>idiocy</u>⁵².

⁵² idiocy /ˈɪdiəsi/ n. 愚蠢行为；蠢事

（33）"You needn't look for it," said Della. "It's sold, I tell you—sold and gone, too. It's Christmas Eve, boy. Be good to me, for it went for you. Maybe the hairs of my head were numbered," she went on with sudden serious sweetness, "but nobody could ever count my love for you.[53] Shall I put the chops on, Jim?"

（34）Out of his trance[54] Jim seemed quickly to wake. He enfolded[55] his Della. For ten seconds let us regard with discreet[56] scrutiny[57] some inconsequential[58] object in the other direction. Eight dollars a week or a million a year—what is the difference? A mathematician or a wit would give you the wrong answer. The magi brought valuable gifts, but that was not among them. This dark assertion[59] will be illuminated[60] later on.

（35）Jim drew a package from his overcoat pocket and threw it upon the table.

（36）"Don't make any mistake, Dell," he said, "about me. I don't think there's anything in the way of a haircut or a shave or a shampoo that could make me like my girl any less. But if you'll unwrap that package you may see why you had me going a while at first."

（37）White fingers and nimble[61] tore at the string and paper. And then an ecstatic[62] scream of joy; and then, alas! a quick feminine change to hysterical[63] tears and wails, necessitating[64] the immediate employment of all the comforting powers of the lord of the flat.

（38）For there lay The Combs—the set of combs, side and back, that Della had worshipped long in a Broadway window. Beautiful combs, pure tortoise shell, with jewelled rims—just the shade[65] to wear in the beautiful vanished[66] hair. They were expensive combs, she knew, and her heart had simply craved[67] and yearned[68] over them without the least hope of possession. And now, they were hers, but the tresses[69] that should have adorned the coveted[70] adornments were gone.

（39）But she hugged them to her bosom, and at length[71] she was able to look up with dim eyes and a smile and say: "My hair grows so fast, Jim!"

53 "……也许我的头发数得清,"德拉突然温柔地说,"但是我对你的爱谁也数不清。……"

54 trance /trɑːns/ n. 出神;发呆

55 enfold /ɪnˈfəʊld/ v. 拥抱;搂抱

56 discreet /dɪˈskriːt/ adj. 谨慎的

57 scrutiny /ˈskruːtəni/ n. 仔细检查

58 inconsequential /ɪnˌkɒnsɪˈkwenʃl/ adj. 不重要的;微不足道的

59 assertion /əˈsɜːʃn/ n. 明确肯定;断言

60 illuminate /ɪˈluːmɪneɪt/ v. 阐明;解释

61 nimble /ˈnɪmbl/ adj. 灵活的;敏捷的

62 ecstatic /ɪkˈstætɪk/ adj. 狂喜的

63 hysterical /hɪˈsterɪkl/ adj. 歇斯底里的

64 necessitate /nəˈsesɪteɪt/ v. 使成为必要

65 shade /ʃeɪd/ n. 色度

66 vanish /ˈvænɪʃ/ v. 突然消失

67 crave /kreɪv/ v. 渴望

68 yearn /jɜːn/ v. 渴望;渴求

69 tress /tres/ n. (女子飘逸的)长发

70 covet /ˈkʌvət/ v. 渴望;贪求

71 at length: 最后;最终

(40) And then Della leaped up like a little singed cat[72] and cried, "Oh, oh!"

(41) Jim had not yet seen his beautiful present. She held it out to him eagerly upon her open palm. The dull precious metal seemed to flash with a reflection of her bright and ardent[73] spirit.

(42) "Isn't it a dandy[74], Jim? I hunted all over town to find it. You'll have to look at the time a hundred times a day now. Give me your watch. I want to see how it looks on it."

(43) Instead of obeying, Jim tumbled down[75] on the couch and put his hands under the back of his head and smiled.

(44) "Dell," said he, "let's put our Christmas presents away and keep'em a while. They're too nice to use just at present. I sold the watch to get the money to buy your combs. And now suppose you put the chops on."

(45) The magi[76], as you know, were wise men—wonderfully wise men—who brought gifts to the Babe in the manger[77]. They invented the art of giving Christmas presents. Being wise, their gifts were no doubt wise ones, possibly bearing the privilege of exchange in case of duplication[78]. And here I have lamely[79] related to you the uneventful[80] chronicle of two foolish children in a flat who most unwisely sacrificed for each other the greatest treasures of their house. But in a last word to the wise of these days let it be said that of all who give gifts these two were the wisest. Of all who give and receive gifts, such as they are wisest. Everywhere they are wisest.[81] They are the magi.

[72] 明喻（simile）。德拉像被烫伤的小猫一样跳了起来。

[73] ardent /'ɑːdnt/ adj. 热烈的；激情的

[74] dandy /'dændi/ adj. 棒的；非常好的

[75] tumble down：倒下

[76] the magi：东方三博士，又称东方三贤士。在耶稣出生后，他们特意从东方来到耶路撒冷朝拜耶稣，将黄金、乳香、殁药作为礼物献给他，被认为是圣诞礼物的发明人。

[77] manger /'meɪndʒə(r)/ n. 马槽

[78] duplication /ˌdjuːplɪ'keɪʃn/ n. 重复

[79] lamely /'leɪmli/ adv. 不具说服力地

[80] uneventful /ˌʌnɪ'ventfl/ adj. 平凡的

[81] 夸张（exaggeration）。三句话都以"wisest"结尾，表现出作者对于两位主人公间真挚爱情的高度赞扬和肯定。

⌐ 精华赏析 ⌐

　　作为短篇小说大师欧·亨利的代表作之一,《麦琪的礼物》有着欧·亨利式小说的典型特征。首先,故事的构思巧妙,有着典型的"欧·亨利式结尾"。其次,在讲述故事时,作者使用的语言幽默,既写出了德拉和吉姆这对夫妻的贫苦生活,又写出了他们生活中的感动和快乐,达到让读者"笑中带泪"的艺术效果。

一、欧·亨利式结尾

在《麦琪的礼物》这个故事中,夫妻双方都卖掉自己最珍爱的宝贝,为对方换得心仪的圣诞礼物,直到故事的结尾,他们才得知,送给双方的礼物都成了无用的东西,这种意外的结局让读者始料不及、嗟叹不已。但是,这种与众不同的结尾反倒让读者印象深刻,能够深化故事的主题,因此其意义不言而喻。在这篇小说中,欧·亨利式的意外结局是通过叙述视角的转换和明线、暗线双故事线的结合达到的。

第一,叙述视角的转换。欧·亨利在他的短篇小说中善于设置悬念,让故事的结局出人意料,而"短篇小说的悬念感在很大程度上来源于小说技巧的叙述视角:叙述视角调控、营造着小说的悬念艺术魅力"(林雪萍,2008)。《麦琪的礼物》这篇小说主要运用了第三人称全知叙述视角,向读者呈现故事的主要情节。因此,读者可以看到,德拉为了攒钱给吉姆买圣诞礼物,跟杂货店、肉铺和菜铺老板软磨硬泡,可直到圣诞节的前一天,也仅仅攒到了1.87美元。由于没有足够的钱给吉姆买礼物,她万般无奈,伤心欲绝地扑倒在破旧的沙发上嚎啕大哭。在嚎哭之后,德拉突然想到一个能快速赚钱的主意,那就是卖掉自己珍爱的漂亮秀发,但是想到这儿她却花容失色,以至于在去发制品店的路上还一直流着眼泪。故事的大部分内容都是用全知叙述视角讲述的,通过这种"上帝视角"的叙述,读者可以看到故事的全貌,得以窥见租住在破旧公寓里这对男女主角贫穷窘迫的生活,了解故事发生的时间、地点、背景等信息,从而迅速了解故事的始末。

但是如果一直采用全知视角,反而会让故事的可信度大打折扣,让读者怀疑故事的真实性。因此,在必要的时候,进行叙述视角的转换是必要的,这样不仅可以增加故事的真实性,还可以起到深化主题的重要作用(王健红,2002)。在故事中,欧·亨利也穿插使用了一些限制叙述视角,如在小说的第26段,吉姆回到家中,看到德拉的短发时,他的"两只眼死死盯着德拉,眼里的表情她看不明白,只觉得害怕。那是既非愤怒,也非惊奇,也非不赞同,也非厌恶的神情,与她预料中的任何一种表情都不一样。他目不转睛地盯着她,脸上的神情异样"(欧·亨利,2003:32)。在描述吉姆看到德拉的头发后的反应时,作者运用了限制叙述视角,让读者仅从德拉的角度看吉姆的反应,而非从全知视角全面、真实地详述吉姆此时此刻的心情和感受,这样既能增加故事的真实性,又能适当留白,从而留下悬念,"让读者因为受困于有限视角而渴望知晓原因或结果,从而构建出悬念效果和阅读紧张感"(林雪萍,2008),为后面出其不意的结局做好铺垫。

第二,明线和暗线双故事线的交相呼应。在《麦琪的礼物》这个故事中,作者详细介绍了女主角德拉在圣诞节前一天的经历和心理变化,从她由于无钱给丈夫买礼物而独自黯然神伤,到伤心地去发制品店卖头发,再到兴奋地去商店四处搜索并最终为吉姆挑选了一条白金表链,直至最后冷静地回到家中边做饭边担心。德拉这一天的经历是这个故事的一条明线。而她的丈夫吉姆这一天的经历则是故事的暗线,因为吉姆在同一天,去卖了自己的金表,给德拉买了她心仪已久的一整套精美发梳。这条暗线与明线交相呼应,到了故事的最后,吉姆说自己为了给德拉买圣诞礼物而卖掉了自己的金表,此时此刻,故事的明线和暗线交会。读者可以想象一下,吉姆这一天又是怎么度过的呢?他是不是也焦虑、挣扎、纠结了许久,最后还是下定决心把金表卖了呢?原来这对夫妻是如此地相爱,他们都愿意付出自己最珍爱的东西,只为给对方送上最好的圣诞节礼物。但是很可惜,阴差阳错,他们给对方买回来的礼物都成为了无用之物。故事的结局让读者始料不及,但确实是既在意料之外,又在情理之中。感动之余,读者可以感受到这对夫妻的纯洁和善良,体会到他们永恒的爱情,与此同时,作者也揭露了社会现实,让读者领会到美国下层人民生活的艰难和辛酸(马兰,2010)。

二、语言幽默

除了欧·亨利式的结局,这篇小说还有一个特色,那就是语言幽默。欧·亨利非常擅长用轻松、幽默的语言描写底层人民的生活,因而被誉为"美国生活的幽默百科全书"。在《麦琪的礼物》这个故事中,幽默主要是通过运用多种修辞手法达到的。作者运用反复、夸张、明喻、暗喻等多种修辞手法,用幽默的方式描写了这对苦命鸳鸯的贫困生活。

比如在小说中,作者反复提及德拉只有1.87美元:

One dollar and eighty-seven cents. (Para. 1)

One dollar and eighty-seven cents. And the next day would be Christmas. (Para. 1)

Tomorrow would be Christmas Day, and she had only $1.87 with which to buy Jim a present. (Para. 6)

Only $1.87 to buy a present for Jim. Her Jim. (Para. 6)

But what could I do—oh! what could I do with a dollar and eighty-seven cents? (Para. 22)

反复强调圣诞节前一天德拉只有1.87美元这个事实,能够营造出一种紧迫感,让读者体会到德拉的焦虑心情,并使得她卖掉头发这一决定成为必然。

而在提及吉姆珍贵的金表时(第9段),作者没有直接说这个表值多少钱,却用了夸张手法,强调吉姆的金表珍贵到会让所罗门王嫉妒地扯胡子的地步。(Had King Solomon been the janitor, with all his treasures piled up in the basement, Jim would have pulled out his watch every time he passed, just to see him pluck at his beard from envy.)读到此处,读者脑海中定会出现这个财富与智慧并存的国王气得吹胡子瞪眼的情形,这一场景让人忍俊不禁,印象深刻。小说中还使用了其他的修辞手法,让故事更加生动有趣,大家可以结合注释部分,思考这些修辞手法达到的艺术效果,体会欧·亨利式的幽默。

总而言之,《麦琪的礼物》这篇小说的两大特色就是典型的"欧·亨利式结尾"和幽默的语言。作者通过叙述视角的转换和明线、暗线双重主线,恰当设置悬念,让故事的情节引人入胜,结尾处夫妇间甜蜜而又苦涩的爱情和无私的奉献精神则扣人心弦,感人肺腑。而在叙述过程中,作者运用了各种修辞手法,讲述故事时语言风趣幽默,让读者笑中带泪,进而产生"含泪的微笑"的艺术效果。

参考文献

[1] 林雪萍.《麦琪的礼物》的叙述视角透视[J]. 广西民族大学学报(哲学社会科学版),2008(S1):82-84.

［2］马兰.《麦琪的礼物》之故事情节探究［J］.兰州教育学院学报,2010(5):36-37,45.

［3］欧·亨利. 麦琪的礼物［M］.张经浩,译. 上海:上海社会科学院出版社,2003.

［4］王健红. 小说叙述视角浅探［J］. 贵州大学学报(社会科学版),2000(2):63-68.

■ 术语解说 ■

　　全知叙述视角:亦称"上帝视角",叙述者大于人物,知道的比文本中任何人物知道的都要多,清晰地知道故事中所有的人物、场景及故事发生的时间、地点、起因、经过等所有具体细节,可以说是无所不知。其优点是可以向读者客观全面地介绍事实真相,缺点在于叙述者过于全能全知,因而会降低文本的可信度。

　　限制叙述视角:亦称"有限视角",是一种受到限制的主观视角,叙述者可由文本中的某一具体人物充当,也可以由几个人轮流充当,仅知道该人物知道的事情,而该人物不知道的事,叙述者无权叙述。其优点在于,从文本中真实角色的角度叙述能够让事件更具真实性,缺点在于因具体人物角度受限,读者不能全方面了解具体情况。

■ 阅读思考 ■

1. 你知道小说的标题"*The Gift of the Magi*"有什么含义吗?

2. 读一读欧·亨利的另外一篇经典短篇小说《警察与赞美诗》(*The Cop and the Anthem*),体会"欧·亨利式结尾"的作用和独特魅力。

Chapter Three　Humanity and Life

So we beat on, boats against the current, borne back ceaselessly into the past.

F. Scott Fitzgerald

The Great Gatsby

于是我们奋力向前划,逆流向上的小舟,不停地倒退,进入过去。

——(美)菲茨杰拉德《了不起的盖茨比》

7

Six Chapters of a Floating Life (Excerpt)

Shen Fu

【作品简介】

《浮生六记》(*Six Chapters of a Floating Life*)为清朝文人沈复的自传体散文,书名典出李白"浮生若梦,为欢几何?"之句。作者用简练生动的语言记录了自己大半生的人生经历,包括婚姻爱情、居家生活、家庭变故、漫游见闻等。原作共六记,现仅存四记,即《闺房记乐》《闲情记趣》《坎坷记愁》和《浪游记快》,另有两记《中山记历》和《养生记道》现已失传。本文选自第二卷《闲情记趣》。

《浮生六记》深受著名学者俞平伯、林语堂等人的推崇。俞平伯在其德译本的序中说:"沈复习幕经商,文学非其专业。今读其文,无端悲喜能移我情,家常言语,反若有胜于宏文巨制者,此无他,真与自然而已。"林语堂说:"素好《浮生六记》,发愿译成英文,使世人略知中国一对夫妇之恬淡可爱生活。"

【作者简介】

沈复(1763—1825),字三白,号梅逸,生于姑苏城南沧浪亭畔一个士族家庭,十八岁时娶舅女陈芸为妻。他一生不慕功名,没有参加过科举考试,家道中落后,曾以卖画维持生计。在妻子去世后,沈复到四川充当幕僚,此后情况不明。

【译者简介】

林语堂(1895—1976),福建龙溪(今漳州)人,著名作家、学者、翻译家、语言学家。早年留学美国、德国,获哈佛大学比较文学硕士、德国莱比锡大学语言学博士。回国后曾在清华大学、北京大学、厦门大学任教。1945年赴新加坡筹建南洋大学,任校长。曾创办《论语》《人间世》《宇宙风》等刊物,提倡幽默、闲适和独抒性灵的小品文创作。1966年定居台湾,1967年受聘为香港中文大学研究教授,主持编撰《林语堂当代汉英词典》。1976年在香港逝世,享年80岁。

林语堂文字功底深厚,尤其擅长英文写作,曾于1940年和1950年先后两度获得诺贝尔文学奖提名。其主要作品包括小说《京华烟云》《风声鹤唳》《朱门》,散文和杂文文集《吾国与吾民》《人生的盛宴》《生活的艺术》以及译著《东坡诗文选》《浮生六记》等。

（1）I remember that when I was a child, I could stare at the sun with wide, open eyes. I could see the tiniest objects, and loved to observe the fine grains and patterns of small things, from which I derived[1] a romantic, unworldly[2] pleasure. When mosquitoes were humming round in summer, I transformed them in my imagination into a company of storks[3] dancing in the air. And when I regarded them that way, they were real storks to me, flying by the hundreds and thousands, and I would look up at them until my neck was stiff. Again, I kept a few mosquitoes inside a white curtain and blew a puff of smoke round them, so that to me they became a company of white storks flying among the blue clouds, and their humming was to me the song of storks singing in high heaven, which delighted me intensely. Sometimes I would squat by a broken, earthen[4] wall, or by a little bush on a raised flower-bed, with my eyes on the same level as the flower-bed itself, and there I would look and look, transforming in my mind the little plot of grass into a forest and the ants and insects into wild animals. The little elevations[5] on the ground became my hills, and the depressed areas[6] became my valleys, and my spirit wandered in that world at leisure.

（2）One day, I saw two little insects fighting among the grass, and while I was all absorbed watching the fight, there suddenly appeared a big monster, overturning my hills and tearing up my forest—it was a little toad[7]. With one lick of his tongue, he swallowed up the two little insects. I was so lost in my young imaginary world that I was taken unawares[8] and quite frightened. When I had recovered myself, I caught the toad, struck it several dozen times and chased it out of the courtyard. Thinking of this incident afterwards when I was grown up, I understood that these two little insects were committing adultery by rape. "The wages of sin is death." so says an ancient proverb, and I wondered whether it was true of the insects also. I was a naughty boy, and once my ball (for we call the genital[9] organ a "ball" in Soochow) was

---

[1] derive /dɪˈraɪv/ v. 获得；得到
[2] unworldly /ʌnˈwɜːldlɪ/ adj. 非尘世的；超凡的
[3] stork /stɔːk/ n. 鹳

[4] earthen /ˈɜːθn/ adj. 泥土做的；土质的

[5] elevation /ˌelɪˈveɪʃn/ n. 高地；高处
[6] 指地势低洼之处。

[7] toad /təʊd/ n. 癞蛤蟆

[8] unawares /ˌʌnəˈweəz/ adv. 出其不意地；不留神地

[9] genital /ˈdʒenɪtl/ adj. 生殖的

bitten by an earthworm and became swollen. [Believing that the duck's saliva[10] would act as an antidote[11] for insect bites,] they held a duck over it, but the maid-servant, who was holding the duck, accidentally let her hand go, and the duck was going to swallow it. I got frightened and screamed. People used to tell this story to make fun of me. These were the little incidents of my childhood days.

(3) When I was grown up, I loved flowers very much and was very fond of training pot flowers and pot plants. When I knew Chang Lanp'o, I learnt from him the secrets of trimming branches and protecting joints, and later the art of grafting[12] trees and making rockeries[13]. The orchid was prized most among all the flowers because of its subdued fragrance[14] and graceful charm, but it was difficult to obtain really good classic varieties. At the end of his days, Lanp'o presented me with a pot of orchids, whose flowers had lotus-shaped petals; the centre of the flowers was broad and white, the petals were very neat and even at the "shoulders," and the stems were very slender. This type was classical, and I prized it like a piece of old jade. When I was working away from home, Yün used to take care of it personally and it grew beautifully. After two years, it died suddenly one day. I dug up its roots and found that they were white like marble, while nothing was wrong with the sprouts, either. At first, I could not understand this, but ascribed[15] it with a sigh merely to my own bad luck, which might be unworthy to keep such flowers. Later on, I found out that some one had asked for some off-shoots[16] from the same pot, had been refused, and had therefore killed it by pouring boiling water over it. Thenceforth[17] I swore I would never grow orchids again.

(4) Next in preference came the azalea[18]. Although it had no smell, its flowers lasted a longer time and were very beautiful to look at, in addition to its being easy to train up. Yün loved these flowers so much that she would not stand for too much cutting and trimming, and,

10 saliva /sə'laɪvə/ n. 唾液

11 antidote /'æntɪdəʊt/ n. 解毒药

12 graft /grɑːft/ v. 嫁接；移植

13 rockery /'rɒkərɪ/ n. 假山；假山庭院

14 subdued fragrance：幽香
(subdue /səb'djuː/ v. 压制；克制)

15 ascribe /ə'skraɪb/ v. 把……归咎于

16 off-shoot：(植物的)旁枝、分枝

17 thenceforth /ˌðens'fɔːθ/ adv. 从那时起；此后

18 azalea /ə'zeɪlɪə/ n. 杜鹃

consequently, it was difficult to make them grow in proper form. The same thing was true of the other flowers.

(5) The chrysanthemum, however, was my passion in the autumn of every year. I loved to arrange these flowers in vases instead of raising them in pots, not because I did not want to have them that way, but because I had no garden in my home and could not take care of them myself. What I bought at the market were not properly trained and not to my liking. When arranging chrysanthemum flowers in vases, one should take an odd, not an even, number and each vase should have flowers of only one colour. The mouth of the vase should be broad, so that the flowers could lie easily together. Whether there be half a dozen flowers or even thirty or forty of them in a vase, they should be so arranged as to come up together straight from the mouth of the vase, neither overcrowded, nor too much spread out, nor leaning against the mouth of the vase. This is called "keeping the handle firm." Sometimes they can stand gracefully erect, and sometimes spread out in different directions. In order to avoid a bare monotonous effect, they should be mixed with some flower buds and arranged in a kind of studied <u>disorderliness</u>[19]. The leaves should not be too thick and the stems should not be too stiff. In using pins to hold the stems up, one should break the long pins off, rather than expose them. This is called "keeping the mouth of the vase clear." Place from three to seven vases on a table, depending on the size of the latter, for if there were too many of them, they would be overcrowded, looking like chrysanthemum screens at the market. The stands for the vases should be of different height, from three or four inches to two and a half feet, so that the different vases at different heights would balance one another and belong intimately to one another as in a picture with unity of composition. To put one vase high in the centre with two low at the sides, or to put a low one in front and a tall one behind, or to arrange them

[19] disorderliness /dɪsˈɔːdəlɪnɪs/ *n.* 混乱;无秩序

in symmetrical[20] pairs, would be to create what is vulgarly called "a heap of gorgeous refuse[21]." Proper spacing and arrangement must depend on the individual who has an understanding of pictorial[22] composition.

(6) In the case of flower bowls or open dishes, the method of making a support for the flowers is to mix pitch[23] and refined[24] resin[25] with elm[26] bark, flour and oil, and heat up the mixture with hot hay ashes until it becomes a kind of glue, and with it glue[27] some nails upside down on to a piece of copper. This copper plate can then be heated up and glued on to the bottom of the bowl or dish. When it is cold, tie the flowers in groups by means of wire and stick them on those nails. The flowers should be allowed to incline sideways and not shoot up from the centre; it is also important that the stems and leaves should not come too closely together. After this is done, put some water in the bowl and cover up the copper support with some clean sand, so that the flowers will seem to grow directly from the bottom of the bowl.

(7) When picking branches from flower-trees for decoration in vases, it is important to know how to trim them before putting them in the vase, for one cannot always go and pick them oneself, and those picked by others are often unsatisfactory. Hold the branch in your hand and turn it back and forth in different ways in order to see how it lies most expressively[28]. After one has made up one's mind about it, lop off[29] the superfluous[30] branches, with the idea of making the twig look thin and sparse[31] and quaintly[32] beautiful. Next think how the stem is going to lie in the vase and with what kind of bend, so that when it is put there, the leaves and flowers can be shown to the best advantage.

(8) If one just takes any old branch in hand, chooses a straight section and puts it in the vase, the consequence will be that the stem will be too stiff, the branches will be too close together and the flowers and leaves will be turned in the wrong direction, devoid of[33]

[20] symmetrical /sɪˈmetrɪkl/ adj. 对称的
[21] 中国传统艺术珍品"锦灰堆",又名"八破图"。
[22] pictorial /pɪkˈtɔːrɪəl/ adj. 图画的
[23] pitch /pɪtʃ/ n. 沥青;柏油
[24] refined /rɪˈfaɪnd/ adj. 精炼的;提纯的
[25] resin /ˈrezɪn/ n. 树脂
[26] elm /elm/ n. 榆树
[27] glue 此处作动词。

[28] 指最能表达出花枝的姿态。
[29] lop off: 砍下;剪去;截掉
[30] superfluous /suːˈpɜːfluəs/ adj. 过多的;多余的
[31] sparse /spɑːs/ adj. 稀疏的
[32] quaintly /ˈkweɪntlɪ/ adv. 古雅别致地;优雅地

[33] devoid of: 缺少;缺乏

all charm and expression. To make a straight twig crooked[34], cut a mark half-way across the stem and insert a little piece of broken brick or stone at the joint; the straight branch will then become a bent one. In case the stem is too weak, put one or two pins to strengthen it. By means of this method, even maple leaves and bamboo twigs or even ordinary grass and thistles[35] will look very well for decoration. Put a twig of green bamboo side by side with a few berries of Chinese matrimony vine[36] or arrange some fine blades of grass together with some branches of thistle. They will look quite poetic, if the arrangement is correct.

(9) In planting new trees, it does not matter if the trunk comes up from the ground at an angle, for if let alone for a year, it will grow upwards by itself. On the other hand, if one lets the stem come up in a perpendicular[37] line, it will be difficult later on for it to have a dynamic posture.

(10) As to the training of pot plants, one should choose those with claw[38]-like roots coming above the surface of the ground. Lop off the first three branches from the ground before allowing the next one to grow up, making a bend at every point where a new branch starts off. There should be seven such bends, or perhaps nine, from the lower end of a tree to its top. It is against good taste to have swollen[39] joints at these bends, or to have two branches growing directly opposite each other at the same point. These must branch off[40] in all directions from different points, for if one only allows those on the right and left to grow up, the effect will be very bare, or "the chest and back will be exposed," as we say. Nor, for instance, should they grow straight from the front or behind. There are "double-trunked" and "treble[41]-trunked" trees which all spring from the same root above the ground. If the root were not claw-shaped, they would look like planted sticks and would on that account be disqualified.

(11) The proper training of a tree, however, takes

[34] crooked /krʊkt/ *adj.* 扭曲的；弯曲的

[35] thistle /ˈθɪsl/ *n.* 蓟（野生植物；叶有刺）

[36] matrimony vine：枸杞藤（matrimony /ˈmætrɪmənɪ/）

[37] perpendicular /ˌpɜːpənˈdɪkjələ(r)/ *adj.* 垂直的

[38] claw /klɔː/ *n.* （动物或禽类的）爪

[39] swollen /ˈswəʊlən/ *adj.* 臃肿的；粗大的（swell 的过去分词）

[40] branch off：分叉

[41] treble /ˈtrebl/ *adj.* 三倍的；三重的

at least thirty to forty years. In my whole life, I have seen only one person, old Wan Ts'aichang of my district, who succeeded in training several trees in his life. Once I also saw at the home of a merchant at Yangchow two pots, one of boxwood[42] and one of cypress[43], presented to him by a friend from Yüshan, but this was like casting pearls before swine[44]. Outside these cases, I have not seen any really good ones. Trees whose branches are trained in different horizontal circles going up like a pagoda[45] or whose branches turn round and round like earthworms are incurably vulgar.

（12） When arranging miniature[46] sceneries with flowers and stones in a pot, design so that a small one could suggest a painting, and a big one the infinite. One should make it so that, with a pot of tea, one could lose oneself in a world of imagination; and only this kind should be kept in one's private studio for enjoyment. Once I planted some narcissus[47] and could not find any pebbles from Lingpi[48] for use in the pot, and I substituted them with pieces of coal that looked like rocks. One can also take five or seven pieces of yellow-brimmed white cabbage of different size, whose core is white like jade, and plant them in sand in an oblong[49] earthen basin, decorated with charcoal[50] instead of pebbles. The black of the charcoal will then contrast vividly with the white of the cabbage, quite interesting to look at. It is impossible to enumerate[51] all the possible variations, but if one exercises one's ingenuity[52], it will be found to be an endless source of pleasure. For instance, one can take some calamus[53] seeds in the mouth, chew them together with cold rice soup, and blow them on to pieces of charcoal. Keep them in a dark damp place and fine little calamus will grow from them. These pieces of charcoal can then be placed in any flower basin, looking like moss-covered rocks. Or one can take some old lotus seeds, grind[54] off slightly both ends, and put them in an egg-shell, making a hen sit on it together with other eggs. When the little chickens are hatched, take the egg out

[42] boxwood: 黄杨木

[43] cypress /'saɪprəs/ n. 柏树

[44] cast pearls before swine: （英语成语）明珠暗投；对牛弹琴

[45] pagoda /pə'ɡəʊdə/ n. 佛塔

[46] miniature /'mɪnətʃə (r)/ adj. 微型的

[47] narcissus /nɑː'sɪsəs/ n. 水仙花

[48] 灵璧石：中国四大观赏石之一，产自安徽省灵璧县，因此得名。

[49] oblong /'ɒblɒŋ/ adj. 长方形的；矩形的

[50] charcoal /'tʃɑːkəʊl/ n. 木炭

[51] enumerate /ɪ'njuːməreɪt/ v. 列举

[52] ingenuity /ˌɪndʒə'njuːətɪ/ n. 创造力；聪明才智

[53] calamus /'kæləməs/ n. 菖蒲

[54] grind /ɡraɪnd/ v. 磨碎；碾碎

also and plant the old lotus seeds in old clay from swallows' nests, prepared with twenty per cent of ground[55] asparagus[56]. Keep these then in a small vessel filled with river water, and expose them to the morning sun. When the flowers bloom, they will be only the size of a wine cup, while the leaves will be about the size of a bowl, very cute and beautiful to look at.

（13） As to the planning of garden pavilions, towers, winding corridors and out-houses, the designing of rockery and the training of flower-trees, one should try to show the small in the big, and the big in the small, and provide for the real in the unreal and for the unreal in the real. One reveals and conceals alternately, making it sometimes apparent and sometimes hidden. This is not just rhythmic[57] irregularity, nor does it depend on having a wide space and great expenditure[58] of labour and material. Pile up a mound[59] with earth dug from the ground and decorate it with rocks, mingled[60] with flowers; use live plum-branches for your fence, and plant creepers[61] over the walls. Thus one can create the effect of a hill out of a flat piece of ground. In the big, open spaces, plant bamboos that grow quickly and train plum-trees with thick branches to screen them off. This is to show the small in the big. When a courtyard is small, the wall should run in a series of convex[62] and concave[63] lines, decorated with green, covered with ivy and inlaid[64] with big slabs[65] of stone with inscriptions[66] on them. Thus when you open your window, you seem to face a rocky hillside, alive with rugged[67] beauty. This is to show the big in the small. Contrive[68] so that an apparently blind alley leads suddenly into an open space and a closet[69]-like door forms the entrance into an unexpected courtyard. This is to provide for the real in the unreal. Let a door lead into a blind courtyard and conceal the view by placing a few bamboo trees and a few rocks before it. Thus you suggest something which is not there. Place low balustrades[70] along the top of a wall so as to suggest a roof garden. This is to provide for the unreal in

---

55 ground /graʊnd/ adj. 磨碎的

56 asparagus /əˈspærəgəs/ n. 天门冬（多年生草本植物，其块根可入药）

57 rhythmic /ˈrɪðmɪk/ adj. 有节奏（或规律）的

58 expenditure /ɪkˈspendɪtʃə(r)/ n. （材料等的）耗费；消耗

59 mound /maʊnd/ n. 土墩；土丘

60 mingle /ˈmɪŋɡl/ v. 使混合；与……结合

61 creeper /ˈkriːpə(r)/ n. 蔓生植物；攀缘植物

62 convex /ˈkɒnveks/ adj. 凸面的

63 concave /kɒnˈkeɪv/ adj. 凹的；凹面的

64 inlaid /ˌɪnˈleɪd/ adj. 镶嵌着图案的；嵌入的（inlay 的过去分词）

65 slab /slæb/ n. （石、木等坚硬物质的）厚板

66 inscription /ɪnˈskrɪpʃən/ n. 铭刻；碑文

67 rugged /ˈrʌɡɪd/ adj. 崎岖的；凹凸不平的；粗犷的

68 contrive /kənˈtraɪv/ v. 巧妙地策划；精巧地设计

69 closet /ˈklɒzɪt/ n. 储藏室；壁橱

the real.

（14）Poor scholars who live in crowded houses should follow the method of the boatmen in our native district who make clever arrangements with their limited space on the sterns[71] of their boats by devising certain modifications[72], such as making a series of successive elevations one after another, and using them as beds, of which there may be three in a little room, and separating them with papered wooden partitions[73]. The effect will be compact[74] and wonderful to look at, like surveying a long stretch of road, and one will not feel the cramping[75] of space. When my wife and I were staying at Yangchow, we lived in a house of only two beams[76], but the two bedrooms, the kitchen and the parlour[77] were all arranged in this method, with an exquisite effect and great saving of space. Yün once said to me laughingly, " The arrangements are exquisite enough, but after all, they lack the luxurious atmosphere of a rich man's house." It was so indeed.

（15）Once I visited my ancestral tombs on the hill and found some pebbles of great beauty, with faint tracings on them. On coming back, I talked it over with Yün, and said, "People mix putty[78] with Hsüanchow stones[79] in white stone basins, because the colours of the two elements blend. These yellow pebbles of this hill, however, are different, and although they are rugged and simple, they will not blend in colour with putty. What can we do?" "Take some of the worse quality," she said, "pound them into small pieces and mix them in the putty before it is dry, and perhaps when it is dry, the colour will be uniform[80]."

（16）So we did as she suggested, and took a rectangular[81] Yi-hsing earthen basin[82], on which we piled up a mountain peak on the left coming down in undulations[83] to the right. On its back, we made rugged square lines in the style of rock paintings of Ni Yünlin[84], so that the whole looked like a rocky precipice[85] overhanging a river. At one corner we made a hollow

[70] balustrade /ˌbælə'streɪd/ n. 栏杆

[71] stern /stɜːn/ n. 船尾

[72] modification /ˌmɒdɪfɪ'keɪʃn/ n. 修改；改进

[73] partition /pɑː'tɪʃn/ n. 隔断；隔扇；隔板墙

[74] compact /kəm'pækt/ adj. 紧凑的；紧密的

[75] cramp /kræmp/ v. 束缚；约束

[76] beam /biːm/ n. （建筑物的）梁

[77] parlour /'pɑːlə(r)/ n. （私人住房的）起居室；客厅

[78] putty /'pʌtɪ/ n. 油灰

[79] 宣石，主要产于安徽省宣城市所辖的宁国市。

[80] uniform /'juːnɪfɔːm/ adj. 一致的；统一的

[81] rectangular /rek'tæŋɡjələ(r)/ adj. 长方形的；矩形的

[82] 宜兴窑在今江苏宜兴丁蜀镇，是我国重要的陶瓷产区，因烧造紫砂器而闻名。

[83] undulation /ˌʌndju'leɪʃn/ n. 波

place, which we filled with mud and planted with multi-leaf white duckweed[86], while the rocks were planted with dodder[87]. This took us quite a few days to finish. In late autumn, the dodder grew all over the hill, like wistarias[88] hanging down from a rock. The red dodder flowers made a striking contrast to the white duckweed, which had grown luxuriantly[89], too, from the pond underneath. Looking at it, one could imagine oneself transported to some fairy region. We put this under the eaves[90], and discussed between ourselves where we should build a covered terrace[91] by the water, where we should put a garden arbour[92], and where we should put a stone inscription: "Where petals drop and waters flow." And Yün further discussed with me where we could build our home, where we could fish, and where we could go up for a better view of the distance, all so absorbed in it as if we were moving to live in that little imaginary universe. One night, two cats were fighting for food and fell down over the eaves and accidentally broke the whole thing into pieces, basin and all. I sighed and said, "The gods seem to be jealous of even such a little effort of ours." And we both shed tears.

(17) To burn incense[93] in a quiet room is one of the cultivated pleasures of a leisurely life. Yün used to burn aloes[94]-wood and *shuhsiang* [a kind of fragrant wood from Cambodia[95]]. She used to steam the wood first in a cauldron[96] thoroughly, and then place it on a copper wire net over a stove, about half an inch from the fire. Under the action of the slow fire, the wood would give out a kind of subtle fragrance without any visible smoke. Another thing, the "buddha's fingers[97]" [a variety of citron[98]] should not be smelt by a drunken man, or it would easily rot. It is also bad for the quince[99] to perspire[100] [as under atmospheric[101] changes], and when it does so, one should wash it with water. The citron alone is easy to take care of, because it is not afraid of handling. There are different ways of taking care of the "buddha's fingers" and the quince which cannot be expressed in so many

浪形

84 倪云林,即倪瓒,元末明初画家、诗人,"元四家"之一。

85 precipice /ˈpresəpɪs/ *n.* 悬崖;绝壁

86 duckweed /ˈdʌkwiːd/ *n.* 浮萍

87 dodder /ˈdɒdə/ *n.* 菟丝子(沈复原文为"茑萝")

88 wistaria /wɪˈstɛərɪə/ *n.* 紫藤

89 luxuriantly /lʌgˈʒʊərɪəntlɪ/ *adv.* 茂盛地;浓密地

90 eave /ɪv/ *n.* 屋檐

91 terrace /ˈterəs/ *n.* 露天平台;看台

92 arbour /ˈɑːbə(r)/ *n.*(花园、院子中由藤蔓在架子上攀缘而成的)棚架;凉棚

93 incense /ˈɪnsens/ *n.* 香(尤指宗教礼仪用的)

94 aloe /ˈæləʊ/ *n.* 芦荟

95 Cambodia /kæmˈbəʊdɪə/ 柬埔寨

96 cauldron /ˈkɔːldrən/ *n.* 大锅

97 即佛手柑。

98 citron /ˈsɪtrən/ *n.* 香橼

99 quince /kwɪns/ *n.* 榅桲(沈复原文为"木瓜")

100 perspire /pəˈspaɪə(r)/ *v.* 出汗

101 atmospheric /ˌætməsˈferɪk/ *adj.* 大气的;大气层的

words. I have seen people who take one of these things, which have been properly kept, and handle or smell it in any old way and put it down again roughly, which shows that they do not know the art of preserving these things.

（18）In my home I always had a vase of flowers on my desk. "You know very well about arranging flowers in vases for all kinds of weather," said Yün to me one day. "I think you have really understood the art, but there is a type of painting commonly called 'insects on grass blades,' which you haven't applied yet. Why don't you try?"

（19）"I'm afraid," I replied, "that I cannot hold the insect's legs still. What can I do?"

（20）"I know a way, except that I am afraid it would be too cruel," said Yün.

（21）"Tell me about it," I asked.

（22）"You know that an insect does not change its colour after death. You can find a mantis[102] or cicada[103] or a butterfly; kill it with a pin and use a fine wire to tie its neck to the flowers, arranging its legs so that they either hold on to the stem or rest on the leaves. It would then look like a live one. Don't you think it is very good?"

（23）I was quite delighted and did as she suggested, and many of our friends thought it very wonderful. I am afraid it is difficult to find ladies nowadays who show such an understanding of things.

（24）When I was staying with my friend Mr. Hua at Hsishan[104] with Yün, Mrs. Hua used to ask Yün to teach her two daughters reading. In that country house, the yard was wide open and the glare of the summer sun was very oppressive. Yün taught them a method of making movable screens of growing flowers. Every screen consisted of a single piece. She took two little pieces of wood about four or five inches long, and laid them parallel like a low stool, with the hollow top filled by four horizontal bars over a foot long. At the four corners, she made little round holes on which she stuck a trellis[105]-work made of bamboo. The trellis was six or seven feet high and on its bottom was placed a pot of peas which

[102] mantis /ˈmæntɪs/ n. 螳螂
[103] cicada /sɪˈkɑːdə/ n. 蝉

[104] 锡山，今江苏省无锡市锡山区。

[105] trellis /ˈtrelɪs/ n.（支撑攀缘植物的）棚；架

would then grow up and entwine[106] round the bamboo trellis. This could be easily moved by two persons.

（25）One can make several of these things and place them wherever one pleases, before windows or doors, and they will look like living plants, casting their green shade into the house, warding off[107] the sun and yet allowing the wind to come through. They can be placed in any irregular formation, adjustable according to time and circumstances, and are, therefore, called "movable flower screens." With this method, one can use any kind of fragrant weeds of the creeper family, instead of peas. It is an excellent arrangement for people staying in the country.

（26）My friend Lu Panfang's name was Chang and his literary name[108] Ch'ünshan. He was very good at painting pine-trees and cypresses, plum blossoms and chrysanthemums, as well as writing the *lishu* style of calligraphy[109], besides specializing in carving seals. I stayed in his home called Hsiaoshuanglou for a year and a half. The house faced east and consisted of five beams, of which I occupied three. From it one could get a beautiful view of the distance in rain or shine. In the middle of the court, there was a tree, the *Osmanthus fragrans*[110], which filled the air with a kind of delicate fragrance. There were corridors and living rooms, and the place was quite secluded[111]. When I went there, I brought along a man-servant and an old woman, who also brought with them a young daughter. The man-servant could make dresses and the old woman could spin; therefore Yün did embroidery[112], the old woman spun and the man-servant made dresses to provide for our daily expenses.

（27）I was by nature very fond of guests and whenever we had a little drinking party, I insisted on having wine-games. Yün was very clever at preparing inexpensive dishes; ordinary foodstuffs[113] like melon, vegetables, fish and shrimps had a special flavour when prepared by her. My friends knew that I was poor, and

---

[106] entwine /ɪnˈtwaɪn/ v. 盘绕；缠绕

[107] ward off: 避开；躲开

[108] literary name：表字，旧时人在本名以外所起的表示德行或本名意义的名字。

[109] 隶书（calligraphy /kəˈlɪɡrəfɪ/ n. 书法艺术）

[110] Osmanthus fragrans：桂花树

[111] secluded /sɪˈkluːdɪd/ adj. 清净的；不受打扰的

[112] embroidery /ɪmˈbrɔɪdərɪ/ n. 刺绣

[113] foodstuff /ˈfuːdstʌf/ n. 食物；食品

often helped pay the expenses in order that we might get together and talk for the whole day. I was very keen on keeping the place spotlessly[114] clean, and was, besides, fond of free and easy ways with my friends.

（28） At this time, there were a group of friends, like Yang Pufan, also called Ch'anghsü, who specialized in portrait sketches; Yüan Shaoyü, also called P'ai, who specialized in painting landscape; and Wang Hsing-lan, also called Yen, good at painting flowers and birds. They all liked the Hsiaoshuanglou because of its seclusion[115], so they would bring their painting utensils[116] to the place and I learnt painting from them. They would then either write "grass-script" or "chüan-script"[117] or carve seals, from which we made some money which we turned over to Yün to defray[118] expenses for teas and dinners. The whole day long, we were occupied in discussing poetry or painting only. There were, moreover, friends like the brothers Hsia Tan-an and Hsia Yishan, the brothers Miao Shanyin and Miao Chihpo, Chiang Yünhsiang, Loh Chühsiang, Chou Hsiaohsia, Kuo Hsiaoyü, Hua Hsingfan, and Chang Hsienhan. These friends came and went as they pleased, like the swallows by the eaves. Yün would take off her hairpin[119] and sell it for wine without a second's thought, for she would not let a beautiful day pass without company. Today these friends are scattered to the four corners of the earth like clouds dispersed[120] by a storm, and the woman I loved is dead, like broken jade and buried incense. How sad indeed to look back upon these things!

（29） Among the friends at Hsiaoshuanglou, four things were tabooed[121]: firstly, talking about people's official promotions; secondly, gossiping about law-suits and current affairs; thirdly, discussing the conventional eight-legged essays[122] for the imperial examinations[123]; and fourthly, playing cards and dice[124]. Whoever broke any of these rules was penalized to provide five catties[125] of wine. On the other hand, there were four things which we all approved: generosity, romantic charm, free and

[114] spotlessly /ˈspɒtləslɪ/ adv. 一尘不染地

[115] seclusion /sɪˈkluːʒn/ n. 清静；与世隔绝

[116] utensil /juːˈtensl/ n. 器皿；家什

[117] 即草篆，汉字书体的一种。

[118] defray /dɪˈfreɪ/ v. 支付；付给

[119] hairpin /ˈheəpɪn/ n. 发夹

[120] disperse /dɪˈspɜːs/ v. （使）分散；驱散

[121] taboo /təˈbuː/ v. 列为禁忌；禁止；避讳

[122] 指八股文。

[123] 指科举考试。

[124] dice /daɪs/ n. 骰子；掷骰游戏（赌博）

[125] catty /ˈkætɪ/ n. 斤（重量单位）

easy ways, and quietness. In the long summer days when we had nothing to do, we used to hold examinations among ourselves. At those parties, there would be eight persons, each bringing two hundred cash along. We began by drawing lots, and the one who got the first would be the official examiner, seated on top by himself, while the second one would be the official recorder, also seated in his place. The others would then be the candidates, each taking a slip of paper, properly stamped with a seal, from the official recorder. The examiner then gave out a line of seven words and one of five words, with which each of us was to make the best couplet[126]. The time limit was the burning of a joss-stick[127] and we were to tease our brains[128] standing or walking about, but were not allowed to exchange words with each other. When a candidate had made the couplets, he placed them in a special box and then returned to his seat. After all the papers had been handed in, the official recorder then opened the box and copied them together in a book, which he submitted to the examiner, thus safeguarding against any partiality[129] on the latter's part.

(30) Of these couplets submitted, three of the seven-word lines[130] and three of the five-word lines[131] were to be chosen as the best. The one who turned in the best of these six chosen couplets would then be the official examiner for the next round, and the second best would be the official recorder. One who had two couplets failing to be chosen would be fined twenty cash, one failing in one couplet fined ten cash, and failures handed in beyond the time limit would be fined twice the amount. The official examiner would get one hundred cash "incense money." Thus we could have ten examinations in a day and provide a thousand cash with which to buy wine and have a grand drinking party. Yün's paper alone was considered special and exempt[132] from fine, and she was allowed the privilege of thinking out her lines on her seat.

(31) One day Yang Pufan made a sketch of Yün and myself working at a garden with wonderful likeness.

126 couplet /ˈkʌplət/ n. 对句（相连的两行长度相等的诗句）；对联
127 joss-stick：线香（中国古代常以燃香作为时间计量的单位，即"一炷香的时间"。）
128 tease one's brains：(= rack one's brains) 绞尽脑汁

129 partiality /ˌpɑːʃiˈælətɪ/ n. 偏袒

130 seven-word lines：七言（诗句）
131 five-word lines：五言（诗句）

132 exempt /ɪgˈzempt/ adj. 免除（责任、付款等）

On that night, the moon was very bright and was casting a wonderfully picturesque[133] shadow of an orchid flower on the white wall. Inspired by some hard drinking, Hsing-lan said to me, "Pufan can paint your portrait sketch, but I can paint the shadows of flowers."

（32）"Will the sketch of flowers be as good as that of a man?" I asked.

（33）Then Hsing-lan took a piece of paper and placed it against the wall, on which he traced the shadow of the orchid flower with dark and light inkings. When we looked at it in the day-time, there was a kind of haziness about the lines of leaves and flowers, suggestive[134] of the moonlight, although it could not be called a real painting. Yün liked it very much and all my friends wrote their inscriptions on it.

（34）There are two places in Soochow called the South Garden and the North Garden. We would go there when the rape flowers[135] were in bloom, but there was no wine shop nearby where we could have a drink. If we brought eatables along in a basket, there was little fun drinking cold wine in the company of the flowers. Some proposed that we should look for some place to get a drink in the neighbourhood, and others suggested that we should look at the flowers first and then come back for a drink, but this was never quite the ideal thing, which should be to drink warm wine in the presence of flowers. While no one could make any satisfactory suggestion, Yün smiled and said, "Tomorrow you people provide the money and I'll carry a stove to the place myself." "Very well," they all said. When my friends had left, I asked Yün how she was going to do it. "I am not going to carry it myself," she said. "I have seen *wonton* sellers in the streets who carry along a stove and a pan and everything we need. We could just ask one of these fellows to go along with us. I'll prepare the dishes first, and when we arrive, all we need is just to heat them up, and we will have everything ready including tea and wine."

[133] picturesque /ˌpɪktʃəˈresk/ *adj.* 优美的；古色古香的；生动的；栩栩如生的

[134] suggestive /səˈdʒestɪv/ *adj.* 使人想起……的；引起联想的

[135] rape flowers：油菜花

（35）"Well, but what about the kettle for boiling tea?"

（36）"We could carry along an earthen pot," she said, "remove the *wonton* seller's pan and suspend the pot over the fire by a spike. This will then serve us as a kettle for boiling tea, won't it?"

（37）I clapped my hands in applause. There was a *wonton* seller by the name of Pao, whom we asked to go along with us the following afternoon, offering to pay him a hundred cash, to which Pao readily consented. The following day my friends, who were going to see the flowers, arrived. I told them about the arrangements, and they were all amazed at Yün's ingenious[136] idea. We started off after lunch, bringing along with us some straw mats and cushions[137]. When we had arrived at the South Garden, we chose a place under the shade of willow trees, and sat together in a circle on the ground. First we boiled some tea, and after drinking it, we warmed up the wine and heated up the dishes. The sun was beautiful and the breeze was gentle, while the yellow rape flowers in the field looked like a stretch of gold, with gaily[138] dressed young men and women passing by the rice fields and bees and butterflies flitting[139] to and fro—a sight which could make one drunk without any liquor. Very soon the wine and dishes were ready and we sat together on the ground drinking and eating. The *wonton* seller was quite a likeable person and we asked him to join us. People who saw us thus enjoying ourselves thought it quite a novel[140] idea. Then the cups, bowls and dishes lay about in great disorder on the ground, while we were already slightly drunk, some sitting and some lying down, and some singing or yelling. When the sun was going down, I wanted to eat congee[141], and the *wanton* seller bought some rice and cooked it for us. We then came back with a full belly.

（38）"Did you enjoy it today?" asked Yün.

（39）"We would not have enjoyed it so much, had it not been for Madame!" all of us exclaimed. Then

[136] ingenious /ɪnˈdʒiːnɪəs/ *adj.* 新颖独特的；巧妙的；心灵手巧的

[137] cushion /ˈkʊʃn/ *n.* 坐垫；软垫

[138] gaily /ˈgeɪlɪ/ *adv.* （着装）艳丽地；华丽地

[139] flit /flɪt/ *v.* 轻快地从一处到另一处；掠过

[140] novel /ˈnɒvl/ *adj.* 新颖的；与众不同的

[141] congee /ˈkɒndʒiː/ *n.* 米粥

merrily we parted.

(40) A poor scholar should try to be economical in the matter of food, clothing, house and furniture, but at the same time be clean and artistic. In order to be economical, one should "manage according to the needs of the occasion," as the saying goes. I was very fond of having nice little suppers with a little liquor, but did not care for many dishes. Yün used to make a tray with a plum-blossom design. It consisted of six deep dishes of white porcelain[142], two inches in diameter, one in the centre and the other five grouped round it, painted grey and looking like a plum flower. Both its bottom and its top were bevelled[143] and there was a handle on the top resembling the stem of a plum flower, so that, when placed on the table, it looked like a regular plum blossom dropped on the table, and on opening, the different vegetables were found to be contained in the petals of the flower. A case like this with six different dishes would be quite enough to serve a dinner for two or three close friends. If second helping was needed, more could be added besides this, we made another round tray with a low border for holding chopsticks, cups and the wine pot. These were easily moved about and one could have the dinner served at any place one wished. This is an example of economy in the matter of food.

(41) Yün also made me my collars, socks and my little cap. When my clothes were torn, she would cut out one piece to mend another, making it always look very neat and tidy. I used to choose quiet colours for my clothes, for the reason that dirty spots would not show easily, and one could wear them both at home and abroad. This is an instance of economy in the matter of dress. When I first took up my residence at the Hsiaoshuanglou, I found the rooms too dark, but after papering the walls with white paper, they were quite bright again. During the summer months, the ground floor was quite open, because the windows had all been taken down, and we felt that the place lacked privacy.

[142] porcelain /ˈpɔːsəlɪn/ n. 瓷器

[143] bevel /ˈbevl/ v. 把（物体的方形边）改成斜面边

"There is an old bamboo screen," suggested Yün. "Why don't we use it and let it serve in place of a railing[144]?"

(42) "But how?" I asked.

(43) "Take a few pieces of bamboo of black colour," she replied, "and make them into a square, leaving room for people to pass out and in. Cut off half of the bamboo screen and fasten it on the horizontal bamboo, about the height of a table, letting the screen come down to the ground. Then put four vertical pieces of short bamboo in the centre, fasten these in place by means of a string, and then find some old strips of black cloth and wrap them up together with the horizontal bar with needle and thread. It would give a little privacy and would look quite well, besides being inexpensive." This is an instance of "managing according to the needs of the occasion." This goes to prove the truth of the ancient saying that "slips of bamboo and chips of wood all have their use."

(44) When the lotus flowers bloom in summer, they close at night and open in the morning. Yün used to put some tea leaves in a little silk bag and place it in the centre of the flower at night. We would take it out the next morning, and make tea with spring water, which would then have a very delicate flavour.

[144] railing /ˈreɪlɪŋ/ n. 围栏；栏杆

🔲 精华赏析 🔲

这里我们谈一谈中国传统文化独特而又重要的一部分——隐逸文化。

很多人非常推崇《浮生六记》中记录的沈复和芸娘的生活，把他们夫妻看成是神仙眷侣，是中国封建社会真正的隐士。他们夫妻二人年龄相当，志趣相投，伉俪情深，琴瑟和鸣；生性淡泊，不喜名利，不问仕途经济；平日里谈诗论赋，品花赏月，充满诗情画意，闲情雅趣，把布衣蔬食的清苦日子过成了世外桃源的生活。林语堂更是在《浮生六记》的译者序里写道："我仿佛看到中国处世哲学的精华在两位恰巧成为夫妇的人身上表现出来"，并盛赞芸娘为"中国文学及中国历史上一个最可爱的女人"。然而，另外一些人则批评他们一味追求精神享受，没有立世养家的本事，没有对父母、子女尽责，只靠父母的供给过日子，是寄生虫；沈复纨绔浪荡，不务正业，芸娘又一味纵容，不加规劝，最终两人遭父母嫌恶，被赶出家门；他们不谙人情世故，不懂人性险恶，愚弱懦弱，受人欺辱，最终只能郁郁寡欢，惨淡收场。

书中的沈复，批评者视其为落魄的浪荡公子，爱慕者则称其为真正的高士。其实，当今世人对沈复夫妇的两种不同的评价,反映了中国传统文化里两种截然相反的人生哲学——积极入世与消极避世。究其思想根源,这两种不同的人生态度与统贯中华文化命脉、培育中华民族精神、铸就中华民族性格的儒、佛、道三家思想有着千丝万缕的联系。

儒家提倡"学而优则仕",强调"修身齐家治国平天下",讲的是"天下兴亡,匹夫有责"的担当,这是一种积极入世的人生哲学。由于儒家思想是我国封建社会的正统思想,这种观念在中国封建社会根深蒂固,影响深远,这就是为什么无心仕途经济的沈复饱受争议的原因。但是,儒家虽然倡导积极入仕,但孔子也说过:"天下有道则见,无道则隐";孟子也说过:"穷则独善其身,达则兼济天下。"因此,儒家并不排斥隐逸。道教是我国唯一的本土宗教,它崇尚自然,提倡无为和不争,追求精神的高度自由。同时,道家重视修炼养生,以此达到长生,羽化登仙。这种致虚守静、与世无争的思想常常被当作是出世之学。佛教自传入中原后逐渐本土化,它宣扬四大皆空,认为世俗生活就是各种烦恼和痛苦滋生的根源,只有放下执念,无欲无求,才能脱离苦海。所以,佛教的思想多被视为遁世哲学。由此可见,中国隐逸文化的形成,受到儒、佛、道三家思想的影响,这种深厚博大的思想根基也赋予了中国隐逸文化独具特色的东方审美。

那么,何为隐士?首先,隐士选择的是一种归隐的生活方式,他们不问仕途经济,不慕富贵荣华,但隐士文化的重点还是在"士",即知识分子,指的是饱读诗书、学识渊博的贤能达士,并非一般的山野樵夫。韩兆琦在《中国古代的隐士》中认为隐士是与"官僚"相对而言的,是指"有道德、有才干,原是个做官的材料,但由于某种客观或主观的原因,没有进入官场;或者本来做官做得好好的,后来由于某种客观或主观的原因而离开官场,找个什么地方'隐'起来"(韩兆琦,1996)的人。

中国历史上隐士众多,历朝历代都有隐士名留青史。他们或者是德行深厚、品行高洁的世外高人,如伯夷、叔齐、颜回等,或者是满腹韬略、才华横溢的旷世奇才,如鬼谷子、黄石公等。我国最早的隐士当属上古时代的许由和与他同时期的巢父,他们的故事为我们留下了"饮犊上流"这个成语。据说尧帝要把君位让给许由,许由推辞不受,并跑到颍水边洗耳,表示不愿听到这些俗言浊语。在旁边牵牛饮水的巢父便讽刺许由隐匿不深,才会被尧找到,更责备许由洗耳的水会脏了自己牛的嘴,便牵牛到上游饮水。许由从此隐居深山,再不出游。中国人最熟悉的古代隐士可能是陶渊明,他归田之后,一边躬耕陇亩,从事农业劳动,一边进行诗歌创作,写下了大量流传千古的名篇佳句,被誉为中国"隐逸诗人之宗""田园诗派之鼻祖"。历史上还有一位非常惨烈的隐士,为了追求隐逸的生活而丢了性命,那就是介子推。介之推是春秋时期晋国人,是晋文公重耳的谋臣。相传重耳早年流亡在外,过着食不果腹、衣不蔽体的生活,追随他的介之推曾有一次割下自己大腿上的肉煮成羹汤送给被饿得奄奄一息的重耳吃,救了他一命。后来重耳做了晋国的国君,大行封赏功臣,却疏漏了救命恩人介之推。介之推不愿争宠,携老母隐居绵山。后来晋文公屡次寻介之推而不得,为了逼他出来,下令火烧绵山,介之推抱树而死。后人为了纪念他"割股奉君"的义举和隐居"不言禄"的气节,便在他死难这天熄火灭烟,只吃冷食,这就是寒食节的来历。

实际上,中国古代文人由于同时受到儒家和道家思想的影响,很难在"入世"和"出世"之间画上清晰的界限。进则朝廷庙堂,退而江湖山野,始终是中国古代文人心头化解不开的情结。中国的隐士,大部分都是仕而后隐,他们曾出仕为官,但终因官场黑暗、人心险恶而萌生退意。这些隐士大多性格耿直,为人刚正不阿,不愿卑躬屈膝、攀附权贵,不得不解冠归去。陶渊明便是这类隐士的典型代表。他早年是颇有远志的,但当时的门阀制度使他很难有大的作为。虽然当初"猛志逸四海",最终无奈"性本爱丘山"。还有些人"以隐求仕",隐居是为了寻找入世的机会,如姜子牙、诸葛亮。姜子牙在遇到周文王姬昌之前,隐居渭水河畔。他日日以直钩钓鱼,以期引起姬昌注意,这便是典故"姜太公钓鱼,愿者上钩"的来源。诸葛亮早年跟随叔父诸葛玄投靠荆州刘表,也是希望有一番作为的。诸葛玄死后,诸葛亮便隐居隆中,等候机会。后得徐庶推荐,刘备三顾茅庐,诸葛亮以《隆中对》最终获得刘备的重视。因此,严格来讲他们并不算是真正意义上的隐士。唐朝还有一个"假隐士"卢藏用,可以说是把"以隐求仕"的套路用得炉火纯青了。《新唐书·卢藏用传》记载,幽州范阳人卢藏用因考中进士后没有被调用,便跑到长安南边的终南山隐居,等待朝廷征召。但他并不老老实实在终南山呆着,而是皇上到哪儿就跟到哪里隐居,时人称之为"随驾隐士"。后来他果然一"隐"成名,被朝廷以高士之名征召入仕,隐居的名声让他谋到了好处。后人以"终南捷径"讥讽他的谋官之道。另有一些隐士,虽身居山林,却心在庙堂。战国时的鬼谷子一生隐居深山,但他教出的弟子却出将入相,左右时局,影响着历史的进程。黄石公三试张良的目的,也是为天下选择贤臣良相。商山四皓隐居了一辈子,汉高祖刘邦多次征召而不应,却在耄耋之年甘愿出山辅佐太子刘盈直至登基。可见,即使无心仕途、潜心修行的高士,也很难真正做到不问世事。

完全归隐的纯粹隐士有没有呢?其实大有人在。这些人一生的追求就是隐没于山林,不愿被俗务牵绊,以维护内心真正的自由和平静,所以大多没有留下名字,因此也就不为人知了。这类隐士里面稍微有点名气的是北宋的林逋,就是写出"疏影横斜水清浅,暗香浮动月黄昏"的那位诗人。据记载,他性孤高,喜恬淡,自甘贫困,后隐居杭州西湖,以湖山为伴。林逋终生不仕不娶,没有子女,他在隐居的西湖孤山广植梅树,豢养了很多鹤,人称"梅妻鹤子"。还有的隐士,即便朝廷多次延请,他们也拒不出仕,如晋宋时期的宗炳、元代的吴镇。林逋以诗才留名,宗炳、吴镇以书画之艺扬名,但他们栖身寒庐,寄意田园,固守着超凡脱俗的人生哲学,甘于清贫的生活而怡然自乐,这才是真正的隐士精神。

参考文献

[1] 韩兆琦. 中国古代的隐士[M]. 北京:商务印书馆,1996.
[2] 沈复. 浮生六记[M]. 林语堂,译. 北京:外语教学与研究出版社,1999.

阅读思考

1. 你还知道中国历史上哪些隐士的故事?
2. 你认为沈复是一个隐士吗?

8

The Selfish Giant

Oscar Wilde

【作品简介】

《自私的巨人》(*The Selfish Giant*)是奥斯卡·王尔德创作的九篇童话作品中最短的一篇,讲述了自私的巨人如何从自私变得慷慨,最终进入天堂的温馨故事。这篇童话出自 1888 年出版的王尔德的童话集《快乐王子及其他故事》(*The Happy Prince and Other Tales*),该童话集还包含另外四篇童话,即《快乐王子》(*The Happy Prince*)、《夜莺与玫瑰》(*The Nightingale and the Rose*)、《忠实的朋友》(*The Devoted Friend*)和《了不起的火箭》(*The Remarkable Rocket*)。

【作者简介】

奥斯卡·王尔德(*Oscar Wilde*,1854—1900),出生于爱尔兰都柏林的一个家世卓越的家庭,英国著名作家,唯美主义先锋作家,因其剧作、诗歌、童话和小说而闻名,代表作品包括剧作《温德密尔夫人的扇子》(*Lady Windermere's Fan*)、《莎乐美》(*Salomé*)和《理想丈夫》(*An Ideal Husband*),诗集《斯芬克斯》(*Sphinx*),童话集《快乐王子及其他故事》(*The Happy Prince and Other Tale*)和《石榴之家》(*A House of Pomegranates*),以及长篇小说《道林·格雷的画像》(*The Picture of Dorian Gray*)。

(1) Every afternoon, as they were coming from school, the children used to go and play in the giant's garden.

(2) It was a large lovely garden, with soft green grass. Here and there over the grass stood beautiful flowers like stars, and there were twelve peach trees that in the springtime broke out into <u>delicate</u>[1] <u>blossoms</u>[2] of pink and pearl, and in the autumn bore rich fruit. The birds sat on the trees and sang so sweetly that the children used to stop their games in order to listen to them. "How happy we are here!" they cried to each other.

[1] delicate /ˈdelɪkət/ *adj.* 精美的
[2] blossom /ˈblɒsəm/ *n.* 花朵

（3）One day the giant came back. He had been to visit his friend the Cornish[3] ogre[4], and had stayed with him for seven years. After the seven years were over he had said all that he had to say, for his conversation was limited, and he determined to return to his own castle. When he arrived he saw the children playing in the garden.

（4）"What are you doing there?" he cried in a very gruff[5] voice, and the children ran away.

（5）"My own garden is my own garden," said the giant, "anyone can understand that, and I will allow nobody to play in it but myself." So he built a high wall all round it, and put up a notice-board[6]:

TRESPASSERS[7]

will be

PROSECUTED[8]

（6）He was a very selfish giant.

（7）The poor children had now nowhere to play. They tried to play on the road, but the road was very dusty and full of hard stone, and they did not like it. They used to wander[9] round the high wall when their lessons were over, and talk about the beautiful garden inside. "How happy we were there!" they said to each other.

（8）Then the spring came, and all over the country there were little blossoms and little birds. Only in the garden of the selfish giant it was still winter. The birds did not care to sing in it as there were no children, and the trees forget to blossom. Once a beautiful flower put its head out[10] from the grass, but when it saw the notice-board it was so sorry for the children that it slipped[11] back into the ground again, and went off to sleep. The only people who were pleased were the snow and the frost. "Spring has forgotten this garden," they cried, "so we will live here all the year round." The snow covered up the grass with her great white cloak[12], and the frost painted all the tree sliver. Then they invited the north wind to stay with them, and he came. He was wrapped in

---

[3] Cornish /ˈkɔːnɪʃ/ *adj.* 康沃尔的

[4] ogre /ˈəʊɡə(r)/ *n.* （传说中的）食人恶魔

[5] gruff /ɡrʌf/ *adj.* 低沉粗哑的；生硬的

[6] notice-board：布告栏

[7] trespasser /ˈtrespəsə(r)/ *n.* 不法进入者

[8] prosecute /ˈprɒsɪkjuːt/ *v.* 起诉；控告

[9] wander /ˈwɒndə(r)/ *v.* 漫步；徘徊

[10] put its head out：把头伸出来

[11] slip /slɪp/ *v.* 悄悄疾行；溜

[12] cloak /kləʊk/ *n.* 斗篷

furs, and he roaded[13] all day about the garden, and blew the chimney-pot down. "This is a delightful spot," he said, "we must ask the hail[14] on a visit." So the hail came, every day for three hours he rattled[15] on the roof of the castle till he broke most of the slates[16], and then he ran round and round the garden as fast as he could go. He was dressed in grey, and his breath was like ice[17].

(9) "I cannot understand why the spring is so late in coming," said the selfish giant, as he sat at the window and looked out at his cold, white garden, "I hope there will be a change in the weather."

(10) But the spring never came, nor the summer. The autumn gave golden fruit to every garden, but to the giant's garden she gave none. "He is too selfish," she said. So it was always winter there, and the north wind and the hail, and the frost and the snow danced about through the trees.

(11) Once morning the giant was lying awake in bed when he heard some lovely music. It sounded so sweet to his ears that he thought it must be the king's musicians passing by. It was really only a little linnet[18] singing outside his window, but it was so long since he had heard a bird sing in his garden that it seemed to him to be the most beautiful music in the world. Then the hail stopped dancing over his head, and the north wind ceased[19] roaring, and a delicious perfume[20] came to him through the open casement. "I believe the spring has come at last," said the giant; and he jumped out of bed and looked out.

(12) What did he see?

(13) He saw a most wonderful sight. Through a little hole in the wall the children had crept in, and they were sitting in the branches of the trees. In every tree that he could see there was a little child. And the trees were so glad to have the children back again that they had covered themselves with blossoms, and were waving their arms gently above the children's heads. The birds were flying about and twittering[21] with delight, and the flowers

---

[13] roar /rɔː(r)/ v. 怒吼；咆哮

[14] hail /heɪl/ n. 冰雹

[15] rattle /ˈrætl/ v. (使)发出震颤(或碰撞)声

[16] slate /sleɪt/ n. (盖房顶的)石板瓦

[17] 明喻(simile)

[18] linnet /ˈlɪnɪt/ n. 赤胸朱顶雀

[19] cease /siːs/ v. 停止；结束

[20] perfume /ˈpɜːfjuːm/ n. 芳香；香味

[21] twitter /ˈtwɪtə(r)/ v. (鸟儿)啁啾

were looking up through the green grass and laughing. It was a lovely scene, only in one corner it was still winter. It was the farthest corner of the garden, and in it was standing a little boy. He was so small that he could not reach up to the branches of the tree, and he was wandering all round it, crying bitterly[22]. The poor tree was still quite covered with frost and snow, and the north wind was blowing and roaring above it. "Climb up! Little boy," said the tree, and it bent its branches down as low as it could; but the boy was too tiny.

(14) And the giant's heart melted as looked out.

(15) "How selfish I have been!" he said, "now I know why the spring would not come here. I will put that poor little boy on the top of the tree, and then I will knock down the wall, and my garden shall be the children's playground for ever and ever." He was really very sorry for what he had done.

(16) So he crept downstairs and opened the front door quite softly, and went out into the garden. But when the children saw him they were so frightened that they all ran away, and the garden became winter again. Only the little boy did not run for his eyes were so full of tears that he did not see the giant coming. And the giant stole up behind him and took him gently in his hand, and put him up into the tree. And the tree broke at once into blossom, and the birds came and sang on it, and the little boy stretched out his two arms and flung them round the giant's neck, and kissed him. And the other children, when they saw that the giant was not wicked[23] any longer came running back, and with them came the spring. "It is your garden now, little children," said the giant, and he took a great axe[24] and knocked down the wall. And when the people were going to market at twelve o'clock they found the giant playing with the children in the most beautiful garden they had ever seen.

(17) All day long they played, and in the evening they came to the giant to bid[25] him goodbye.

[22] bitterly /'bɪtəli/ *adv.* 伤心地

[23] wicked /'wɪkɪd/ *adj.* 邪恶的;危险的

[24] axe /æks/ *n.* 斧头

[25] bid /bɪd/ *v.* 向(某人)问候、道别等

（18）"But where is your little companion?" he said, "the boy I put into the tree." The giant loved him the best because he had kissed him.

（19）"We don't know," answered the children, "he has gone away."

（20）"You must tell him <u>to be sure</u>[26] and come here tomorrow," said the giant. But the children said that they did not know where he lived, and had never seen him before; and the giant felt very sad.

（21）Every afternoon, when school was over, the children came and played with the giant. But the little boy whom the giant loved was never seen again. The giant was very kind to all the children, yet he longed for his first little friend, and often spoke of him. "How I would like to see him!" he used to say.

（22）Years went over, and the giant grew very old and <u>feeble</u>[27]. He could not play about any more, so he sat in a huge armchair, and watched the children at their games, and admired his garden. "I have many beautiful flowers," he said, "but the children are the most beautiful flowers of all."

（23）One winter morning he looked out of his window as he dressing. He did not hate the window now, for he knew that it was merely the spring asleep, and that the flowers were resting.

（24）Suddenly he rubbed his eyes in wonder and looked and looked. It certainly was a <u>marvellous</u>[28] sight. In the farthest corner of the garden was a tree quite covered with lovely white blossom. Its branches were golden, and silver fruit hung down from them, and <u>underneath</u>[29] it stood the little boy he had loved.

（25）Downstairs ran the giant in great joy, and out into the garden. He <u>hastened</u>[30] across the grass, and came near to the child. And when he came quite close his face grew red with anger, and he said, "Who <u>hath</u>[31] dared to wound <u>thee</u>[32]?" For on the palms of the child's hands were the prints of two nails, and the prints of two nails were on the little feet.

[26] to be sure：当然

[27] feeble /ˈfiːbl/ *adj.* 虚弱的

[28] marvellous /ˈmɑːvələs/ *adj.* 极好的

[29] underneath/ˌʌndəˈniːθ/ *prep.* 在……下面

[30] hasten /ˈheɪsn/ *v.* 赶往；加速

[31] hath /hæθ/ *aux.* 古英语中 have 的第三人称单数形式

[32] thee /ðiː/ *pron.*（古英语第二人称单数的宾格）你

（26）"Who hath dared to wound thee?" cried the giant, "Tell me, that I may take my big sword and slay³³ him!"

（27）"Nay³⁴!" answer the child, "but these are the wounds of love!"

（28）"Who art thou?³⁵" said the giant, and a strange awe³⁶ fell on him, and he knelt before the little child.

（29）And the child smiled on the giant, and said to him, "you let me play once in your garden, today you shall come with me to my garden, which is Paradise."

（30）And when the children ran in that afternoon, they found the giant lying dead under the tree, all covered with white blossom.

³³ slay /sleɪ/ v. 杀死

³⁴ nay /neɪ/ int. （古英语中的 no）不

³⁵ 即 "Who are you?"

³⁶ awe /ɔː/ n. 敬畏

▸ 精华赏析 ◂

唯美主义是 19 世纪末流行于西欧的文艺思潮,唯美主义者主张"为艺术而艺术",即艺术应追求单纯的美,旨在为人类提供感观上的愉悦,而非传递某种道德或情感的信息。作为唯美主义的代表人物和倡导者,王尔德在其作品中践行了唯美主义的原则,认为不是艺术再现生活,而是"生活模仿艺术";他认为艺术与道德无关,文学作品的"形式"重于"主题",因为主题常与道德相关联。唯美主义理论在王尔德的作品中得到了很大程度的实践,在《自私的巨人》这篇童话故事中,王尔德也摒弃了童话故事教条式的说教,而是极力追求故事形式上的美和语言上的美。

一、形式美

王尔德认为形式上的美重于道德说教,他独具匠心地设计了《自私的巨人》的结构。在故事的一开始,巨人离家去看食人魔朋友,孩子们在巨人的花园里快乐地玩耍。紧接着,巨人回到家中,发现有人闯入他的私人花园,自私的他不愿意和别人分享自己的花园,便粗暴地将所有孩子赶走。由于孩子们不来花园,即使春天到了,鸟儿也不来拜访,花儿也不再开放,原本美丽的花园被北风和冰雹笼罩,没有了春天、夏天和秋天,陷入永恒的冬季。最后,一群孩子偷偷地从一个小洞爬进院子,随着孩子们的到来,园子里也由寒转暖,鸟儿开始歌唱,花儿努力绽放。只有在园子的一角,有一棵树仍然被白雪覆盖,树下有个小男孩因为爬不上去而哭泣。看到这一场景,巨人的心软了,他悄悄抱起孩子,放到树枝上,这棵树马上就开了花。受到触动的巨人摒弃了内心的自私,拆毁了花园的围墙,允许孩子们到他的花园自由玩耍,而巨人也因此收获了春天和快乐。在这则童话故事中,王尔德没有进行空洞的道德说教，教育人们必须无私分享，他只是通过精心设计故事结构，呈现三个不同的场景，来揭示故事的主题，那就是独乐乐不如众乐乐，人不能太自私，要懂得分享，自私而拒绝分享的人则会失去很多快乐。

　　除了精心设计的结构，故事的悲剧结尾也体现了王尔德"为艺术而艺术"和"艺术与道德无关"的理念。《自私的巨人》没有落入俗套，像传统的童话故事一样，以变得无私的巨人和孩子们在花园里开心、幸福地玩耍为结局。王尔德把结尾设置为巨人苦寻当初亲吻感化自己的小男孩而不得，在多年之后，巨人老去，受了伤的小男孩来找巨人，邀请他去自己的花园（即天堂），最后巨人死在了一棵树下，身上盖满白花。没有完美的大团圆结局，没落入"善有善报，恶有恶报"的传统道德说教，王尔德给读者展示了一个更为残酷的现实世界（蔡玲燕，2012），而这个悲剧结局却能让故事的寓意升华，让读者更为震撼，进而反思故事的主题。

二、语言美

　　除了精心构建故事结构，王尔德讲述故事时还使用了大量优美的语言和修辞手法，让故事读起来生动有趣，充满美感。

　　首先，从词汇层面来看，故事的叙述语言符合儿童特点。虽然句子和用词都比较简单，但是王尔德精心选择了一些美好的词语，为简单的场景创造出了一种意境美。如在故事的第二段，介绍巨人不在家的时候花园的场景："这是一个可爱的大花园，园里长满了柔嫩的青草，草丛中到处露出星星似的美丽花朵；还有十二棵桃树，在春天开出淡红色和珍珠色的鲜花，在秋天结着丰富的果子。"（王尔德，2006:26）（It was a large lovely garden, with soft green grass. Here and there over the grass stood beautiful flowers like stars, and there were twelve peach trees that in the springtime broke out into delicate blossoms of pink and pearl, and in the autumn bore rich fruit.）虽然这段话的用词都比较口语化，描写的也是生活中常见的场景，但作者用了很多美感十足的词语，如"lovely"（可爱的）、"soft"（柔软的）、"beautiful"（美丽的）、"delicate"（娇嫩的）、"rich"（丰富的）等对花园、青草、花朵和果子进行修饰，创造了一幅栩栩如生的花园美景图，仿佛春光明媚的景象就在眼前。

　　其次，在故事中，作者还使用了大量拟人、比喻等修辞手法，使叙述的语言更加形象、优美。如故事第 2 段中将花儿比喻成"星星"（Here and there over the grass stood beautiful flowers like stars...），第 8 段中说冰雹的呼吸"像冰一样"（...his breath was like ice...），第 22 段中将孩子比喻成"花朵"（but the children are the most beautiful flowers of all）。读到这些形象的比喻，读者在脑海中便会浮现出星星般美丽的花朵，感受到冬天肆虐的花园里寒冷的气息和巨人眼中孩子的可爱。优美的比喻将"花儿""冰雹"和"孩子"的形象描述得更加生动、具体，更容易引发读者的联想和想象，给读者留下深刻的印象。

　　在这个故事中，作者用得最多的修辞手法是拟人，这一修辞手法出现在故事的诸多地方，尤其是在描写花园景象的时候。比如第 8 段提到一朵美丽的花儿看到巨人竖的写着"TRESPASSERS will be PROSECUTED"的牌子后，就缩回地里，"继续睡觉了"（went off to sleep）；第 10 段描写孩子们被赶出去后，花园里就再也没有春天、夏天和秋天，一年到头只剩下冬天，"北风、冰雹、霜和雪就在树木间跳舞"（the north wind and the hail, and the frost and the snow danced about through the trees）；第 13 段描写孩子们回到花园后，园子里的树都十分高兴，"在孩子们头上挥舞着胳膊"（waving their arms gently above the children's heads），而花儿们也"从绿草中伸出头来，开心地大笑"（the flowers were looking up through the green grass and laughing）；第 16 段中，巨人把哭泣的孩子放到树枝上之后，树马上开了花，"鸟儿们飞到枝头歌唱"（the birds came and sang on it）。拟人的使用使得原本没有生命的东西变得生动活泼起来，花儿、树、草和鸟儿们似乎都有了生命，就像可爱的孩子一样，会笑会唱；即使是冬天里给人们带来寒冷的北风、冰雹、霜和雪，也像一群调皮的孩子一样，淘气地在园子里跳舞。这种拟人化的描写让文章更加优美，使无趣的生活场景变得活泼可爱，也非常符合孩子们的想象规律。

《自私的巨人》这篇童话故事无论是结构上还是语言上，都体现了王尔德"为艺术而艺术"的理念，别出心裁的故事结构、不落俗套的悲剧结尾和用心选择的优美语言，使这个故事充满了美感，能够让读者在看完整个故事后仍然回味无穷。

📖 参考文献 📖

[1] 蔡玲燕. 论唯美主义在王尔德的童话中的体现[J]. 文学界，2012（5）：153-154.
[2] 王尔德. 快乐王子集[M]. 巴金，译. 北京：人民文学出版社，2006.

📖 阅读思考 📖

1. 你喜欢《自私的巨人》这篇童话故事吗？为什么呢？
2. 读一读王尔德的另外一篇童话故事《快乐王子》，试着分析这篇童话是如何体现他"为艺术而艺术"这一理念的。

Love of Life (Excerpt)

Jack London

【作品简介】

Love of Life(《热爱生命》)是杰克·伦敦发表于 1907 年的中篇小说,是他"北方故事"中最著名的一篇。小说讲述了一个悲壮的故事:一位淘金者在返乡途中被朋友抛弃,在近乎残忍的恶劣环境中独自在广袤的荒原上跋涉。主人公在与寒冷、饥饿、伤病和野兽的抗争中,在生与死的抉择中,最终生存了下来,充分展现了生命的坚韧与顽强。

《热爱生命》的发表曾轰动了欧美文坛,小说中表现出来的勇敢和冒险的浪漫精神,对生命的热爱和敬畏,深陷绝境中的坚强意志,受到了全世界读者的喜爱,并得到了列宁的称赞,在生命的最后时刻,病榻上的列宁曾特意请人朗读《热爱生命》。

【作者简介】

杰克·伦敦(Jack London,1876—1916),美国著名的现实主义作家。他的少年时代充满坎坷,自幼从事体力劳动,当过童工,装卸工和水手,当过劫取牡蛎的贼,一度沦为流浪汉,也曾加入过到阿拉斯加淘金的行列。他早年这些坎坷的生活经历为他后来从事文学创作提供了丰富的源泉。杰克·伦敦从 24 岁开始写作,一生著述颇丰,总共创作了 19 部长篇小说,197 篇短篇小说,3 部剧作,还有一些随笔、纪实文学作品等,其中最著名的有《马丁·伊登》《野性的呼唤》《海狼》《白牙》《热爱生命》等小说。杰克·伦敦的创作思想较为复杂,受到过马克思、斯宾塞、尼采等人的影响,在他的作品中,读者时常能感受到英雄主义情结,对生命本身的崇拜,对生存意义的追求。但是到了晚期,他逐渐脱离社会斗争,为了迎合出版商的需要和满足个人的物质享受也写了不少粗制滥造的作品。1916 年,杰克·伦敦在精神极度空虚和悲观失望中自杀身亡,终年 40 岁。

(1) Another day of fog. Half of his last blanket had gone into foot-wrappings.[1] He failed to pick up Bill's trail. It did not matter. His hunger was driving him too compellingly[2]—only—only he wondered if Bill, too, were lost. By midday the irk[3] of his pack became too oppressive. Again he divided the gold, this time merely

[1] 他最后一条毯子的一半都用来包脚了。

[2] 饥饿令他无法抗拒。

[3] irk /ɜːk/ n. 厌倦;苦恼

spilling half of it on the ground. In the afternoon he threw the rest of it away, there remaining to him only the half-blanket, the tin bucket, and the rifle.

(2) An hallucination[4] began to trouble him. He felt confident that one cartridge[5] remained to him. It was in the chamber of the rifle and he had overlooked it. On the other hand, he knew all the time that the chamber was empty. But the hallucination persisted. He fought it off for hours, then threw his rifle open and was confronted with emptiness. The disappointment was as bitter as though he had really expected to find the cartridge.

(3) He plodded[6] on for half an hour, when the hallucination arose again. Again he fought it, and still it persisted, till for very relief he opened his rifle to unconvince himself[7]. At times his mind wandered farther afield[8], and he plodded on, a mere automaton, strange conceits[9] and whimsicalities[10] gnawing[11] at his brain like worms. But these excursions out of the real were of brief duration[12], for ever the pangs[13] of the hunger-bite called him back. He was jerked back abruptly once from such an excursion by a sight that caused him nearly to faint. He reeled and swayed, doddering[14] like a drunken man to keep from falling. Before him stood a horse. A horse! He could not believe his eyes. A thick mist was in them, intershot with sparkling points of light. He rubbed his eyes savagely to clear his vision, and beheld[15], not a horse, but a great brown bear. The animal was studying him with bellicose[16] curiosity.

(4) The man had brought his gun halfway to his shoulder before he realized. He lowered it and drew his hunting-knife from its beaded sheath[17] at his hip. Before him was meat and life. He ran his thumb along the edge of his knife.[18] It was sharp. The point was sharp. He would fling himself upon the bear and kill it. But his heart began its warning thump, thump, thump. Then followed the wild upward leap and tattoo of flutters[19], the pressing as of an iron band about his forehead, the creeping of the dizziness into his brain.

[4] hallucination /hə,luːsɪˈneɪʃn/ n. 幻觉

[5] cartridge /ˈkɑːtrɪdʒ/ n. 子弹;弹药筒

[6] plod /plɒd/ v. 艰难地行走;吃力地行进

[7] 为了摆脱(幻觉带来的)焦虑,他再次打开枪膛让自己不要相信(枪膛里有子弹)。

[8] afield /əˈfiːld/ adv. 在(向)远处

[9] conceit /kənˈsiːt/ n. 自负;骄傲自大

[10] whimsicality /ˌwɪmzɪˈkælətɪ/ n. 异想天开;怪诞的行为或想法

[11] gnaw /nɔː/ v. 咬;啃;啮

[12] 这些非现实的思维旅行是短暂的。

[13] pang /pæŋ/ n. 突然的疼痛(或痛苦)

[14] dodder /ˈdɒdə/ v. 摇摆;蹒跚

[15] behold /bɪˈhəʊld/ v. 看见

[16] bellicose /ˈbelɪkəʊs/ adj. 好斗的

[17] sheath /ʃiːθ/ n. (刀、剑等的)鞘

[18] 他用大拇指试了试刀刃。

[19] 然后心脏向上猛的一紧,接着砰砰地一阵狂跳。(tattoo /təˈtuː/ n. 连续急促的敲击)

（5）His desperate courage was evicted[20] by a great surge of fear. In his weakness, what if the animal attacked him? He drew himself up to his most imposing stature, gripping the knife and staring hard at the bear. The bear advanced clumsily a couple of steps, reared up[21], and gave vent to[22] a tentative[23] growl. If the man ran, he would run after him; but the man did not run. He was animated now with the courage of fear. He, too, growled, savagely, terribly, voicing the fear that is to life germane and that lies twisted about life's deepest roots[24].

（6）The bear edged away to one side, growling menacingly[25], himself appalled[26] by this mysterious creature that appeared upright and unafraid. But the man did not move. He stood like a statue till the danger was past, when he yielded to a fit of trembling and sank down into the wet moss.

（7）He pulled himself together[27] and went on, afraid now in a new way. It was not the fear that he should die passively from lack of food, but that he should be destroyed violently before starvation had exhausted the last particle of the endeavor in him that made toward surviving. There were the wolves. Back and forth across the desolation drifted their howls, weaving the very air into a fabric of menace that was so tangible that he found himself, arms in the air, pressing it back from him as it might be the walls of a wind-blown tent.[28]

（8）Now and again the wolves, in packs of two and three, crossed his path. But they sheered clear of him.[29] They were not in sufficient numbers, and besides they were hunting the caribou[30], which did not battle, while this strange creature that walked erect might scratch and bite.

（9）In the late afternoon he came upon scattered bones where the wolves had made a kill. The debris[31] had been a caribou calf an hour before, squawking[32] and running and very much alive. He contemplated[33] the bones, clean-picked and polished, pink with the cell-life in them which had not yet died[34]. Could it possibly be

[20] evict /ɪ'vɪkt/ v. 驱逐；赶出

[21] 后腿直立起来

[22] give vent to：发出（声音）

[23] tentative /'tentətɪv/ adj. 不确定的；犹豫不决的；试探性的

[24] 喊出了生死攸关、与生命之根紧密相连的恐惧。（germane /dʒɜː'meɪn/ adj. 与……有密切关系）

[25] menacingly /'menəsɪŋlɪ/ adv. 胁迫地；恐吓地

[26] appal /ə'pɔːl/ v. 使大为震惊；使惊骇

[27] pull oneself together：振作起来；恢复镇定

[28] 整个荒原上回荡着狼嚎声，那声音与空气交织在一起，构成一张危险的大网。这张网如此真实，以至于他发现自己不自觉地举起手来，像推一顶被风吹得鼓起来的帐篷一样，想把这张网从身边推开。

[29] 但是它们都避开他。

[30] caribou /'kærɪbuː/ n. 驯鹿

[31] debris /'debriː/ n. 残骸；残渣

[32] squawk /skwɔːk/ v. 尖声高叫

[33] contemplate /'kɒntəmpleɪt/ v. 沉思；凝视

[34] 骨头上没死的细胞仍泛着粉红色。

that he might be that ere³⁵ the day was done! Such was life, eh? A vain and fleeting thing. It was only life that pained. There was no hurt in death. To die was to sleep. It meant cessation³⁶, rest. Then why was he not content to die?

（10）But he did not moralize³⁷ long. He was squatting in the moss, a bone in his mouth, sucking at the shreds of life that still dyed it faintly pink. The sweet meaty taste, thin and elusive almost as a memory³⁸, maddened him. He closed his jaws on the bones and crunched. Sometimes it was the bone that broke, sometimes his teeth. Then he crushed the bones between rocks, pounded them to a pulp³⁹, and swallowed them. He pounded his fingers, too, in his haste, and yet found a moment in which to feel surprise at the fact that his fingers did not hurt much when caught under the descending rock.

（11）Came frightful days of snow and rain. He did not know when he made camp, when he broke camp⁴⁰. He travelled in the night as much as in the day. He rested wherever he fell, crawled on whenever the dying life in him flickered up and burned less dimly. He, as a man, no longer strove. It was the life in him, unwilling to die, that drove him on. He did not suffer. His nerves had become blunted, numb, while his mind was filled with weird⁴¹ visions and delicious dreams.

（12）But ever he sucked and chewed on the crushed bones of the caribou calf, the least remnants⁴² of which he had gathered up and carried with him. He crossed no more hills or divides, but automatically followed a large stream which flowed through a wide and shallow valley. He did not see this stream nor this valley. He saw nothing save visions.⁴³ Soul and body walked or crawled side by side, yet apart, so slender was the thread that bound them.

（13）He awoke in his right mind⁴⁴, lying on his back on a rocky ledge. The sun was shining bright and warm. Afar off⁴⁵ he heard the squawking of caribou

---

³⁵ ere /eə(r)/ *conj.* 在……之前

³⁶ cessation /se'seɪʃn/ *n.* 停止；终止

³⁷ moralize /'mɒrəlaɪz/ *v.* 进行道德说教

³⁸ 像回忆一样模糊而无法捉摸。（elusive /ɪ'luːsɪv/ *adj.* 难找的；难以解释的；难以捉摸的）

³⁹ pulp /pʌlp/ *n.* 浆状物

⁴⁰ break camp：拔营

⁴¹ weird /wɪəd/ *adj.* 怪诞的；离奇的

⁴² remnant /'remnənt/ *n.* 残余部分

⁴³ 除了幻象，他什么都看不到。（save /seɪv/ *prep.* 除……外）

⁴⁴ 他醒来时神志清醒。

⁴⁵ afar off：远处

calves. He was aware of vague memories of rain and wind and snow, but whether he had been beaten by the storm for two days or two weeks he did not know.

（14）For some time he lay without movement, the <u>genial</u>[46] sunshine pouring upon him and <u>saturating</u>[47] his miserable body with its warmth. A fine day, he thought. Perhaps he could manage to locate himself. By a painful effort he rolled over on his side. Below him flowed a wide and <u>sluggish</u>[48] river. Its unfamiliarity puzzled him. Slowly he followed it with his eyes, winding in wide sweeps among the bleak, bare hills, bleaker and barer and lower-lying than any hills he had yet encountered. Slowly, deliberately, without excitement or more than the most casual interest, he followed the course of the strange stream toward the sky-line and saw it <u>emptying into</u>[49] a bright and shining sea. He was still unexcited. Most unusual, he thought, a vision or a <u>mirage</u>[50]—more likely a vision, <u>a trick of his disordered mind</u>[51]. He was confirmed in this by sight of a ship lying at anchor in the midst of the shining sea. He closed his eyes for a while, then opened them. Strange how the vision persisted! Yet not strange. He knew there were no seas or ships in the heart of the barren lands, just as he had known there was no cartridge in the empty rifle.

（15）He heard a snuffle behind him—a half-choking gasp or cough. Very slowly, because of his exceeding weakness and stiffness, he rolled over on his other side. He could see nothing near at hand, but he waited patiently. Again came the snuffle and cough, <u>and outlined between two jagged rocks not a score of feet away he made out the gray head of a wolf</u>[52]. The sharp ears were not pricked so sharply as he had seen them on other wolves; the eyes were <u>bleared</u>[53] and bloodshot, the head seemed to <u>droop</u>[54] <u>limply</u>[55] and <u>forlornly</u>[56]. The animal blinked continually in the sunshine. It seemed sick. As he looked, it snuffled and coughed again.

（16）This, at least, was real, he thought, and turned on the other side so that he might see the reality of

[46] genial /ˈdʒiːnɪəl/ adj. 友好的；（气候）温暖的

[47] saturate /ˈsætʃəreɪt/ v. 浸透；使充满

[48] sluggish /ˈslʌgɪʃ/ adj. 缓慢的；迟缓的

[49] empty into: 流入；汇入

[50] mirage /ˈmɪrɑːʒ/ n. 幻景；海市蜃楼
[51]（看到的景象）是他错乱的神经捣的鬼。

[52] 不到二十英尺外，在两块四凸不平的岩石间，他看见一只灰狼的头。（jagged /ˈdʒægɪd/ adj. 凹凸不平的）
[53] blear /blɪə/ v. 使……模糊不清
[54] droop /druːp/ v. 垂落；垂下；垂头丧气
[55] limply /ˈlɪmplɪ/ adv. 四肢无力地；疲惫地
[56] forlornly /fəˈlɔːnlɪ/ adv. 孤独凄凉地

the world which had been veiled from him before by the vision. But the sea still shone in the distance and the ship was plainly discernible[57]. Was it reality, after all? He closed his eyes for a long while and thought, and then it came to him. He had been making north by east[58], away from the Dease Divide and into the Coppermine Valley. This wide and sluggish river was the Coppermine. That shining sea was the Arctic Ocean. That ship was a whaler[59], strayed east, far east, from the mouth of the Mackenzie, and it was lying at anchor in Coronation Gulf. He remembered the Hudson Bay Company chart[60] he had seen long ago, and it was all clear and reasonable to him.

（17）He sat up and turned his attention to immediate affairs. He had worn through the blanket-wrappings, and his feet were shapeless lumps of raw meat. His last blanket was gone. Rifle and knife were both missing. He had lost his hat somewhere, with the bunch of matches in the band[61], but the matches against his chest were safe and dry inside the tobacco pouch[62] and oil paper. He looked at his watch. It marked eleven o'clock and was still running. Evidently he had kept it wound[63].

（18）He was calm and collected[64]. Though extremely weak, he had no sensation of pain. He was not hungry. The thought of food was not even pleasant to him, and whatever he did was done by his reason alone. He ripped off his pants' legs to the knees and bound them about his feet. Somehow he had succeeded in retaining the tin bucket. He would have some hot water before he began what he foresaw was to be a terrible journey to the ship.

（19）His movements were slow. He shook as with a palsy[65]. When he started to collect dry moss, he found he could not rise to his feet. He tried again and again, then contented himself with crawling about on hands and knees. Once he crawled near to the sick wolf. The animal dragged itself reluctantly out of his way, licking its

[57] discernible /dɪˈsɜːnəbl/ adj. 看得清的；辨别得出的

[58] 他一直朝北偏东的方向走。

[59] whaler /ˈweɪlə(r)/ n. 捕鲸船

[60] chart /tʃɑːt/ n. 图表；海图

[61] 藏在帽檐里的火柴也一并丢了。

[62] pouch /paʊtʃ/ n. 小袋子；荷包

[63] wound /waʊnd/ v. 给（钟表等）上发条（wind 的过去分词）

[64] collected /kəˈlektɪd/ adj. 镇静；冷静

[65] palsy /ˈpɔːlzɪ/ n. 瘫痪；麻痹

chops⁶⁶ with a tongue which seemed hardly to have the strength to curl. The man noticed that the tongue was not the customary healthy red. It was a yellowish brown and seemed coated with a rough and half-dry mucus⁶⁷.

（20）After he had drunk a quart of hot water the man found he was able to stand, and even to walk as well as a dying man might be supposed to walk. Every minute or so he was compelled to rest. His steps were feeble and uncertain, just as the wolf's that trailed him were feeble and uncertain; and that night, when the shining sea was blotted out⁶⁸ by blackness, he knew he was nearer to it by no more than four miles.

（21）Throughout the night he heard the cough of the sick wolf, and now and then the squawking of the caribou calves. There was life all around him, but it was strong life, very much alive and well, and he knew the sick wolf clung to the sick man's trail in the hope that the man would die first. In the morning, on opening his eyes, he beheld it regarding⁶⁹ him with a wistful and hungry stare. It stood crouched, with tail between its legs, like a miserable and woe-begone⁷⁰ dog. It shivered in the chill morning wind, and grinned dispiritedly⁷¹ when the man spoke to it in a voice that achieved no more than a hoarse whisper.

（22）The sun rose brightly, and all morning the man tottered⁷² and fell toward the ship on the shining sea. The weather was perfect. It was the brief Indian Summer⁷³ of the high latitudes⁷⁴. It might last a week. Tomorrow or next day it might be gone.

（23）In the afternoon the man came upon a trail. It was of another man, who did not walk, but who dragged himself on all fours. The man thought it might be Bill, but he thought in a dull, uninterested way. He had no curiosity. In fact, sensation and emotion had left him. He was no longer susceptible⁷⁵ to pain. Stomach and nerves had gone to sleep. Yet the life that was in him drove him on. He was very weary, but it refused to die. It was because it refused to die that he still ate muskeg⁷⁶

⁶⁶ chop /tʃɒp/ n. 颌；颚

⁶⁷ mucus /'mjuːkəs/ n. 黏液

⁶⁸ blot out: 挡住；遮蔽

⁶⁹ regard /rɪ'gɑːd/ v. 注视；凝视

⁷⁰ woe-begone /'wəʊbɪgɒn/ adj. 忧愁的；悲伤的

⁷¹ dispiritedly /dɪ'spɪrɪtɪdlɪ/ adv. 没精神地；气馁地

⁷² totter /'tɒtə(r)/ v. 跌跌撞撞；蹒跚

⁷³ Indian Summer: 北美地区一种特别的天气现象，冬天来临前忽然回暖。

⁷⁴ latitude /'lætɪtjuːd/ n. 纬度（区）

⁷⁵ susceptible /sə'septəbl/ adj. 易受影响（或伤害等）；敏感的

⁷⁶ muskeg /'mʌskeg/ n. （北美北部和北欧的）沼泽地

berries and minnows[77], drank his hot water, and kept a wary[78] eye on the sick wolf.

（24）He followed the trail of the other man who dragged himself along, and soon came to the end of it—a few fresh-picked bones where the soggy[79] moss was marked by the foot-pads of many wolves. He saw a squat[80] moose-hide sack, mate to his own[81], which had been torn by sharp teeth. He picked it up, though its weight was almost too much for his feeble fingers. Bill had carried it to the last. Ha! ha! He would have the laugh on Bill. He would survive and carry it to the ship in the shining sea. His mirth[82] was hoarse and ghastly[83], like a raven's croak[84], and the sick wolf joined him, howling lugubriously[85]. The man ceased suddenly. How could he have the laugh on Bill if that were Bill; if those bones, so pinky-white and clean, were Bill?

（25）He turned away. Well, Bill had deserted him; but he would not take the gold, nor would he suck Bill's bones. Bill would have, though, had it been the other way around, he mused[86] as he staggered on.

（26）He came to a pool of water. Stooping over in quest of minnows, he jerked his head back as though he had been stung. He had caught sight of his reflected face. So horrible was it that sensibility awoke long enough to be shocked.[87] There were three minnows in the pool, which was too large to drain; and after several ineffectual[88] attempts to catch them in the tin bucket he forbore[89]. He was afraid, because of his great weakness, that he might fall in and drown. It was for this reason that he did not trust himself to the river astride[90] one of the many drift-logs which lined its sand-spits.

（27）That day he decreased the distance between him and the ship by three miles; the next day by two—for he was crawling now as Bill had crawled; and the end of the fifth day found the ship still seven miles away and him unable to make even a mile a day. Still the Indian Summer held on, and he continued to crawl and faint, turn and turn about; and ever the sick wolf coughed and

---

[77] minnow /ˈmɪnəʊ/ *n.* 一种小淡水鱼

[78] wary /ˈweərɪ/ *adj.* 小心的；谨慎的

[79] soggy /ˈsɒgɪ/ *adj.* 潮湿的

[80] squat /skwɒt/ *adj.* 矮而宽的

[81] 和他自己的那条一样。

[82] mirth /mɜːθ/ *n.* 欢笑；欢乐

[83] ghastly /ˈgɑːstlɪ/ *adj.* 恐怖的；可怕的

[84] croak /krəʊk/ *n.* 低沉沙哑的声音

[85] lugubriously /ləˈguːbrɪəslɪ/ *adv.* 悲哀地；伤心地

[86] muse /mjuːz/ *v.* 沉思；冥想

[87] 这张脸如此可怕，他一下子恢复了理智，惊愕了好久。

[88] ineffectual /ˌɪnɪˈfektʃuəl/ *adj.* 无用的；不起作用的

[89] forbear /fɔːˈbeə(r)/ *v.* 克制；忍住（不说话或不做某事）（过去式：forbore；过去分词：forborne）

[90] astride /əˈstraɪd/ *prep.* 跨（或骑）在……上

wheezed at his heels. His knees had become raw meat like his feet, and though he padded them with the shirt from his back it was a red track he left behind him on the moss and stones. Once, glancing back, he saw the wolf licking hungrily his bleeding trail, and he saw sharply what his own end might be—unless—unless he could get the wolf. Then began as grim a tragedy of existence as was ever played[91]—a sick man that crawled, a sick wolf that limped, two creatures dragging their dying carcasses[92] across the desolation and hunting each other's lives.

(28) Had it been a well wolf, it would not have mattered so much to the man; but the thought of going to feed the maw[93] of that loathsome[94] and all but dead thing was repugnant[95] to him. He was finicky[96]. His mind had begun to wander again, and to be perplexed by hallucinations, while his lucid[97] intervals grew rarer and shorter.

(29) He was awakened once from a faint by a wheeze close in his ear. The wolf leaped lamely back, losing its footing[98] and falling in its weakness. It was ludicrous[99], but he was not amused. Nor was he even afraid. He was too far gone for that. But his mind was for the moment clear, and he lay and considered. The ship was no more than four miles away. He could see it quite distinctly when he rubbed the mists out of his eyes, and he could see the white sail of a small boat cutting the water of the shining sea. But he could never crawl those four miles. He knew that, and was very calm in the knowledge. He knew that he could not crawl half a mile. And yet he wanted to live. It was unreasonable that he should die after all he had undergone. Fate asked too much of him. And, dying, he declined to die. It was stark[100] madness, perhaps, but in the very grip of Death he defied Death and refused to die[101].

(30) He closed his eyes and composed himself with infinite precaution[102]. He steeled himself[103] to keep above the suffocating[104] languor[105] that lapped like a rising tide

[91] 于是，一场残酷的求生悲剧开始了，其残忍程度不亚于以前上演过的任何一场。
[92] carcass /ˈkɑːkəs/ n. 动物的尸体
[93] maw /mɔː/ n. (动物的)胃
[94] loathsome /ˈləʊðsəm/ adj. 令人厌恶的
[95] repugnant /rɪˈpʌɡnənt/ adj. 使人极度反感的
[96] finicky /ˈfɪnɪkɪ/ adj. 过分讲究的；过分挑剔的
[97] lucid /ˈluːsɪd/ adj. (尤指糊涂状态中或过后)头脑清晰的；清醒的
[98] lose one's footing: 跌倒
[99] ludicrous /ˈluːdɪkrəs/ adj. 滑稽的；可笑的
[100] stark /stɑːk/ adj. 完全的；十足的
[101] 但是当被死神攥到手里时，他奋起反抗，不愿赴死。
[102] precaution /prɪˈkɔːʃn/ n. 预防；防备

through all the wells of his being. It was very like a sea, this deadly languor, that rose and rose and drowned his consciousness bit by bit. Sometimes he was all but submerged[106], swimming through oblivion[107] with a faltering[108] stroke; and again, by some strange alchemy[109] of soul, he would find another shred of will and strike out more strongly.

(31) Without movement he lay on his back, and he could hear, slowly drawing near and nearer, the wheezing intake and output of the sick wolf's breath. It drew closer, ever closer, through an infinitude[110] of time, and he did not move. It was at his ear. The harsh dry tongue grated like sandpaper against his cheek.[111] His hands shot out—or at least he willed them to shoot out. The fingers were curved like talons[112], but they closed on empty air[113]. Swiftness and certitude require strength[114], and the man had not this strength.

(32) The patience of the wolf was terrible. The man's patience was no less terrible. For half a day he lay motionless, fighting off unconsciousness and waiting for the thing that was to feed upon him and upon which he wished to feed[115]. Sometimes the languid sea rose over him[116] and he dreamed long dreams; but ever through it all, waking and dreaming, he waited for the wheezing breath and the harsh caress[117] of the tongue.

(33) He did not hear the breath, and he slipped slowly from some dream to the feel of the tongue along his hand. He waited. The fangs[118] pressed softly; the pressure increased; the wolf was exerting its last strength in an effort to sink teeth in the food for which it had waited so long. But the man had waited long, and the lacerated[119] hand closed on the jaw. Slowly, while the wolf struggled feebly and the hand clutched feebly, the other hand crept across to a grip. Five minutes later the whole weight of the man's body was on top of the wolf. The hands had not sufficient strength to choke the wolf, but the face of the man was pressed close to the throat of the wolf and the mouth of the man was full of hair. At the

[103] steel oneself: 下定决心，坚强面对

[104] suffocating /ˈsʌfəkeɪtɪŋ/ adj. 令人窒息的

[105] languor /ˈlæŋɡə(r)/ n. 倦怠

[106] submerge /səbˈmɜːdʒ/ v. 淹没

[107] oblivion /əˈblɪviən/ n. 沉睡；昏迷；无意识状态

[108] faltering /ˈfɔːltərɪŋ/ adj. (动作)犹豫的；彷徨的

[109] alchemy /ˈælkəmɪ/ n. 神秘力量；魔力

[110] infinitude /ɪnˈfɪnɪtjuːd/ n. 无限

[111] 狼粗糙干燥的舌头像砂纸一样舔舐着他的脸颊。

[112] talon /ˈtælən/ n. (猛禽的)爪

[113] 但是什么也没抓到。

[114] 想要抓得又快又准需要力气。
(certitude /ˈsɜːtɪtjuːd/ n. 确信；确定)

[115] 等着那只想吃掉他，而他也想吃掉的狼。

[116] 有时候，倦怠像海水一样袭来。
(languid /ˈlæŋɡwɪd/ adj. 倦怠的)

[117] caress /kəˈres/ n. 抚摩

[118] fang /fæŋ/ n. (尤指狗的)尖牙

[119] lacerate /ˈlæsəreɪt/ v. 划破；割裂(皮或肉)

end of half an hour the man was aware of a warm trickle in his throat. It was not pleasant. It was like <u>molten</u>[120] <u>lead</u>[121] being forced into his stomach, and it was forced by his will alone. Later the man rolled over on his back and slept.

[120] molten /ˈməultən/ *adj.* 熔化的
[121] lead /liːd/ *n.* 铅

精华赏析

在美国文学史上,杰克·伦敦的小说创作特色明显,独树一帜。和同时代的美国作家相比,杰克·伦敦的作品更多地关注人自身的存在,展现人类在恶劣的环境中寻求生存和发展的顽强生命力。他成功地塑造了一批极具代表性的人物形象:他们虽身处险恶的环境,但凭借着坚强的意志,最终克服困难,成长为一个个"超人",这就是铸就了杰克·伦敦创作风格的"超人"题材小说。下面我们以《热爱生命》为例,分析杰克·伦敦的"超人"主题在该小说中的体现,并探寻"超人"主题产生的根源。

"超人"小说中的主人公往往置身于极其严酷、复杂的自然或社会环境中,这是杰克·伦敦此类主题小说的模式化情节设置,而本故事的主人公就是如此。他是一个返乡的淘金人,刚刚被同伴抛弃,独自跋涉在广袤而荒凉的荒原之上。不久他发现自己迷路了,他的脚踝扭伤,尖利的石头刺破他的裤子,在膝盖上划出一道道血痕。鞋子磨破了,他只能在地上一点点艰难爬行。食物吃完了,只能靠沼泽地里的小浆果和灯芯草聊以果腹。饥饿和伤痛让他渐渐丧失了意识,他产生了幻觉。更可怕的是,这奄奄一息的淘金人,先后被一只熊和一只饿狼盯上,而他根本没有力气与这些野兽搏斗……恶劣的自然环境、饥饿和伤痛的折磨、恶兽的威胁,在这种艰难、恶劣的环境里,常人是无法生活的。

面对如此残酷的生存条件,主人公几次想要放弃,但都凭借坚强的意志一次次坚持了下去。为了生存和恢复体力,他开始像野兽一样,生吃水坑里的小鱼,把刚孵出来的雏鸟几口吞进肚子,甚至吸吮狼啃食过的驯鹿骨头。为了活下去,他拼尽全身的力气,咬死了那匹令他作呕的病狼,喝了狼的血,最终在人与兽的较量中赢得了胜利。他获救了,成功生存了下来,在一次次历练中,成长为一名"超人"。杰克·伦敦并没有花很多笔墨描写淘金人在每一次抗争时的内心活动,他的每一次坚持,每一次生命力量的勃发,都源自他对生命的渴望。这种对生命的坚持,与其说是信念,不如说是一种本能的驱动。

杰克·伦敦对此类具备"超人"人格的人物形象如此痴迷,一方面与他个人的人生经历不无关系,另一方面也受到了尼采的"超人"哲学和斯宾塞的社会达尔文进化论思想的深刻影响。

杰克·伦敦是旧金山一个破产农民家庭的私生子,出身卑微,从小就饱尝贫穷和饥饿的艰辛。因家境贫困,他自幼从事体力劳动,当过童工、装卸工、水手、牡蛎贼、淘金者,还因流浪被捕入狱。但他并没有向命运低头,他决心通过自学和个人努力彻底改变自己的命运。在最初尝试写作的过程中,杰克·伦敦屡遭退稿,但他毫不气馁,终于靠坚强的意志和不懈的努力成为了享誉全球的著名作家。可以说,他自己坎坷的经历是他进行小说创作的源泉,他笔下的每一个"超人"形象,都有他自己的影子。

杰克·伦敦在广泛的阅读中,接触到了马克思、尼采、斯宾塞等人的思想,特别是尼采的"超人"哲学思想,这对他的创作风格产生了巨大的影响。"超人"哲学是尼采在1883年出版的《查拉图斯特拉如是说》一书中首次提出的,他认为西方文明在2000多年来一直宣扬"理想国""天堂"等"更好的世界"的存在,从而否认现世的价值和真实性,是自欺欺人的谎言。所以尼采用"上帝死了!"来重估价值,构建新的价值体系。他认为人类的进化没有停止,未来的人一定是能超越现在的自我的"超人"。"超人"是天才,拥有最坚强的意志和最高的智慧,是集全人类智慧于一身的"真理的化身"。他们是生活中的强者,具有强大、旺盛的生命本能;他们最能忍受痛苦的折磨,又能从痛苦中崛起;他们与不幸命运抗争,把人类社会的悲剧当做人生的历程。

尼采所推崇的这种"强力意志"成了促进杰克·伦敦不断创作、不断超越的精神支柱,他在自己的文学作品中践行了这种"超人"哲学思想,除了《热爱生命》,其他作品如《野性的呼唤》《海狼》《白牙》《北方的奥德赛》以及他的长篇自传体小说《马丁·伊登》都深刻反映了这种哲学。

◪ 阅读思考 ◪

1. 以《热爱生命》为例,总结杰克·伦敦小说中的"超人"形象的特征。
2. 查阅资料,讨论尼采的"超人"哲学思想的现实意义。

Because I Could Not Stop for Death

Emily Dickinson

【作品简介】

艾米莉·狄金森从 30 多岁开始了自己的隐居生活,鲜少与外界联系,其诗作的独特魅力是在她逝世后才被人们发现和认识的。在其创作的 1700 多首诗歌中,关于死亡主题的诗歌将近 600 首,约占三分之一。狄金森如此关注死亡这一主题是与她的生活有着密切联系的。她的家位于人们送葬去公墓的必经之路上,在她那个年代,年轻人的死亡率很高,她经常看到送葬队伍从自家门前经过;另外狄金森的家人和朋友相继去世,她一生经历了数次所爱的人的离世,这使得她不得不一直思考着死亡。《因为我不能停步等待死亡》(*Because I Could Not Stop for Death*)是狄金森死亡诗歌的代表作之一,诗歌中的意象很奇特,把死亡比作一位绅士驾着马车而来,在诗歌中死亡并不可怕,诗人面对死亡也是冷静、平和的,因为在诗人看来死亡是通向永恒的必经之路。从诗歌中可以看出狄金森对死亡的独特理解,她并不惧怕死亡,死亡于她而言不是终结而是永恒。

【作者简介】

艾米莉·狄金森(Emily Dickinson)被视为世界抒情短诗的大师,二十世纪现代主义诗歌的先驱之一,狄金森的作品在她生前发表的只有几篇,绝大多数是在她去世后发表的,她的诗歌公开出版后得到了越来越高的评价,她在美国诗歌史上的地位仅次于惠特曼。1984 年美国文学界纪念"美国文学之父"华盛顿·欧文诞辰两百周年时,在纽约圣·约翰教堂同时开辟了"诗人角",入选的只有惠特曼和狄金森两人。

狄金森生于 1830 年 12 月 10 日。她的祖父是马萨诸塞州阿姆斯特学院的主要创始人。狄金森的父亲和兄弟曾为该学院管理财务达 59 年之久。她的父亲爱德华还是一位在法学界颇有声望的律师。

狄金森在 19 岁以前先后在阿姆斯特学院及离该学院不远的霍利奥克山女子学校求学。她对《圣经》十分熟悉,喜爱约翰·济慈(John Keats)、布朗宁夫人(E. B. Browning)、艾米莉·勃朗特(Emily Bronte)、乔治·艾略特(George Eliot)等人的作品。在学校里,她除了文学作品外,也接触数学、天文学等自然科学方面的基本知识,这些在她的创作题材和技巧上都有所反映。

狄金森在 25 岁以前与小城镇上的人交往颇多,和他们一起享受青年人的欢乐、跳舞、写诗、去郊外欣赏大自然的美景等,偶尔也离开小城镇去波士顿、费城游览。1858 年至 1862 年,由于生活中的苦闷,不愉快的经历,青年时期女伴的相继成婚、离去以及一些至今不明的原因,她的生活道路有了明显的改变。1860 年(也就是她 30 岁的那年)起,她开始了一种几乎与世隔绝的生活,靠书信以及有限的窗外自然景象保持着与外界的联系。

狄金森的一生是在具有浓厚的清教徒生活传统的新英格兰地区度过的。她的父母亲和兄弟姐妹都在 19 世纪上半叶新英格兰连续不断的信仰复兴运动高潮中被卷入了宗教的热潮。但狄金森却不愿盲目接受牧师的说教和训诫,对正统的加尔文教派的教义常常表示疑惑,喜欢玄思冥想,对各种问题常常带着反叛性的独特见解。她和以康科德为中心的知识界没有直接来往,和他们之间唯一的联系只是阅读爱默生的作品。她相信个人思考,相信直觉知识,与他们所追求的目标不谋而合。在这个意义上她也是一个超验主义者。所不同的是爱默生以高亢的激情陈述了自己的观点,梭罗进行了社会实践,而狄金森却过着一种修女式的生活,在孤寂和静思中追求自己的理想。和她同时代的惠特曼以奔放的激情讴歌了美国的民主精神,讴歌了千千万万的普通人,把自己和人民大众融为一体;而狄金森则是远离繁忙而喧嚣的世界,在僻静的小屋里探索人生、自然、死亡和天国的真正含义,为自己开拓了一条她认为是走向永生、进入真正的艺术创作的道路。除了她生前发表的几篇作品外,现在我们看到的 1775 首诗篇都是在其去世后,狄金森的姐姐在她的抽屉里找到的。1955 年,约翰逊根据诗人笔迹的变化大致推断出作品的写作年代,并做了编号,出版了一些狄金森的作品。

狄金森的生活天地狭小,脱离社会,她的诗歌往往神秘朦胧,较难理解。按照不同的题材,人们把狄金森的诗歌分为了爱情、人生的苦闷、死亡永生、上帝、大自然、诗歌创作等方面。狄金森诗歌的形式多为民歌体和圣经圣歌体,而后者是继英国前浪漫主义诗人威廉·布莱克(William Blake)以来极少被人使用的诗体;诗行基本上由三音步和四音步抑扬格及其各种变体构成。狄金森在诗歌创作中有许多独特的创造,她巧妙安排声与义的关系,变换使用头韵、半韵、不完全韵的声音效果,独创性地使用逗号、破折号及其他标点,读者们在阅读诗歌的时候忽而戛然而止,忽而异峰突起,忽而急转直下,忽而婉转曲折,别有一番神韵。

(1) Because / I could / not stop / for Death—
　　~ V/ ~ V/ ~ V/ ~ V

(2) He¹ kind / ly stopped / for me—
　　~ V/ ~ V/ ~ V

(3) The Ca / rriage held / but just / Ourselves—
　　~ V/ ~ V / ~ V / ~ V

(4) And Immor / tality².
　　V ~ ~/V ~ ~

(5) We slow / ly drove / —He knew / no haste
　　~ V/ ~ V/ ~ V/ ~ V

(6) And I / had put / away

(1) Iamb(抑扬格)

(2) Iamb(抑扬格)

(3) Iamb(抑扬格)

(4) Dactyl(扬抑抑格)

¹ 这里 He 指的是死神,第一句说"我不能停下来等待死亡",说明人并不能决定自己何时死亡,而第二句"他殷勤地停车接我",说明每个人都要面临死亡,到了要离开这个世界的时候,死神自然会来接他们走。

² immortality /ˌɪmɔːˈtæləti/ n. 永生

(5) Iamb(抑扬格)

~ V/ ~ V/ ~ V

　(7) My la / bor and / my lei / sure too,
　　　 ~ V/ ~ V/ ~ V / ~ V

　(8) For His Ci / vility[3] —
　　　 V ~ ~/V ~ ~ /

　(9) We passed / the School[4], / where Chil / dren strove
　　　 ~ V/ ~ V/ ~ V/~ V

　(10) At Recess— / in the Ring—
　　　 ~ ~ V/ ~ ~ V

　(11) we passed / the Fields of Ga / zing Grain[5] —
　　　 ~ V/ ~ V/ ~ V/ ~ V

　(12) We passed / the Se tting Sun[6]—
　　　 ~ V/ ~ V/ ~ V

　(13) Or ra / ther—He / passed Us—
　　　 ~ V/ ~ V/ ~ V

　(14) The Dews[7]/ drew qui / vering[8]/ and chill—
　　　 ~ V / ~ V / ~ ~ / ~ V

　(15) For on / ly Go / ssamer[9], / my Gown[10] —
　　　 ~ V/ ~ V/ ~ V / ~ V

　(16) My Tip / pet[11]—on / ly Tulle[12] —
　　　 ~ V/ ~ V/ ~ V

　(17) We paused / before / a House[13]/ that seemed
　　　 ~ V/ ~ V/ ~ V/ ~ V

　(18) A Swe / lling[14] of / the Ground—
　　　 ~ V/ ~ V/ ~ V

　(19) The Roof / was scarce / ly vi / sible—
　　　 ~ V / ~ V / ~ V / ~ ~

　(20) The Cor / nice[15]—in / the Ground—
　　　 ~ V / ~ V / ~ V

　(21) Since then / —'tis Cen / turies / — and yet
　　　 ~ V/ ~ V/ ~ ~/ ~ V

　(22) Feels shor / ter than / the Day
　　　 ~ V/ ~ V/ ~ V

（6）Iamb（抑扬格）

（7）Iamb（抑扬格）

（8）Dactyl（扬抑抑格）

[3] 诗歌中的死神不是恐怖狰狞的样子,而是谦谦君子的模样(civility / səˈvɪləti/ n.彬彬有礼的行为;礼貌;客气)

（9）Iamb（抑扬格）

（10）Anapest（抑抑扬格）

（11）Iamb（抑扬格）

（12）Iamb（抑扬格）

[4] 学校象征人的童年阶段

[5] 成熟的庄稼地象征人的成年阶段

[6] 夕阳象征人的晚年阶段

（13）Iamb（抑扬格）

（14）Iamb（抑扬格）/Pyrrhic（抑抑格）

（15）Iamb（抑扬格）/Pyrrhic（抑抑格）

（16）Iamb（抑扬格）

[7] dews /djuːz/ n.露;露水

[8] quiver /ˈkwɪvə(r)/ v.颤抖;哆嗦

[9] gossamer /ˈɡɒsəmə(r)/ n.蛛丝;薄纱

[10] gown /ɡaʊn/ n.长袍;礼服;长衫

[11] tippet /ˈtɪpɪt/ n.旧时的女士披巾

[12] tulle /tjuːl/ n.绢网

（17）Iamb（抑扬格）

（18）Iamb（抑扬格）

（19）Iamb（抑扬格）/Pyrrhic（抑抑格）

（20）Iamb（抑扬格）

[13] 房子隆起于地面,屋顶勉强可见,屋檐低于地面,可以看出这个房子就是坟墓。

[14] swelling /ˈswelɪŋ/ n.膨胀

[15] cornice /ˈkɔːnɪs/ n.檐板;飞檐

（21）Iamb（抑扬格）/Pyrrhic（抑抑

(23) I first / surmised[16]/ the Hor / ses' Heads
~ V / ~ V / ~ V / ~ V

(24) Were toward / Eter / nity[17]—
~ ~ V/ ~ V/ ~ ~

格）

(22) Iamb（抑扬格）

(23) Iamb（抑扬格）

(24) Anapest（抑抑扬格）/Iamb（抑扬格）/Pyrrhic（抑抑格）

[16] surmise /səˈmaɪz/ v. 推测；猜测
[17] eternity /ɪˈtɜːnəti/ n. 永恒；不朽

在这一节中我们看到死亡的马车是朝向永恒的，在永恒之后以破折号结尾，更形象地彰显出永恒的状态，暗示这种状态将永远持续，没有终点，不断向远方延伸。

ᴸ 精华赏析 ᴿ

艾米莉·狄金森绝对算是美国屈指可数的优秀女作家的代表。她出生在1830年，此时美国的文学之父——华盛顿·欧文已经完成他的杰作《征服格拉纳》，可是当比华盛顿·欧文年轻的狄金森的诗歌被发现并出版后，西方评论家对她的生平、作品及艺术技巧的关注和研究超乎寻常，不少评论家都认为她的文学成就堪比华盛顿·欧文。如果说，华盛顿·欧文用一支"蜡笔"描绘了美国的山水、平原、瀑布等风物，那么狄金森就用一支"工笔"精致地刻画了美国人的"灵魂"，这灵魂比大海更广阔，难怪亨利·詹姆斯称她的诗歌是"灵魂的风景画"，威廉·卡洛斯·威廉斯更是称她为"圣恩主"，以表示对她的崇敬（常耀信，2006）。在狄金森探索灵魂的旅途中，死亡是她主要关注的话题，*Because I Could Not Stop for Death* 是狄金森死亡主题诗歌中的一首代表作品。诗歌中的死神是一位绅士，他驾着马车来邀请对方入座与他同行，这一路上他们来到了学校，来到了田野，看见了夕阳西下，他们从生走向了死，又从死走向了永生。

一、诗歌的节奏与韵律

这首诗歌诗行基本上由三音步和四音步抑扬格（Iamb）构成，但是还有一些其他的变体，如扬抑抑格（Dactyl）、抑抑扬格（Anapest）和抑抑格（Pyrrhic）。狄金森通过这些不同的节奏表达了不同的意境和情感。规律的抑扬格（Iamb）听起来就像是"滴答滴答"的马蹄声，"我不能停下来等待死亡"，死神驾着马车停在"我"的身边，他亲切、和善地邀请"我"坐上他的马车，于是伴随着马蹄声载着"我"一起前行。扬抑抑格（Dactyl）出现在头两个诗节的结尾处，一处是 And Immortality，一处是 For His Civility。扬抑抑格（Dactyl）在这里的使用表达了一种意愿和决心，她决定跟着这位绅士一起前行，一起走向死亡。使用抑抑扬格（Anapest）的时候，诗歌的情绪发生了变化，变得激动热烈起来。"At Recess—in the Ring—"这句中马车经过了学校,孩子们正在操场上玩耍、喧闹,之前低沉压抑的氛围被打破,通过格律的变化我们感受到孩子们在操场上玩耍、肆意奔跑,开怀大笑的欢乐气氛。而抑抑格(Pyrrhic)出现在最后三个诗节中,此时已经离死亡、离坟墓越来越近,阳光已经消失,美好的景象也消失了,露水让人浑身颤抖、发凉,因为衣服穿得单薄更强化了寒冷的感觉。眼前出现的是一座低矮的房子,只能勉强看到屋顶,这里的抑抑格(Pyrrhic)是非重读音节,表达了一种悲凉压抑的情绪。我们可以深深地感受到即将面临死亡的人是被动绝望的,眼看着自己一步步走向坟墓,对即将发生的一切都无力改变。

随着全诗不断变化的格律,我们可以感受到这一路上坐在马车上的人的情绪在不断变化,有过一开始的坚定,有过坦然和平静,也有过偶尔的轻松与欢快,还有过走向人生终点的悲伤与绝望。在狄金森的诗歌中,情绪的起伏伴随着格律的变化,时而高昂,时而低沉,时而平缓,读来别有一番味道。

二、诗歌中的隐喻

"诗歌是语言的艺术,通过语词新的组织,意义在诗中流动起来。通过语词的'反常'使用,诗歌显得含糊、怪异、不合逻辑。在诸种'反常'方式中,隐喻占据重要地位"(王胜男,2021)。诗歌的语言与日常用语的区别明显,日常用语以交际为目的,一般需避免意义含混,而诗歌的语言更重视言外之意,通过创造丰富、新颖的意义空间来展现语言的独特韵味。可以说对诗歌语言的生命力和创造力而言,隐喻在其中起到了重要的作用。德里达认为诗在本质上是隐喻性的(雅克·德里达,2005)。

这首诗歌也使用了不少隐喻,我们不妨一起来分析。诗歌一开始就是一个驾着马车来的人,这里的 Carriage Ride"乘坐马车的旅行"指的是人从生到死的旅程。在第三诗节中连续有几个隐喻:他们先经过了学校,看见了在操场上玩耍的孩子们,这里的 the School 指的是人的童年阶段,嬉戏玩耍是童年时代生活的主旋律,童年阶段是美好快乐的;之后他们又经过了一块田地,这里的 the Field of Gazing Grain 指的是人的成年阶段,在成年阶段,人们需要辛勤劳作,人们变得成熟,人们获得各种收获和成果;最后他们又看见了夕阳西下,这里的 the Setting Sun 指的是人的晚年阶段,晚年阶段的人生就像夕阳一样即将落幕,死神驾着马车带着车上的人回顾了他的一生,从童年到成年再到晚年。在诗歌的倒数第二节中,马车在一个房子前停了下来,房子微微隆起于地面,屋顶勉强可见,屋檐低于地面,这样的 House 其实指的是坟墓。把坟墓比做房子,一来坟墓看起来就像一个小房子,另外也暗指死亡是人的最终归宿。

狄金森在这首诗歌中使用的隐喻并不过分新奇,她用贴近生活的隐喻带读者回顾了人的一生,同时将坟墓比做房子,死亡也不再那么可怖。

三、诗歌中的词汇

这首诗歌中使用的词汇有两类,一类是简单朴素的词汇,如 labor, leisure, school, children, ring, grain, sun 等,另一类则是庄重严肃的词汇,如 immortality, civility, eternity 等。在诗歌中,简单朴素的词汇用来描写人们朴实平淡的日常生活,而庄重严肃的词汇用来描写死亡与永恒。这两类词给读者描绘了两个不同的画面,一边是人们平平淡淡的生活,虽然没有波澜壮阔但却真真切切;另一边是人类挥之不去,不断要思考的庄严而恒久的话题:死亡与永恒。这两类词语在诗歌中交织与碰撞,让我们意识到这两个不同的场景不是决然分开的,它们有时会交织在一起,在平凡的生活中不时会有死神来敲门,在平静祥和的生活场景中突然会有冰冷的坟墓闯入眼帘。两种词汇的对立与交融撞击着读者的心灵,让人意识到生与死也是这般对立和交融的。

四、诗歌中的标点符号

诗歌中的标点符号也是比较有特色的,比如原本应该用逗号和句号的地方,却用了大量的破折号。在分析诗歌中破折号的作用前,我们先来回顾一下"陌生化"的概念。什克洛夫斯基提出了"陌生化"的概念来阐释语言所具有的文学性效果,他认为只有"陌生化"的语言才具有文学性可言。"陌生化"又被译为"奇特化",是与"无意识化""自动化"相对的,它是使人感到惊异、新鲜和陌生的具有审美特征的语言(邱运华,2006)。什克洛夫斯基在《艺术作为手法》中说:

为了恢复对生活的感觉,为了感觉到事物,为了使石头成为石头,存在着一种名为艺术的东西。艺术的目的是提供作为视觉而不是作为识别的事物的感觉;艺术的手法就是使事物奇特化的手法,是使形式变得模糊、增加感觉的困难和时间的手法,因为艺术中的感觉行为本身就是目的,应该延长;艺术是一种体验事物的制作的方法,而"制作"成功的东西对艺术来说是无关紧要的(茨维坦·托多罗夫,1989)。

简单说来,习以为常不是艺术,奇特变形才是艺术。艺术就是通过各种手法打破惯例。艺术需要感知和理解,沉淀和深思,常常使用一些手段和方法延长人们感知的时间。这首诗歌在标点符号的选择和使用上就打破了常规。大量的破折号出现在诗歌中产生了一种陌生化的效果。这些破折号的使用是出人意料的,自然会引起读者的注意,"这里不是该用逗号或句号吗?""作者使用破折号的意图是什么?"伴随着这样的提问,诗歌也就有了更丰富的意蕴。读者在看到破折号的时候会自然而然地停留和思考,各种想法在脑海里翻腾,这就延长了读者的感知时间。

对狄金森使用的破折号可以有好几个层面的理解,比如表示作者在创作时思绪万千,难以言尽;表示诗歌的意义未完结;表示死亡不是终点,它只是通往永恒的必经之路;刻画了永恒的状态,从一点出发不断延伸,没有终点等。

狄金森在这首诗歌中表达了自己对死亡的独特理解:死亡不是可怕的事情,它是每个人都要经历的一段旅程,死亡不是终结,死亡即重生,死亡即永恒。

▣ 参考文献 ▣

[1] 常耀信. 美国文学选读[M]. 天津:南开大学出版社,2006.

[2] 邱运华. 文学批评方法与案例[M]. 北京:北京大学出版社,2006.

［3］茨维坦·托多罗夫编选. 俄苏形式主义文论选［M］. 北京:中国社会科学出版社,1989.

［4］王胜男. 纳尔逊·古德曼隐喻理论视野下的诗歌隐喻新探［J］.文艺评论,2021(6):91-97.

［5］雅克·德里达. 论文字学［M］.汪家堂,译. 上海:上海译文出版社,2005.

▣ 阅读思考 ▣

1. 你还读过狄金森的其他诗歌吗？请与大家分享。
2. 爱默生的哪些思想影响了狄金森？请举例说明。
3. 你是否认为使人感到惊异、新鲜和陌生的事物是具有审美特征的？请举例证明你的观点。
4. 中国儒释道各家思想中的生死观是什么？请比较分析。

Chapter Four   Human and Nature

We must pursue the harmonious coexistence between humanity and nature. Humanity and nature are a community of life. There is no substitute for the current eco-environment. When we use it, we take it for granted. But once damaged, it will struggle to recover. "Heaven and earth coexist with me; all things and I are one." "Heaven and earth do not speak, yet the seasons change and all things grow." When human beings make rational use of nature and protect it, the rewards of nature are often generous; when human beings rudely exploit and plunder nature, the punishment is bound to be merciless. It is an immutable law that harm caused by human actions to nature will eventually hurt human beings themselves. "All things must be in harmony with nature to grow, and obtain from nature to thrive."

Xi Jinping

Xi Jinping: The Governance of China

坚持人与自然和谐共生。人与自然是生命共同体。生态环境没有替代品,用之不觉,失之难存。"天地与我并生,而万物与我为一。""天不言而四时行,地不语而百物生。"当人类合理利用、友好保护自然时,自然的回报常常是慷慨的;当人类无序开发、粗暴掠夺自然时,自然的惩罚必然是无情的。人类对大自然的伤害最终会伤及人类自身,这是无法抗拒的规律。"万物各得其和以生,各得其养以成"。

——习近平《习近平谈治国理政》第三卷

Autumn in Peiping

Yu Dafu

【作品简介】

1934 年 8 月,受到国民党白色恐怖威胁的郁达夫辗转来到北平(今北京),当时中国正处于抗日战争时期,国家前途未卜。作者颠沛流离来到故都,目睹了北平悲凉的秋天,回想起曾于 1926 年病逝于北平的儿子,心中有无尽的感叹,故而创作了《故都的秋》(*Autumn in Peiping*)一文。在这篇散文中,作者赞美了北方的秋天,表达了对故都的无限眷恋,流露出对国家和民族命运深深的忧虑。本文选自 1999 年由上海外语教育出版社出版的张培基译本《英译中国现代散文选》,注释中出现的中文原文出自 2015 年人民文学出版社出版的《郁达夫散文》。

【作者简介】

郁达夫(1896—1945),原名郁文,字达夫,出生于浙江富阳,中国现代著名小说家、散文家、诗人、革命烈士。他曾于 1913 年赴日本留学,1921 年参与成立创造社,1922 年毕业后回国参加各种形式的抗日爱国运动,1938 年远赴新加坡从事报刊编辑和抗日救亡工作,1942 年流亡到苏门答腊,1945 年被日军秘密杀害。受到自身经历和社会大环境的影响,郁达夫的作品有一种深深的"孤独感",给人一种略带颓废的美,其代表作有《沉沦》《故都的秋》《春风沉醉的晚上》《迟桂花》等。

(1) Autumn, wherever it is, always has something to recommend itself. In North China, however, it is particularly limpid[1], serene[2] and melancholy[3]. To enjoy its atmosphere to the full in the onetime capital, I have, therefore, made light of[4] travelling a long distance from Hangzhou to Qingdao, and thence to Peiping.

(2) There is of course autumn in the South too, but over there plants wither[5] slowly, the air is moist, the sky pallid[6], and it is more often rainy than windy. While muddling along[7] all by myself among the urban dwellers[8] of

[1] limpid /ˈlɪmpɪd/ *adj.* 清澈的;透明的

[2] serene /səˈriːn/ *adj.* 平静的

[3] melancholy /ˈmelənkəli/ *adj.* 忧郁的;令人忧伤的

[4] make light of: 对……不在乎

[5] wither /ˈwɪðə(r)/ *v.* 枯萎;凋谢

[6] pallid /ˈpælɪd/ *adj.* 暗淡的

[7] muddle along: 得过且过

[8] dweller /ˈdwelə(r)/ *n.* 居民;居住者

Suzhou, Shanghai, Xiamen, Hong Kong or Guangzhou, I feel nothing but a little chill[9] in the air, without ever relishing[10] to my heart's content the flavour, colour, mood and style of the season. Unlike famous flowers which are most attractive when half opening, or good wine which is most tempting[11] when one is half drunk, autumn, however, is best appreciated in its entirety[12].

(3) It is more than a decade since I last saw autumn in the North. When I am in the South, the arrival of each autumn will put me in mind of Peiping's Tao Ran Ting with its reed[13] catkins[14], Diao Yu Tai with its shady[15] willow trees, Western Hills with their chirping[16] insects, Yu Quan Shan Mountain on a moonlight evening and Tan Zhe Si with its reverberating[17] bell. Suppose you put up in a humble rented house inside the bustling[18] imperial city[19], you can, on getting up at dawn, sit in your courtyard sipping a cup of strong tea, leisurely[20] watch the high azure[21] skies and listen to pigeons circling overhead. Saunter[22] eastward under locust trees[23] to closely observe streaks[24] of sunlight filtering[25] through their foliage[26], or quietly watch the trumpet-shaped blue flowers of morning glories[27] climbing half way up a dilapidated[28] wall, and an intense feeling of autumn will of itself well up inside you. As to morning glories, I like their blue or white flowers best, dark purple ones second best, and pink ones third best. It will be most desirable to have them set off by some tall thin grass planted underneath here and there.

(4) Locust trees in the North, as a decorative embellishment[29] of nature, also associate us with autumn. On getting up early in the morning, you will find the ground strewn[30] all over with flower-like pistils[31] fallen from locust trees. Quiet and smelless, they feel tiny and soft underfoot. After a street cleaner has done the sweeping under the shade of the trees, you will discover countless lines left by his broom in the dust, which look so fine and quiet that somehow a feeling of forlorness[32] will begin to creep up on you. The same depth of implication[33] is found

9 chill /tʃɪl/ n. 寒冷；寒意
10 relish /ˈrelɪʃ/ v. 享受
11 tempting /ˈtemptɪŋ/ adj. 吸引人的
12 entirety /ɪnˈtaɪərəti/ n. 整体；全部
13 reed /riːd/ n. 芦苇
14 catkin /ˈkætkɪn/ n. 柔荑花序（如柳絮等）
15 shady /ˈʃeɪdi/ adj. 阴凉的
16 chirp /tʃɜːp/ v.（发）啁啾声
17 reverberate /rɪˈvɜːbəreɪt/ v. 回荡
18 bustling /ˈbʌslɪŋ/ adj. 繁忙的
19 imperial city: 皇城
20 leisurely /ˈleʒəli/ adv. 悠闲地
21 azure /ˈæʒə(r)/ adj. 天蓝色的
22 saunter /ˈsɔːntə(r)/ v. 漫步
23 locust tree: 槐树
24 streak /striːk/ n. 条纹；条痕
25 filter /ˈfɪltə(r)/ v.（光或声）隐约透过
26 foliage /ˈfəʊliɪdʒ/ n. 树叶
27 morning glories: 牵牛花
28 dilapidated /dɪˈlæpɪdeɪtɪd/ adj. 破旧的
29 embellishment /ɪmˈbelɪʃmənt/ n. 装饰；修饰
30 strew /struː/ v. 布满；撒满
31 pistil /ˈpɪstɪl/ n. 雌蕊
32 forlorn /fə(r)ˈlɔː(r)n/ adj. 凄凉的
33 implication /ˌɪmplɪˈkeɪʃn/ n. 含义

in the ancient saying that a single fallen leaf from the *wutong* tree is more than enough to inform the world of autumn's presence[34].

(5) The sporadic[35] feeble chirping of cicadas[36] is especially characteristic of autumn in the North. Due to the abundance of trees and the low altitude[37] of dwellings in Peiping, cicadas are audible[38] in every nook[39] and cranny[40] of the city. In the South, however, one cannot hear them unless in suburbs or hills. Because of their ubiquitous[41] shrill noise, these insects in Peiping seem to be living off every household like crickets or mice.

(6) As for autumn rains in the North, they also seem to differ from those in the South, being more appealing[42], more temperate[43].

(7) A sudden gust[44] of cool wind under the slaty[45] sky, and raindrops will start pitter-pattering[46]. Soon when the rain is over, the clouds begin gradually to roll towards the west and the sun comes out in the blue sky. Some idle townsfolk, wearing lined or unlined clothing made of thick cloth, will come out pipe in mouth and, loitering[47] under a tree by the end of a bridge, exchange leisurely conversation with acquaintances with a slight touch of[48] regret at the passing of time:

(8) "Oh, real nice and cool —"

(9) "Sure! Getting cooler with each autumn shower!"

(10) Fruit trees in the North also make a wonderful sight in autumn. Take jujube[49] tree for example. They grow everywhere — around the corner of a house, at the foot of a wall, by the side of a latrine[50] or outside a kitchen door. It is at the height of autumn that jujubes, shaped like dates or pigeon eggs, make their appearance in a light yellowish-green amongst tiny elliptic[51] leaves. By the time when they have turned ruddy[52] and the leaves fallen, the north-westerly wind will begin to reign supreme[53] and make a dusty world of the North. Only at the turn of July and August when jujubes, persimmons[54], grapes are 80—90 percent ripe will the North have the

[34] presence /ˈprezns/ n. 存在；出现

[35] sporadic /spəˈrædɪk/ adj. 偶尔的

[36] cicada /sɪˈkɑːdə/ n. 蝉

[37] altitude /ˈæltɪtjuːd/ n. 高度；海拔

[38] audible /ˈɔːdəbl/ adj. 听得见的

[39] nook /nʊk/ n. 幽静的角落

[40] cranny /ˈkræni] / n. 缝隙

[41] ubiquitous /juːˈbɪkwɪtəs/ adj. 普遍的；无所不在的

[42] appealing /əˈpiːlɪŋ/ adj. 吸引人的

[43] temperate /ˈtempərət/ adj. 温和的

[44] gust /gʌst/ n. 一阵强风；一阵狂风

[45] slaty /ˈsleɪti/ adj. 深灰色的

[46] pitter-patter /ˈpɪtə pætə(r)/ v. (尤指下雨时) 发出啪啪声

[47] loiter /ˈlɔɪtə(r)/ v. 游荡；闲逛

[48] touch of: 一点儿；少许

[49] jujube /ˈdʒuːdʒuːb/ n. 枣子

[50] latrine /ləˈtriːn/ n. 厕所；茅厕

[51] elliptic /ɪˈlɪptɪk/ adj. 椭圆的

[52] ruddy /ˈrʌdi/ adj. 红色的

[53] reign supreme: 主宰；称雄

[54] persimmon /pəˈsɪmən/ n. 柿子

best of autumn — the golden days in a year.

（11）Some literary critics say that Chinese literati[55], especially poets, are mostly disposed[56] to be decadent[57], which accounts for predominance[58] of Chinese works singing the praises of autumn. Well, the same is true of foreign poets, isn't it? I haven't read much of foreign poetry and prose, nor do I want to enumerate[59] autumn-related poems and essays in foreign literature. But, if you browse[60] through collected works of English, German, French or Italian poets, or various countries' anthologies[61] of poetry or prose, you can always come across a great many literary pieces eulogizing[62] or lamenting[63] autumn. Long pastoral[64] poems or songs about the four seasons by renowned poets are mostly distinguished by beautiful moving lines on autumn. All that goes to show that all live creatures and sensitive humans alike are prone to[65] the feeling of depth, remoteness, severity and bleakness. Not only poets, even convicts[66] in prison, I suppose, have deep sentiments in autumn in spite of themselves. Autumn treats all humans alike, regardless of nationality, race or class. However, judging from Chinese idiom qiushi[67] (autumn scholar, meaning an aged scholar grieving over frustrations in his life) and frequent selection in textbooks of Ouyang Xiu's *On the Autumn Sough*[68] and Su Dongpo's *On the Red Cliff*[69], Chinese men of letters[70] seem to be particularly autumn-minded. But, to know the real flavour of autumn, especially China's autumn, one has to visit the North.

（12）Autumn in the South also has its unique features, such as the moon-lit[71] Ershisi Bridge in Yangzhou, the flowing sea tide at the Qiantangjiang River, the mist-shrouded[72] Putuo Mountain and lotuses[73] at the Lizhiwan Bay. But they all lack strong colour and lingering[74] flavour. Southern autumn is to Northern autumn what yellow rice wine is to *kaoliang* wine, congee to steamed buns, perches to crabs, yellow dogs to camels. [75]

（13）Autumn, I mean Northern autumn, if only it could be made to last forever! I would be more than

---

55 literati /ˌlɪtəˈrɑːti/ n. 文人

56 disposed /dɪˈspəʊzd/ adj. 倾向于

57 decadent /ˈdekədənt/ adj. 堕落的

58 predominance /prɪˈdɒmɪnəns/ n. 主导地位；支配地位

59 enumerate /ɪˈnjuːməreɪt/ v. 列举

60 browse /braʊz/ v. 浏览；翻阅

61 anthology /ænˈθɒlədʒi/ n.（不同作家的作品的）选集

62 eulogize /ˈjuːlədʒaɪz/ v. 讴歌

63 lament /ləˈment/ v. 哀叹；痛惜

64 pastoral /ˈpɑːstərəl/ adj. 田园的

65 prone to：易于

66 convict /kənˈvɪkt/ n. 罪犯

67 qiushi：秋士，指迟暮不遇之士。

68 *On the Autumn Sough*：欧阳修的《秋声赋》

69 *On the Red Cliff*：苏东坡的《赤壁赋》

70 man of letters：文人墨客；文人

71 moon-lit：明月照耀的

72 mist-shrouded：云雾缭绕的

73 lotus /ˈləʊtəs/ n. 荷花；莲花

74 linger /ˈlɪŋɡə(r)/ v. 流连；逗留

75 类比（analogy）。（原文：比起北国的秋来，正象是黄酒之与白干，稀饭之与馍馍，鲈鱼之与大蟹，黄犬之与

willing to keep but one-third of my life-span and have two-thirds of it <u>bartered</u>[76] for the <u>prolonged</u>[77] stay of the season !

骆驼。)

[76] barter /ˈbɑː(r)tə(r)/ v. 以物易物；交换

[77] prolong /prəˈlɒŋ/ v. 延长

◪ 精华赏析 ◪

郁达夫在《故都的秋》一文中，颇含感情地赞美了中国北方秋天的美，但是这种美是略带忧伤的。其实，中国传统文人都有着一种悲秋情结，在古诗词中，秋天多与悲伤、疾病、衰老、失意联系在一起，无论是《汉乐府·长歌行》中的"常恐秋节至，焜黄华叶衰"，还是杜甫《登高》里的"万里悲秋常作客，百年多病独登台"，秋天都是让人感到悲伤的季节。因为人类的生命与大自然相似，都是一个循环往复的过程，都有着生长、成熟、衰老和死亡四个阶段。一年有四季——春、夏、秋、冬，而人生有四个阶段——青年、成年、老年、死亡，因此大自然的秋天对应的是人类的老年，其悲哀是不难想象的(刘正光，1988)。在秋天，夏日里的红花谢了，绿树枯黄，秋风萧瑟，秋雨绵绵，落花随风飘落，寒蝉凄切哀鸣，这些景象让文人们不禁感叹，人生一世，草木一秋，生命即将结束，寒冷的冬季即将到来，怎能让人不心生惆怅呢？而文人的悲秋情结，多用"意象"表达。在《故都的秋》这篇散文中，郁达夫也略带感伤地回忆了北国的秋，其中不乏"悲秋"的意象，主要有落蕊、秋蝉、秋风、秋雨、秋草和破屋等。下面让我们来看一看古诗词中落蕊和秋蝉这两个典型的"悲秋"意象吧！

一、落蕊

落蕊是花儿凋谢后自然飘落的花蕊，在文学作品中与落叶给人的感觉相似。

落花多代表萧瑟、凄凉，与盛开的花儿相比，它们更容易让人联想到人生中的失意与落魄。比如唐代落第秀才严恽在《落花》这首诗中，就用花开与花儿零落喻人生的得意与失意，一句"尽日问花花不语，为谁零落为谁开"传递出诗人再次落第后的失意和忧伤。

落花会让人联想到暮年。在《江畔独步寻花七绝句·其七》一诗中，诗圣杜甫不禁感叹道，"不是爱花即肯死，只恐花尽老相催。繁枝容易纷纷落，嫩叶商量细细开。"落花让人联想到春光易逝，老之将至，所以花儿啊，你们别着急，慢慢开。

落花会让人想到死亡。花儿会枯萎凋谢，人也会衰老飘零。落花让黛玉这个闺中少女联想到死亡，体弱多病的她深感自己命薄，花儿易落，红颜易老，少女也会慢慢老去，终有一天如花儿一样凋零。正因为如此，黛玉才如此怜惜落花，不忍它们被人践踏，边葬花边感叹："侬今葬花人笑痴，他年葬侬知是谁？试看春残花渐落，便是红颜老死时。一朝春尽红颜老，花落人亡两不知！"(《葬花吟》)

每年到了秋季，由于天气转凉，很多花儿开始凋谢。在萧瑟的秋风中，残败的花儿窸窣掉落，尤其是在一夜秋雨之后，在大街小巷里，人们总会看到一地的落蕊，这给人一种悲凉和感伤的情绪。因此，落花便成了"悲秋"的一个重要意象。

二、秋蝉

　　蝉的寿命很长，但是其发育要经过卵、若虫、成虫三个阶段，其中幼虫阶段占据了绝大部分时间。蝉的前半生都会在地下蛰伏，经过数年的等待之后，在六月份，大量幼虫开始羽化为成虫，之后，成年的雄蝉开始鸣奏高歌，其目的就是吸引雌蝉交配，繁衍后代。（雌蝉是不会叫的，它们的腹部也有发声器，但是已经退化，不能发出声音，所以在夏天鸣叫的都是雄蝉。）在交配产卵之后，完成传宗接代使命的雌蝉会马上死去，而这个时候，雄蝉的寿命也所剩无几了。

　　多数蝉会在初夏羽化，夏天即将结束时纷纷死去，因此，蝉被认为是夏天的使者，"微月初三夜，新蝉第一声。"（唐·白居易《六月三日夜闻蝉》）蝉鸣声响起，就预示着夏天到来了。化为成虫后的雄蝉便开始高歌，天气越是炎热，它们唱得越响亮，"泉溜潜幽咽，琴鸣乍往还。长风剪不断，还在树枝间。"（唐·卢仝《新蝉》）在炎炎夏日的午后，你能听到蝉热闹而欢乐的歌唱，蝉鸣声既绵长又高亢，此起彼伏，在树枝间回绕不绝。夏天的蝉是聒噪的，歌声嘹亮，在《昆虫记》中，法布尔就将它们称作"夏日里的音乐家"。

　　由群蝉召开的盛大音乐会在盛夏达到高潮，之后随着气温降低，天气转凉，蝉逐渐消亡。到了秋天，仅存的蝉也无力长鸣了，正如宋代词人柳永描写的："寒蝉凄切，对长亭晚，骤雨初歇。"（《雨霖铃·寒蝉凄切》）秋季里的蝉声变得低沉，听起来急促而凄凉，"秋来吟更苦，半咽半随风。"（自唐·姚合《闻蝉寄贾岛》）秋蝉的吟唱显得更为愁苦，一半因哽咽而断断续续，一半随风而逝。情感丰富的诗人们经常用秋蝉隐喻自己的愁苦心情，"此树开花簌簌黄，秋蝉鸣破雨徐凉。"（宋·董嗣杲《槐花》）在暮秋时节，秋寒阵阵，秋风萧瑟，秋雨连绵，此时再听到凄切的蝉鸣声，悲凉之情便会油然而生，秋蝉便成了"悲秋"的又一个重要意象。

　　在古诗词里，"落蕊"和"秋蝉"作为悲秋意象比比皆是，那"秋风""秋雨""秋草"和"破屋"这些有没有作为"悲秋"的意象呢？一起读读古诗词，找一找，然后跟彼此分享吧！

📖 参考文献 📖

刘正光. 共是悲秋客，哪知此路分——中英诗歌"悲"秋意象探源[J]. 湖南大学学报，1998（2）：39-42.

📖 阅读思考 📖

1. 英语中有没有"悲秋"主题的诗歌？英美的诗人们有没有"悲秋"情结呢？
2. 在《故都的秋》中，作者为什么会提到枣树呢？"秋枣"这一意象，与"悲秋"有关吗？

12

Rural Life in England

Washington Irving

【作品简介】

《英国的乡村生活》(*Rural Life in England*)是美国文学家华盛顿·欧文创作的一篇散文。华盛顿·欧文的散文作品华美清新、笔调优雅、轻松诙谐,其代表作《见闻札记》一书中描写了英美两国风光旖旎的自然景色和地域人物的传奇故事。《英国的乡村生活》是《见闻札记》的第七篇,描写了英国乡村的美丽风物和园林景观,被誉为"记叙历历如画,具有英国水彩画般的鲜明色彩"(高健,2000)。

【作者简介】

华盛顿·欧文(Washington Irving)出生在一个富裕的商人家庭。年少时期,欧文就开始广泛阅读书籍,并且创作了一些诗歌、散文、戏剧等。之后他学习过法律,当过一段时间的律师,但是他发现自己还是更喜欢写作。欧文使用笔名 Diedrich Knickerbocker 写的第一本书是《纽约外史》(*A History of New York from the Beginning of the World to the End of the Dutch Dynasty*)(1809),这本书获得了成功,为欧文带了广泛的赞誉。之后欧文去英国接管自己的家族企业,在生意失败后,他不得不用写作来维持生活。之后出版的《见闻札记》(*The Sketch Book of Geoffrey Crayon, Gent*)(1819—1820)使欧文获得了国际认可。1826 年,欧文作为外交官被派往西班牙,在那里他收集了关于《哥伦布传》(*The History of the Life and Voyages of Christopher Columbus*)(1828)、《征服格拉纳》(*A Chronicle of the Conquest of Granada*)(1829)、《阿尔罕伯拉》(*The Alhambra*)(1832)这些作品的相关资料。1829 年至 1832 年,他是美国驻伦敦公使馆的秘书。在五十岁左右的时候,欧文回到了美国,在哈德逊河畔买下了一处宅院 sunnyside,除了其中四年在西班牙担任外交使节离开过一段时间,他一直住在那里,写下了《歌尔德斯密斯传》(*Life of Goldsmith*)、《华盛顿传》(*Life of Washington*)和其他的一些作品。欧文于 1859 年去世,一生未婚。

华盛顿·欧文被称为"美国文学之父",因为他是美国独立后第一位具有国际影响力的美国作家。在他之前有名的美国作家有本杰明·富兰克林、托马斯·潘恩和菲利普·弗伦诺(富兰克林的主要作品是《富兰克林自传》和《穷理查年鉴》,潘恩的是《常识》,弗伦诺的是一些诗作)。他们的作品总的来说影响力不是很大。只有到了欧文这里,美国文学才引起世界的关注,无论是作品数量还是作品的文学性,欧文都远远超过了他的前辈们。他的《纽约外史》曾轰动一时,受到了欧洲读者的普遍欢迎,美国文学从此迈出了走向世界的第一步。从 1819 年起,欧文陆续发表了许多散文、随笔和故事,1820 年汇集成了《见闻札记》,在英国出版后得到极大关注,使他成为第一个获得国际声誉的美国作家。斯各特、拜伦等人成为他的知交,萨克雷称其为"新世界文坛送往旧世界的第一位使节"。欧文的作品创造性地运用民间文学题材,为美国"童年"时期描绘出浪漫主义画像,对后来的美国文学产生了重要影响。他的作品中有不少是富有想象力、具有传奇色彩的故事,比较著名的有《瑞普·凡·温克尔》《睡谷的传说》《幽灵新郎》,这些作品都构思奇特,耐人寻味。欧文的这些作品也标志着美国浪漫主义的开端。

（1）*Oh*！*Friendly to the best pursuits of man*，

（2）*Friendly to thought*，*to* <u>virtue</u>[1]，*and to peace*，

（3）*Domestic life in rural pleasures past*！

COWPER[2]

（4）The stranger who would form a correct opinion of the English character must not confine his observations to the metropolis. He must go forth into the country; he must <u>sojourn</u>[3] in villages and <u>hamlets</u>[4]; he must visit castles, villas, farmhouses, cottages; he must wander through parks and gardens; along <u>hedges</u>[5] and green lanes; he must <u>loiter</u>[6] about country churches; attend <u>wakes and fairs</u>[7] and other rural festivals; and cope with the people in all their conditions, and all their habits and humors.[8]

（5）In some countries the large cities absorb the wealth and fashion of the nation; they are the only fixed <u>abodes</u>[9] of elegant and intelligent society, and the country is inhabited almost entirely by <u>boorish</u>[10] peasantry. In England, on the contrary, the metropolis is a mere gathering place, or general <u>rendezvous</u>[11], of the polite classes, where they devote a small portion of the year to a hurry of gaiety and <u>dissipation</u>[12], and, having indulged this kind of carnival, return again to the apparently more <u>congenial</u>[13] habits of rural life. The various orders of society are therefore <u>diffused</u>[14] over the whole surface of the kingdom, and the more retired neighborhoods afford specimens of the different ranks.

[1] virtue /'vɜːtʃuː/ n. 德行;美德

[2] 即 William Cowper 威廉·考珀（1731—1800）,英国诗人。

[3] sojourn /'sɒdʒən/ v. 寄居;旅居

[4] hamlet /'hæmlət/ n. 小村庄

[5] hedge /hedʒ/ n. 树篱

[6] loiter /'lɔɪtə(r)/ v. 游荡;徘徊;闲逛

[7] wakes and fairs: 这里指的是节庆和集市。

[8] 欧文认为要想了解英国人的性格,需要深入到英国的乡村中去。

[9] abode /ə'bəʊd/ n. 住所;家

[10] boorish /'bʊərɪʃ/ adj. 粗鲁讨厌的

[11] rendezvous /'rɒndɪvuː/ n. 约会;约会地点;(酒吧等)热门聚会场所

[12] dissipation /ˌdɪsɪ'peɪʃn/ n. 消散;驱散;花天酒地

[13] congenial /kən'dʒiːniəl/ adj. 意气相投的;合意的

[14] diffuse /dɪ'fjuːs/ v. 使分散;散布

（6）The English, in fact, are strongly gifted with the rural feeling. They possess a quick sensibility to the beauties of nature and a keen relish[15] for the pleasures and employments of the country. [16] This passion seems inherent in them. Even the inhabitants of cities, born and brought up among brick walls and bustling[17] streets, enter with facility into rural habits and evince a tact[18] for rural occupation. The merchant has his snug[19] retreat in the vicinity of the metropolis, where he often displays as much pride and zeal in the cultivation of his flower garden and the maturing of his fruits as he does in the conduct of his business and the success of a commercial enterprise. Even those less fortunate individuals, who are doomed to pass their lives in the midst of din[20] and traffic contrive to have something that shall remind them of the green aspect of nature. In the most dark and dingy[21] quarters of the city, the drawing-room window resembles frequently a bank of flowers; every spot capable of vegetation has its grassplot and flowerbed; and every square its mimic[22] park, laid out with picturesque taste and gleaming with refreshing verdure[23].

（7）Those who see the Englishman only in town are apt[24] to form an unfavorable opinion of his social character. He is either absorbed in business, or distracted by the thousand engagements that dissipate[25] time, thought, and feeling, in this huge metropolis. [26] He has, therefore, too commonly a look of hurry and abstraction. Wherever he happens to be, he is on the point of going somewhere else; at the moment he is talking on one subject, his mind is wandering to another; and while paying a friendly visit, he is calculating how he shall economize time so as to pay the other visits allotted[27] to the morning. An immense[28] metropolis, like London, is calculated to make men selfish and uninteresting. In their casual and transient[29] meetings, they can but deal briefly in commonplaces. They present but the cold superfices of character — its rich and genial[30] qualities have no time to

[15] relish /'relɪʃ/ n.享受；乐趣

[16] 这句话的主干是 They possess a sensibility and a relish.

[17] bustling /'bʌslɪŋ/ adj.繁忙的；熙熙攘攘的

[18] tact /tækt/ n.老练；圆通

[19] snug /snʌg/ adj.舒适的

[20] din /dɪn/ n.喧嚣声；嘈杂声

[21] dingy /'dɪndʒi/ adj.又黑又脏的；昏暗的

[22] mimic /'mɪmɪk/ adj.模仿的

[23] verdure /'vɜːdʒə(r)/ n.青葱的草木；郁郁葱葱的植物

[24] apt /æpt/ adj.易于……；有……倾向

[25] dissipate /'dɪsɪpeɪt/ v.浪费；消磨（时间、金钱等）

[26] 在大都会里，要么他的身心都深陷在事务当中，要么就被许多耗费时间、思想和感情的约会弄得心神不宁。

[27] allot /ə'lɒt/ v.分配（时间、钱财等）

[28] immense /ɪ'mens/ adj.极大的；巨大的

[29] transient /'trænziənt/ adj.转瞬即逝的；短暂的

[30] genial /'dʒiːniəl/ adj.和蔼的

be warmed into a flow.

（8）It is in the country that the Englishman gives scope to his natural feelings. He breaks loose gladly from the cold formalities and negative civilities of town, throws off his habits of shy reserve, and becomes joyous and freehearted. He manages to collect around him all the conveniences and elegancies of polite life, and to banish[31] its restraints. His countryseat abounds[32] with every requisite, either for studious retirement, tasteful gratification, or rural exercise. Books, paintings, music, horses, dogs, and sporting implements of all kinds are at hand. He puts no constraint either upon his guests or himself, but in the true spirit of hospitality provides the means of enjoyment, and leaves everyone to partake[33] according to his inclination.

（9）The taste of the English in the cultivation of land and in what is called landscape gardening, is unrivaled[34]. They have studied Nature intently, and discovered an exquisite sense of her beautiful forms and harmonious combinations. Those charms, which in other countries she lavishes[35] in wild solitudes, are here assembled around the haunts of domestic life. They seem to have caught her coy[36] and furtive[37] graces and spread them, like witchery, about their rural abodes.[38]

（10）Nothing can be more imposing than the magnificence of English park scenery. Vast lawns that extend like sheets of vivid green, with here and there clumps[39] of gigantic trees, heaping up rich piles of foliage[40]; the solemn pomp[41] of groves[42] and woodland glades, with the deer trooping[43] in silent herds across them, the hare, bounding away to the covert[44], or the pheasant, suddenly bursting upon the wing; the brook, taught to wind in natural meanderings or expand into a glassy lake; the sequestered[45] pool, reflecting the quivering trees, with the yellow leaf sleeping on its bosom,[46] and the trout roaming fearlessly about its limpid waters while some rustic[47] temple or sylvan[48] statue, grown green and dank with age, gives an air of classic sanctity[49] to the seclusion.[50]

[31] banish /ˈbænɪʃ/ v. 赶走；驱除
[32] abound /əˈbaʊnd/ v. 大量；大量存在
[33] partake /pɑːˈteɪk/ v. 享用；参与
[34] unrivaled /ʌnˈraɪvld/ adj. 无与伦比的
[35] lavish /ˈlævɪʃ/ v. 浪费
[36] coy /kɔɪ/ adj. 害羞的
[37] furtive /ˈfɜːtɪv/ adj. 偷偷摸摸的；遮遮掩掩的
[38] 这句话中使用了明喻（simile）。他们似乎把自然界的一切不轻易示人的优美仪态全都捕捉在手，然后犹如凭借魔力一般使之展现在自己的乡居住宅周围。
[39] clump /klʌmp/ v. 聚集
[40] foliage /ˈfəʊliɪdʒ/ n. 树叶；枝叶
[41] pomp /pɒmp/ n. 盛况；排场
[42] grove /grəʊvz/ n.小树林；果园
[43] troop /truːp/ v. 成群结队而行
[44] covert /ˈkʌvət/ n. 灌木林
[45] sequestered /sɪˈkwestəd/ adj. 僻静的；与外界隔绝的
[46] 这里使用了两个拟人（personification），树木摇曳的身影，落叶静静安睡在水面上。

（11）These are but a few of the features of park scenery; but what most delights me is the creative talent with which the English decorate the unostentatious[51] abodes of middle life. The rudest habitation, the most unpromising and scanty portion of land, in the hands of an Englishman of taste becomes a little paradise. With a nicely discriminating[52] eye, he seizes at once upon its capabilities and pictures in his mind the future landscape. The sterile[53] spot grows into loveliness under his hand; and yet the operations of art which produce the effect are scarcely to be perceived. The cherishing and training of some trees, the cautious pruning[54] of others, the nice distribution of flowers and plants of tender and graceful foliage, the introduction of a green slope of velvet turf[55], the partial opening to a peep of blue distance or silver gleam of water, all these are managed with a delicate tact, a pervading yet quiet assiduity[56], like the magic touchings with which a painter finishes up a favorite picture.

（12）The residence of people of fortune and refinement[57] in the country has diffused a degree of taste and elegance in rural economy that descends to the lowest class. The very laborer, with his thatched[58] cottage and narrow slip of ground, attends to their embellishment[59]. The trim hedge, the grass plot before the door, the little flower bed bordered with snug box, the woodbine trained up against the wall and hanging its blossoms about the lattice[60]; the pot of flowers in the window, the holly[61], providently[62] planted about the house to cheat winter of its dreariness and to throw in a semblance of green summer to cheer the fireside, all these bespeak the influence of taste, flowing down from high sources and pervading the lowest levels of the public mind. If ever Love, as poets sing, delights to visit a cottage, it must be the cottage of an English peasant.

（13）The fondness for rural life among the higher classes of the English has had a great and salutary[63] effect upon the national character. I do not know a finer race of

---

47 rustic /ˈrʌstɪk/ adj. 乡村的;纯朴的

48 sylvan /ˈsɪlvən/ adj. 森林的;树木的

49 sanctity /ˈsæŋktəti/ adj. 神圣的

50 这段话是对英国园林景物的描写,细节丰满,动静结合,写得十分传神。

51 unostentatious /ˌʌnɒstəˈteʃəs/ adj. 朴素的;不夸耀的

52 discriminating /dɪˈskrɪmɪneɪtɪŋ/ adj. 有鉴赏力的;有识别力的

53 sterile /ˈsteraɪl/ adj. 无生气的

54 prune /pruːn/ v. 修剪树枝

55 turf /tɜːf/ n. 草皮

56 assiduity /ˌæsɪˈdjuːəti/ n. 勤勉

57 refinement /rɪˈfaɪnmənt/ n. 精炼;提炼

58 thatched /θætʃt/ adj. (房屋或屋顶)用茅草铺盖的

59 embellishment /ɪmˈbelɪʃmənt/ n. 装饰;修饰

60 lattice /ˈlætɪs/ n. 格子木架;格栅

61 holly /ˈhɒli/ n. 冬青

62 providently /ˈprɒvɪdəntli/ adv. 有远虑地

63 salutary /ˈsæljətri/ adj. 有益的

men than the English gentlemen. Instead of the softness and effeminacy[64] which characterize the men of rank in most countries, they exhibit a union of elegance and strength, a robustness of frame and freshness of complexion which I am inclined to attribute to their living so much in the open air and pursuing so eagerly the invigorating recreations of the country. These hardy exercises produce also a healthful tone of mind and spirits, and a manliness and simplicity of manners, which even the follies[65] and dissipations of the town cannot easily pervert and can never entirely destroy. In the country, too, the different orders of society seem to approach more freely, to be more disposed to blend and operate favorably upon each other. The distinctions between them do not appear to be so marked and impassable[66] as in the cities. The manner in which property has been distributed into small estates and farms has established a regular gradation from the noblemen, through the classes of gentry, small landed proprietors, and substantial farmers, down to the laboring peasantry; and while it has thus banded the extremes of society together, has infused into each intermediate rank a spirit of independence. This, it must be confessed, is not so universally the case at present as it was formerly; the larger estates having, in late years of distress, absorbed the smaller, and, in some parts of the country, almost annihilated[67] the sturdy[68] race of small farmers. These, however, I believe, are but casual breaks in the general system I have mentioned.

(14) In rural occupation there is nothing mean and debasing. It leads a man forth among scenes of natural grandeur and beauty; it leaves him to the workings of his own mind, operated upon by the purest and most elevating of external influences. Such a man may be simple and rough, but he cannot be vulgar. The man of refinement, therefore, finds nothing revolting[69] in an intercourse with the lower orders in rural life, as he does when he casually mingles with the lower orders of cities. He lays aside his distance and reserve and is glad to

[64] effeminacy /ɪˈfemɪnəsi/ n. 柔弱

[65] folly /ˈfɒli/ n. 愚蠢

[66] impassable /ɪmˈpɑːsəbl/ adj. 不能通行

[67] annihilate /əˈnaɪəleɪt/ v. 消灭；毁灭
[68] sturdy /ˈstɜːdi/ adj. 强壮的；顽强的

[69] revolting /rɪˈvəʊltɪŋ/ adj. 极其讨厌的

waive the distinctions of rank and to enter into the honest, heartfelt enjoyments of common life. Indeed, the very amusements of the country bring men more and more together; and the sound hound and horn blend all feelings into harmony. I believe this is one great reason why the nobility and gentry are more popular among the inferior orders in England than they are in any other country, and why the latter have endured so many excessive pressures and extremities without repining[70] more generally at the unequal distribution of fortune and privilege.

(15) To this mingling of cultivated and rustic society may also be attributed the rural feeling that runs through British literature; the frequent use of illustrations from rural life; those incomparable descriptions of nature that abound in the British poets, that have continued down from "The Flower and the Leaf" of Chaucer[71] and have brought into our closets all the freshness and fragrance of the dewy landscape. The pastoral writers of other countries appear as if they had paid Nature an occasional visit, and become acquainted with her general charms; but the British poets have lived and reveled with her — they have wooed[72] her in her most secret haunts[73] — they have watched her minutest caprices[74]. A spray could not tremble in the breeze, a leaf could not rustle to the ground, a diamond drop could not patter in the stream, a fragrance could not exhale from the humble violet, nor a daisy unfold its crimson[75] tints to the morning, but it has been noticed by these impassioned and delicate observers, and wrought up into some beautiful morality.

(16) The effect of this devotion of elegant minds to rural occupations has been wonderful on the face of the country. A great part of the island is rather level, and would be monotonous were it not for the charms of culture; but it is studded[76] and gemmed[77], as it were, with castles and palaces, and embroidered[78] with parks and gardens. It does not abound in grand and sublime[79] prospects, but rather in little home scenes of rural repose and sheltered quiet. Every antique farmhouse and moss-

70 repine /rɪˈpaɪn/ v. 抱怨

71 乔叟(1343—1400),英国小说家、诗人,主要作品有《坎特伯雷故事集》。乔叟于 1400 年在伦敦去世,被葬在威斯敏斯特教堂的"诗人之角"。乔叟被公认为是中世纪英国最伟大的诗人之一,英国诗歌的奠基人,被后人誉为"英国诗歌之父"。

72 woo /wuː/ v. 寻求……的赞同;争取……的支持

73 haunt /hɔːnt/ n. 常去的场所;消磨时光的去处

74 caprice /kəˈpriːs/ n. 反复无常;任性善变

75 crimson /ˈkrɪmzn/ adj. 深红色的;暗红色的

76 stud /stʌd/ v. 装饰

77 gem /dʒem/ v. 点缀;用宝石装饰

78 embroider /ɪmˈbrɔɪdə(r)/ v. 加以渲染(或润色)

79 sublime /səˈblaɪm/ adj. 宏伟的;壮

grown cottage is a picture; and as the roads are continually winding, and the view is shut in by groves and hedges, the eye is delighted by a continual succession of small landscapes of captivating[80] loveliness.

（17）The great charm, however, of English scenery is the moral feeling that seems to pervade it. It is associated in the mind with ideas of order, of quiet, of sober, well-established principles, of hoary[81] usage and reverend custom.[82] Everything seems to be the growth of ages of regular and peaceful existence. The old church of remote architecture, with its low, massive portal, its gothic tower, its windows rich with tracery[83] and painted glass in scrupulous preservation, its stately monuments of warriors and worthies of the olden time, ancestors of the present lords of the soil, its tombstones, recording successive generations of sturdy yeomanry[84], whose progeny[85] still plow the same fields and kneel at the same altar; the parsonage[86], a quaint, irregular pile, partly antiquated, but repaired and altered in the tastes of various ages and occupants; the stile and foot-path leading from the churchyard, across pleasant fields, and along shady hedgerows, according to an immemorial right of way; the neighboring village, with its venerable cottages, its public green sheltered by trees, under which the forefathers of the present race have sported; the antique family mansion, standing apart in some little rural domain, but looking down with a protecting air on the surrounding scene: all these common features of English landscape evince a calm and settled security, a hereditary[87] transmission of home-bred virtues and local attachments that speak deeply and touchingly for the moral character of the nation.

（18）It is a pleasing sight of a Sunday morning, when the bell is sending its sober melody across the quiet fields, to behold the peasantry in their best finery, with ruddy faces and modest cheerfulness, thronging tranquilly[88] along the green lanes to church; but it is still more pleasing to see them in the evenings, gathering about their cottage doors

丽的

80 captivating /ˈkæptɪveɪtɪŋ/ adj. 迷人的；有魅力的；有吸引力的

81 hoary /ˈhɔːri/ adj. 陈旧的
82 它的风景之美让人们在心中联想到秩序、宁静、合理构建的原则，以及久远的习惯与自古尊崇的风俗。欧文在这里对英国乡村景色的赞美上升了一个层面，美景不只是视觉的享受，不只影响了英国人的性格，这里的风景还代表着秩序、原则和风俗等。
83 tracery /ˈtreɪsəri/ n. 窗花格（某些教堂窗户顶部的石制花饰）；精美花饰图案
84 yeomanry /ˈjəʊmənri/ n.（英国旧时的）自耕农；携马当兵的农民
85 progeny /ˈprɒdʒəni/ n. 后代；子孙
86 parsonage /ˈpɑːsənɪdʒ/ n. 教区牧师的住所

87 hereditary /həˈredɪtri/ adj. 遗传的；世袭的

88 tranquilly /ˈtræŋkwɪli/ adv. 安静地；平静地

and appearing to exult in the humble comforts and embellishments which their own hands have spread around them.

(19) It is this sweet home feeling, this settled repose of affection in the domestic scene, that is, after all, the parent of the steadiest virtues and purest enjoyments; and I cannot close these desultory[89] remarks better, than by quoting the words of a modern English poet, who has depicted it with remarkable felicity:

(20) Through each gradation, from the castled hall,

(21) The city dome, the villa crown'd with shade,

(22) But chief from modest mansions numberless,

(23) In town or hamlet, shelt'ring middle life,

(24) Down to the cottaged vale, and straw-roof'd shed;

(25) This western isle has long been famed for scenes

(26) Where bliss domestic finds a dwelling-place;

(27) Domestic bliss, that, like a harmless dove,

(28) (Honor and sweet endearment keeping guard,)

(29) Can center in a little quiet nest

(30) All that desire would fly for through the earth;

(31) That can, the world eluding, be itself

(32) A world enjoyed; that wants no witnesses

(33) But its own sharers, and approving Heaven;

(34) That, like a flower deep hid in rock cleft,

(35) Smiles, though 't is looking only at the sky.[90]

[89] desultory /ˈdesəltri/ adj. 漫无目的的；随意的

[90] 无论什么等级，从城堡内的殿堂，都市的拱顶，绿荫密布的别墅，特别是那无数的朴素邸宅，从中产阶级生活的乡镇村庄，直到山谷间的农舍和茅屋；这西方岛屿因风光而久享盛名，家庭幸福在这里得以栖居；而家庭幸福，像一只纯洁无邪的白鸽，（光荣与甜美的爱抚一直将它呵护，）它能把飞遍人间去寻觅的欲望，全都聚集在一个宁静的小窝里；它能在世界逃逸时，自享一个世界；无须别的见证，而由共享者自成天堂它就像深藏在悬崖里的一朵花，独自微笑，尽管只仰望着天空。

精华赏析

　　《英国的乡村生活》是《见闻札记》中的一篇。使华盛顿·欧文闻名于世的《见闻札记》是一部集"讽刺与异想、事实与虚构、杂写新旧世界"的游记散文作品。欧文在欧洲访古探幽，沉醉在青山翠谷间，流连于宫殿楼宇中，穿梭于古塔教堂里，他通过敏锐的观察，优美流畅的文字把目之所及的美好景色与事物呈现出来。

一、文学、旅行与自然

美国文学产生于一种特殊的人文和自然背景之下，从一开始就与自然有着天然的联系。17 世纪第一批移民从新大陆漂洋过海来到美洲大陆，他们被这里的美景所震撼，这块大陆广袤无垠，物产丰富，景色秀丽。这一时期的美国作家对自己国家的壮美景色从内心深处是热爱和赞美的，另外早期移民也需要在这片蛮荒之地中寻求生存，所以他们十分关注人和自然的关系。不少作家都倾心于描写大自然的宏伟与神奇，他们在自己的作品中反复探讨人与自然的关系，爱默生、惠特曼和梭罗都是歌唱自然的代表作家。美国文学是"一种与地理环境紧密结合的文学。在他们的著作中，我们第一次感受到自我与大自然的融合、个性与环境的交融"（埃默里·埃利奥特，1994）。

华盛顿·欧文是早期的浪漫主义作家。从他的作品中我们看到了文学与旅行、自然之间密不可分的关系。他的不少散文都是游记散文，除了《见闻札记》以外，还有《欧美见闻录》《布雷斯布里奇庄园》《阿尔罕伯拉宫》等不少游记佳作。欧文游览过美国的很多地方，还曾三次去往欧洲，在英、法、德、西等国度过了 17 年，无论是在美国还是在异国他乡，他都会访问当地的名胜古迹，观赏自然风景。他在《见闻札记》的开篇就说到自己从小就非常热爱旅行。他是这样描述自己这个爱好的："I was always fond of visiting new scenes, and observing strange characters and manners. Even when a mere child I began my travel, and made many tours of discovery into foreign parts and unknown regions of my native city, to the frequent alarm of my parents, and the emolument of the town crier. As I grew into boyhood, I extended the range of my observations. My holiday afternoons were spent in rambles about the surrounding country. I made myself familiar with all its places famous in history or fable. I knew every spot where a murder or robbery had been committed, or a ghost seen. I visited the neighboring villages, and added greatly to my stock of knowledge, by nothing their habits and customs, and conversing with their sages and great men. I even journeyed one long summer's day to the summit of the most distant hill, whence I stretched my eye over many a mile of terra incognita, and was astonished to find how vast a globe I inhabited"（华盛顿·欧文，2015）。（我总是喜爱游览没有去过的新地方，去观察奇异的风土人情。我甚至在孩提时代就开始游历了，在我故乡之城的生疏与未知的区域里多次进行过探索之旅，时常让我的父母担惊受怕，也让巡查街道的人为找寻我而获得一点酬金。到长大一些的时候，我的观察范围也有所扩大，我把假日的下午都耗费在周围乡村间的漫游中。我逐渐熟悉了乡村的历史和传说中那些著名的地方；我知道每一处发生谋杀和抢劫的现场，或者出现过鬼怪的地方。我探访过临近的村庄，通过留意人们的风俗习惯以及同当地的贤达人士和著名人物交谈，我极大地增加了自己的见识。在一个漫长的夏日里，我甚至爬上了最远处的一座小山的山顶，从那里极目远眺好几英里之外的无名之地，惊异地发现自己栖身的地球是多么辽阔无边）（华盛顿·欧文，2014）。

无论是田园风光还是古堡废墟都对欧文有着强大的吸引力，因为他不仅仅在领略美景，还试着深入地去了解风土人情，挖掘传说习俗，探索历史文明。正是在这些旅行的过程中欧文积累了大量的写作素材，同时也写下了很多优美的游记。欧文认为，如果只是看自然风光，没有哪个国家可与美国相比。他盛赞美国风景的壮丽雄奇，曾这样写道："I visited various parts of my own country, and had I been merely a lover of fine scenery, I should have felt little desire to seek elsewhere its gratification, for on no country had the charms of nature been more prodigally lavished. Her mighty lakes, like oceans of liquid silver; her mountains, with their bright aerial tints; her valley, teeming with wild fertility; her tremendous cataracts, thundering in their solitudes; her boundless plains, waving with spontaneous verdure; her broad, deep river, rolling in solemn silence to the ocean; her trackless forests, where vegetation puts forth all its magnificence; her skies, kindling with the magic of summer clouds and glorious sunshine; — no, never need an American look beyond his own country for the sublime and beautiful of natural scenery"（华盛顿·欧文，2015）。（我游览过自己国家的各个地方；假如我仅仅是喜爱美丽的风景，那我就不会有多大的欲望到别的地方去寻求满足了，因为再没有别的国家比美国拥有更丰富奇异的大自然的魅力。她巨大的湖泊就像银光闪烁的海洋；她的群山映照着大气明亮的色调；她的山谷布满了丰盈的野生之物；她的大瀑布在幽寂之地发出雷鸣般的轰响；她无边无际的大草原自然地涌动翠绿色的波浪；她的河流既深且广，庄严静穆地滚滚流入海洋；她那人迹罕至的森林草木丰茂，景色壮丽；她的天空，燃烧着魔幻般的夏日云彩和灿烂阳光——不，一个美国人绝不需要到祖国之外去寻找雄伟壮丽的自然景色）（华盛顿·欧文，2014）。

既然欧文认为美国的自然风光已经胜过世界上任何一个地方，那么他想从英国的风景古迹中寻找到什么呢？他崇尚的是欧洲的历史和艺术，"在那儿可以看到艺术的杰作，高度文明社会的优美精致，古代和地方性习俗的奇异特点。我的祖国有青春的美好前景；欧洲有世代积聚的丰富宝藏"（华盛顿·欧文，2014）。有人认为欧文的作品带有英国的烙印，甚至在他的一些作品中表达了对欧洲文明、欧洲历史、欧洲社会人伦的崇尚，算不上纯正的美国文学。与库珀和爱伦·坡等早期的作家相比，欧文的一些作品中的美国特色确实没有那么鲜明。可是我们可以这样去看待欧文，他作为美国文学的奠基人，正是起到了承上启下的作用，他试图从欧洲的文学和历史中汲取营养，从而开辟出美国文学自己的道路。

二、生态批评

我们知道了欧文的作品与旅行和自然密不可分的关系后，来了解下什么是生态批评。生态批评是20世纪七八十年代初盛行于美国的一种关注文学外部研究的文学批评方法，其背景是在全球日趋严重的环境危机下人与自然的关系不断恶化，人类的生存受到了威胁。1962年，美国当代生态学家瑞切尔·卡森（Rachel Carson）的著作《寂静的春天》（*The Silent Spring*）问世，在美国社会引起了广泛的关注，掀起了一场生态运动，并促使建立了第一个地球日。卡森将人的伦理关怀广泛运用到整个自然界，打破人类中心主义，对后来"大地伦理""荒野伦理""动物伦理"等生态主义思想观念的提出具有重要的启发意义。1972年，生态批评家约瑟夫·米可（Joseph Meeker）在他的具有开创性的理论著作《生存喜剧：文学生态学研究》（*The Comedy of Survival: Studies in Literary Ecology*）中指出，文学生态学的研究对象是文学作品中出现的所有生物主题。总之，生态批评旨在通过探讨文学与自然环境之间的关系，以文学的形式启迪人类形成一种新的思维方式，即"作为一个物种的人只是他们所栖居的生物圈的一部分，并使这一事实在所有思维活动中留下印记"（朱新福，2015），主要目的"是从文学领域开始来促使人们认识到环境问题的重要性和迫切性"(Cheryll Glotfelty,1996)。此后美国生态文学批评以强劲之势迅速发展,文学批评家对生态的关注有增无减。1989 年,美国西部文学会议召开,切瑞尔·葛罗特菲尔地(Cheryll Glotfelty)要求将生态批评运用到"自然书写研究"之中。

文学艺术除了满足审美需求外,是有着社会意义的。作家在文学作品中提供更为合理的思维模式,在文学作品中探讨社会问题的解决方法,在文学作品中构想更完美的社会形态等。约翰·洛克(John Locke)在其著作《人类理解论》中认为,人类有权利拿走"自然资源",面对自然和其他生物,人类处于优势的统治地位,自然资源满足人类需求,人类有任意掠夺自然资源的权利。但是进入 20 世纪以来,各种生态问题层出不穷,极端天气、温室效应、冰川融化、物种灭绝,洛克的观点显然需要批判和反思。生态批评强调人和自然应当建立和谐的关系,强调人也是自然的一部分。尊重自然、敬畏自然,人类才能更长久地生存下去,因为人类与自然是相互依存的关系。文学作品通过其特有的方式从方方面面去呈现和反思人与自然的关系,如展示人类任意掠夺自然资源带来的恶果,倡导人与自然界的其他生物建立平等对话和交流的关系,共同营造和谐稳定的生态环境。

在中国的社会主义建设中,生态文明建设是"五位一体"总体布局和"四个方面"战略布局的重要内容。习近平在主持中共十八届中央政治局第四十一次集体学习时就曾指出,"人类发展活动必须尊重自然、顺应自然、保护自然,否则就会遭到大自然的报复。这个规律谁也无法抗拒。人因自然而生,人与自然是一种共生关系,对自然的伤害最终会伤及人类自身。只有尊重自然规律,才能有效防止在开发利用自然上走弯路"(习近平,2017)。"推动形成绿色发展方式和生活方式,是发展观的一场深刻革命。这就要坚持和贯彻新发展理念,正确处理经济发展和生态环境保护的关系,像保护眼睛一样保护生态环境,像对待生命一样对待生态环境,坚决摒弃损害甚至破坏生态环境的发展模式,坚决摒弃以牺牲生态环境换取一时一地经济增长的做法,让良好生态环境成为人民生活的增长点、成为经济社会持续健康发展的支撑点、成为展现我国良好形象的发力点,让中华大地天更蓝、山更绿、水更清、环境更优美"(习近平,2017)。

三、乡村与城市

华盛顿·欧文的《英国的乡村生活》比较了乡村和城市两种不同的生活场景和生活在其中的人的状态。乡村生活是回归自然的生活,在乡村生活场景中,我们随时能看到郁郁葱葱的树木、湍流不息的小河、成群结队的麋鹿、活蹦乱跳的兔子。乡村生活能让人欣赏到自然的美丽和神奇,人和自然能够和谐相处。城市生活则是工业文明的产物,大城市的繁华街道和钢筋混凝土的建筑缺少了大自然的生机盎然,缺少了生活的趣味,甚至可以这样说,城市的发展常常是以牺牲自然环境为代价的,田野树林被高楼大厦所替代了。

欧文还比较了乡村和城市两种生活场景下人的不同。人不是孤立存在的,而是生活在自然环境中,在与自然环境的互动中发展的,自然环境对人会产生影响。乡村和城市两种不同的环境也就孕育出不同性格的人。欧文认为城市中的人"通常是匆匆忙忙、心不在焉的模样"(He has, therefore, too commonly a look of hurry and abstraction),"特别像伦敦这样的大城市,简直是刻意要把人变得自私而无趣"(An immense metropolis, like London, is calculated to make men selfish and uninteresting)。与城市的人们相比,乡村的人们更加热情好客,随心所欲,具有健壮体格与鲜活气质,"他欣然从城市冷漠消极的礼仪客套中摆脱出来,抛开沉默含蓄的习惯,变得欢欣和开放起来"(He breaks loose gladly from the cold formalities and negative civilities of town, throws off his habits of shy reserve, and becomes joyous and freehearted)。在乡村和城市的对比中,显然欧文更崇尚自然的田园生活,因为这种生活是自由和健康的,是和谐与融洽的,是真诚与淳朴的。

从《英国的乡村生活》中我们可以看到乡村生活中人与自然是和谐相处的。人和自然的和谐应该是建立在相互尊重的基础之上的,是一种主体间性关系。与建立在主客二元对立基础之上的主体性哲学不同,"主体间性哲学则消除了主客二元对立,把存在确认为自我主体与世界主体的交往和融合……人与世界的和谐共处才能获得自由"(杨春时,2004)。人与自然不断进行交流互动,在交流和互动中人的身心变得更加丰盈和充实,对自然的情感也愈发真诚和浓烈。欧文这样写道:"其他国家的田园作家似乎对大自然只是偶然光顾,对他一般的美丽魅力只不过稍有领略;但英国诗人却是与大自然一起生活、共享欢乐——他们在她最常去的隐秘地追寻——观察她最细微的变幻无定的风貌。一枝在微风中摇曳的枝条——一片扑簌坠地的落叶——一滴鸣溅于溪涧的钻石般的水滴——一缕发自野生紫罗兰的幽香——一朵在清晨绽放出猩红色花蕾的雏菊——这一切无不被多情而细腻的观察者注意到,精心锤炼成优美而富于意蕴的景象"(华盛顿·欧文,2014)。人与自然的关系既不能是主体和客体、主人和仆人、统治者和臣民的关系,也不能是人把自然当作神灵一样来崇拜和敬畏,两者之间的关系应该是彼此相等、互相尊重的,为了更好地维护彼此间的利益而对话。

乡村生活除了人与自然的和谐相处,人和人也是和谐相处的。欧文认为,在英国的乡村不同阶层的人不再泾渭分明,他们能够更加和谐地相处。第一个原因是无论富人还是穷人都有一个共同的爱好就是对生活环境加以美化,不管是富人的乡间居所还是穷人的一间茅屋,他们都会修剪树木,种上花草,让周围的环境变得美丽起来,所有人都有着相似的审美情趣和爱好,这就拉近了人和人的距离。第二个原因是乡村的生活空间广阔,在广阔的空间不同阶层的人更能自由地相互接近,因此也就更容易融洽和谐地相处。第三个原因是乡村生活中有更多开放式的娱乐活动,它也使不同阶层的人紧密地聚集在一起,在欢歌笑语中人和人也更有了亲密感。第四个原因就是乡村自然环境对人的熏陶,富人变得平易近人,穷人虽简单粗鲁但不会低俗,在这样和谐环境的影响下,即使不同阶层的人交谈往来也不会觉得有身份地位的差异,他们都愿意去享受普通生活中的真诚与淳朴。

一个热爱旅行的欧文,一个崇尚自然的欧文,驻足于英国的乡村,对这里的物与人都极为欣赏,他崇尚乡村生活中人与自然和谐相处的状态,人与人和谐相处的状态。乡村中的环境赏心悦目,人们淡泊宁静,社会秩序井然,欧文认为乡村的这种纯朴之风经世代相传,已成为一个民族的道德风尚。

▣ 参考文献 ▣

[1] Cheryll Glotfelty & Harold Fromm （eds.）. *The Ecocriticism Reader*[M]. Athens：University of Georgia Press，1996.

[2] 埃默里·埃利奥特. 哥伦比亚美国文学史[M].朱通伯，译. 成都：四川辞书出版社,1994.

[3] 高健. 英文散文一百篇[M]. 北京：中国对外出版翻译公司,2000.

[4] 华盛顿·欧文. 睡谷传说：英伦见闻录[M].盛世教育西方名著翻译委员会，译. 上海：世界图书出版公司,2015.

[5] 华盛顿·欧文. 见闻札记[M].伍厚恺，译. 成都：四川文艺出版社,2014.

[6] 习近平. 习近平谈治国理政[M].北京：外文出版社,2017.

[7] 杨春时.论生态美学的主体间性[J].贵州师范大学学报,2004(1):82.

[8] 朱新福.美国经典作家的生态视域和自然思想[M].上海：上海外语教育出版社,2015.

▣ 阅读思考 ▣

1. 你认为人和自然是一种什么样的关系,我们该如何处理好人和自然的关系?

2. 你还知道哪些文学作品中反映出了较为明显的生态意识? 请举例说明。

3. 请在《习近平谈治国理政》(英文版)中找到关于保护生态环境的相关论述,并与同伴进行讨论和学习。

13

Nature (Excerpt)

Ralph Waldo Emerson

【作品简介】

爱默生于 1836 年发表了他阐述超验主义的第一篇重要论著 Nature(《论自然》)。爱默生的超验主义思想体系中一个重要的部分是自然观。他认为大自然本身就是一种象征,人们可以从中看到上帝的存在;在宇宙表面的纷繁多样中存在根本统一,正是由于这种统一,世界是和谐的,人和大自然是统一的。《论自然》分为八个章节,分别是自然(Nature)、商品(Commodity)、美(Beauty)、语言(Language)、纪律(Discipline)、唯心主义(Idealism)、精神(Spirit)和远景(Prospects)。本文是《论自然》第一章节的内容。

【作者简介】

拉尔夫·沃尔多·爱默生(Ralph Waldo Emerson)于 1803 年出生在波士顿附近的康科德。他的父亲是一位牧师,先辈也都是新英格兰地区有名的教会人士。他小时候家族没落,因此经历了评论家所说的"上流社会的贫困生活"。爱默生 1825 年进入哈佛神学院学习,在那里经历了一场精神上的"冒险旅行",大学里的文学氛围令他开始重新审视自己从小接受的加尔文教的信仰,吸收了开明论派的思想,1829 年成为一位论派牧师,但是不久他发现上帝一位论太重理性,于是辞去职务,而后去欧洲旅行,与柯勒律治、克莱尔和华兹华斯等人成为了朋友。爱默生的超验主义思想正是美国清教主义、欧洲浪漫主义思想以及康德先验论哲学相结合的产物。

1836 年出版的《论自然》一书包括了爱默生的基本哲学思想和他对大自然的观点。爱默生认为"从哲学上考虑,宇宙是由自然和心灵组合而成的"。"当心灵向所有的自然物体敞开之后,它们给人的印象却是息息相关、彼此沟通的。大自然从不表现出贫乏单一的面貌"(爱默生,2015)。

1837 年爱默生发表了《论美国学者》的演说,指出美国学者应受教于自然界、书本和行动,学者的任务就是鼓舞人、提高人和引导人。他强调独立思考、行动的重要性和劳动的必要性。

1838 年爱默生应邀给哈佛神学院学生做演讲。这篇《神学院致辞》的精神和《论美国学者》一致,不过其内容偏重宗教。在《论美国学者》中爱默生呼吁依靠自己第一手的思想经验;在《神学院致辞》中他则呼吁依靠自己的精神经验,真理只能通过直觉而不是通过第二手材料获得的。爱默生反对把耶稣当作圣人膜拜、把上帝当作死人供奉,反对形式主义和毫无生气的、教条式的布道,认为传道者的职责是把生活转变成真理,探索人的道德本性。这篇演说对传统基督教的批评激怒了不少卫道士,他们认为这是异端邪说,爱默生也因此有三十年被禁止再到哈佛去发表演说。

爱默生的作品以散文为主,也有诗歌。他的重要著作大多收集在《论文集》(*Essays*)和《论文集:第二辑》(*Essays: Second Series*)中。他的两本诗集分别于 1847 年和 1867 年出版。1845 年后的一些演讲收集在《代表人物》(*Representative Men*)、《英国人的性格》(*English Traits*)和《为人之道》(*The Conduct of Life*)等书中。但这时期的作品已不如前期的那样气势磅礴。在此后的岁月里,他的记忆力开始衰退,人和思想逐渐老化,作品也不出色,但人们永远不会忘记爱默生三四十年代的作品所起到的解放人们思想的巨大作用。爱默生促进了美国的文化革命和民族文学的建立和发展。他的思想对 19 世纪的梭罗、惠特曼和狄金森以及 20 世纪的德莱塞、罗伯特·佛罗斯特、华莱士·史蒂文斯和拉尔夫·埃利森都有不同程度的影响。他的乐观主义精神、对个人意志的推崇和对人性的信心也激起霍桑和梅尔维尔对人性的进一步探讨。

(1) To go into solitude[1], a man needs to retire as much from his chamber as from society. I am not solitary[2] whilst I read and write, though nobody is with me. But if a man would be alone, let him look at the stars. The rays that come from those heavenly worlds will separate between him and what he touches. One might think the atmosphere was made transparent[3] with this design, to give man, in the heavenly bodies, the perpetual[4] presence of the sublime[5]. Seen in the streets of cities, how great they are! If the stars should appear one night in a thousand years, how would men believe and adore; and preserve for many generations the remembrance of the city of God which had been shown! But every night come out these envoys of beauty, and light the universe with their admonishing[6] smile.

(2) The stars awaken a certain reverence[7], because though always present, they are inaccessible[8]; but all natural objects make a kindred[9] impression, when the mind is open to their influence. Nature never wears a mean appearance. Neither does the wisest man extort[10] her secret, and lose his curiosity by finding out all her perfection. Nature never became a toy to a wise spirit. The flowers, the animals, the mountains, reflected the

[1] solitude /ˈsɒlətjuːd/ *n.* 孤独;独处
[2] solitary /ˈsɒlətri/ *adj.* 孤独的;孤零零的
[3] transparent /trænsˈpærənt/ *adj.* 透明的;清澈的;易看穿的;显而易见的
[4] perpetual /pəˈpetʃuəl/ *adj.* 永恒的
[5] sublime /səˈblaɪm/ *n.* 崇高的事物;壮丽的景象
[6] admonish /ədˈmɒnɪʃ/ *v.* 责备;告诫;警告
[7] reverence /ˈrevərəns/ *n.* 尊敬;崇敬
[8] inaccessible /ˌɪnækˈsesəbl/ *adj.* 无法接近的;难以达到的;不可得到的
[9] kindred /ˈkɪndrəd/ *adj.* 相似的;相关的
[10] extort /ɪkˈstɔːt/ *v.* 敲诈;勒索;强夺

wisdom of his best hour, as much as they had delighted the simplicity of his childhood.

(3) When we speak of nature in this manner, we have a distinct but most poetical sense in the mind. We mean the integrity[11] of impression made by manifold natural objects. It is this which distinguishes the stick of timber of the wood-cutter from the tree of the poet. The charming landscape which I saw this morning is indubitably[12] made up of some twenty or thirty farms. Miller owns this field, Locke that, and Manning the woodland beyond. But none of them owns the landscape. There is a property in the horizon which no man has but he whose eye can integrate all the parts, that is, the poet. This is the best part of these men's farms, yet to this their warranty-deeds give no title.

(4) To speak truly, few adult persons can see nature. Most persons do not see the sun. At least they have a very superficial seeing. The sun illuminates[13] only the eye of the man, but shines into the eye and the heart of the child. The lover of nature is he whose inward and outward senses are still truly adjusted to each other; who has retained the spirit of infancy even into the era of manhood. His intercourse with heaven and earth becomes part of his daily food. In the presence of nature a wild delight runs through the man, in spite of real sorrows. Nature says, — he is my creature, and maugre all his impertinent[14] griefs, he shall be glad with me. Not the sun or the summer alone, but every hour and season yields its tribute[15] of delight; for every hour and change corresponds to and authorizes[16] a different state of the mind, from breathless noon to grimmest[17] midnight. Nature is a setting that fits equally well a comic or a mourning piece. In good health, the air is a cordial[18] of incredible virtue. Crossing a bare common, in snow puddles, at twilight, under a clouded sky, without having in my thoughts any occurrence of special good fortune, I have enjoyed a perfect exhilaration[19]. I am glad to the brink of fear. In the woods, too, a man casts off his

---

[11] integrity /ɪnˈtegrəti/ *n.* 诚实正直；完整；完好

[12] indubitably /ɪnˈdjuːbɪtəbli/ *adv.* 不容置疑地；毫无疑问地

[13] illuminate /ɪˈluːmɪneɪt/ *v.* 照明；照亮

[14] impertinent /ɪmˈpɜːtɪnənt/ *adj.* 粗鲁无礼的；不敬的

[15] tribute /ˈtrɪbjuːt/ *n.* 贡品；颂词

[16] authorize /ˈɔːθəraɪz/ *v.* 批准；授权

[17] grim /grɪm/ *adj.* 阴冷的；凄凉的

[18] cordial /ˈkɔːdiəl/ *adj.* 热情友好的

[19] exhilaration /ɪgˌzɪləˈreɪʃn/ *n.* 兴高采烈

years, as the snake his slough[20], and at what period soever of life is always a child. In the woods is perpetual youth. Within these plantations of God, a decorum[21] and sanctity reign, a perennial[22] festival is dressed, and the guest sees not how he should tire of them in a thousand years. In the woods, we return to reason and faith. There I feel that nothing can befall me in life, — no disgrace, no calamity (leaving me my eyes), which nature cannot repair. Standing on the bare ground, — my head bathed by the blithe[23] air and uplifted into infinite space, — all mean egotism vanishes. I become a transparent eyeball; I am nothing; I see all; the currents of the Universal Being circulate through me; I am part or parcel of God. The name of the nearest friend sounds then foreign and accidental: to be brothers, to be acquaintances, master or servant, is then a trifle and a disturbance. I am the lover of uncontained and immortal beauty. In the wilderness, I find something more dear and connate than in streets or villages. In the tranquil[24] landscape, and especially in the distant line of the horizon, man beholds somewhat as beautiful as his own nature.

(5) The greatest delight which the fields and woods minister is the suggestion of an occult[25] relation between man and the vegetable. I am not alone and unacknowledged. They nod to me, and I to them. The waving of the boughs[26] in the storm is new to me and old. It takes me by surprise, and yet is not unknown. Its effect is like that of a higher thought or a better emotion coming over me, when I deemed I was thinking justly or doing right.

(6) Yet it is certain that the power to produce this delight does not reside in nature, but in man, or in a harmony of both. It is necessary to use these pleasures with great temperance. For nature is not always tricked in holiday attire[27], but the same scene which yesterday breathed perfume and glittered as for the frolic[28] of the nymphs[29] is overspread with melancholy today. Nature always wears the colors of the spirit. To a man laboring under calamity, the heat of his own fire hath sadness in

[20]slough /slʌf, slaʊ/ v. 蜕皮
这句话中使用了明喻(simile),把人比作像蛇蜕皮一样一年一年长大。
[21]decorum /dɪˈkɔːrəm/ n. 端庄得体
[22]perennial /pəˈreniəl/ adj. 长久的;反复出现的
[23]blithe /blaɪð/ adj. 快乐的;无忧无虑的
[24]tranquil /ˈtræŋkwɪl/ adj. 宁静的
[25]occult /ˈɒkʌlt/ adj. 神秘的;超自然的
[26]bough /baʊ/ n. 大树枝
[27]attire /əˈtaɪə(r)/ n. 服装
[28]frolic /ˈfrɒlɪk/ n. 欢乐的活动
[29]nymphs /nɪmfs/ n. (古希腊、罗马神话中居于山林水泽的)仙女

it. Then there is a kind of contempt of the landscape felt by him who has just lost by death a dear friend. The sky is less grand as it shuts down over less worth in the population.

▪ 精华赏析 ▪

1836 年出版的爱默生的《论自然》对美国文学界产生了重大影响。这本书将美国的浪漫主义带到了一个新的阶段,即浪漫主义的顶点——新英格兰超验主义,书中包括爱默生的基本哲学观点,这些观点如一股新风潮影响了人们的观念。爱默生认为:"从哲学上考虑,宇宙是由自然和心灵组合而成的。严格地说,所有那些与我们分开的东西,所有被哲学界定为'非我'的事物——这包括自然与艺术,所有的他人和我自己的身体——因此统统都必须归纳到自然的名下"(爱默生,2015)。

一、新英格兰超验主义

何谓超验主义?爱默生在他的文章《超验主义者》中给出了答案:"现在流行的超验主义就是理想主义,1842 年的理想主义。"《论自然》可以说是超验主义的非正式宣言,这本书出版几天后,爱默生的家里就有了经常性的聚会,爱默生、梭罗、玛格丽特·福勒等人聚在一起讨论哲学、文学等问题,这就是"超验主义俱乐部"。他们反对物质利益至上的生活,反对商人的价值观,反对刻板的上帝一位论理性主义。除了聚会、讨论和发表意见,他们还成立了杂志《日晷》。"超验"这个词源于康德哲学,表示"属于哲学的任何事物"。

新英格兰的超验主义有以下几个特征:其一,超验主义认为精神或"超灵"是宇宙中最重要之物。超灵代表善良,它无处不在,无所不能,是一切事物的来源,所有事物都是它的组成部分。它存在于自然和人类之间,是构成宇宙的主要元素。显然这是一种看待世界的全新观念,是对 19 世纪牛顿宇宙观的颠覆:18 世纪的人们认为世界是物质构成的。这种观念同样反对美国忽视精神世界而插手世界事务,从而走上一条机械资本主义道路的趋势。其二,超验主义者注重个人。对他们而言,人是社会最重要的元素,社会的再生只能通过人类的再生来完成,因此人生的主要目标应该是自我完善、自我修养和自我进步,而不是想方设法致富。完美的人应该是自立的,这是爱默生一生都在宣扬的观点。像爱默生和梭罗这样的超验主义者一直在教导着人们,如果想要为完善自己而付出努力,那么就必须依靠自身的力量,这是因为在他们看来,每个人的灵魂都因为和超灵的联系而变得神圣。这种重视个人的观念显然是一种全新对待个人的方法。它和加尔文教的观点完全不同。加尔文教认为人类是堕落的、有罪的,除非上帝大发慈悲,否则人类不可能得到救赎。超验主义反对为了发展资本主义而磨灭人性。新英格兰的工业化使人丧失了人性,人们没有了各自独立的特征而趋于统一化。看到这种趋势,超验主义者一再重申个人的重要性,以及恢复个性的意义。其三,超验主义认为自然是超灵或上帝的象征。对他们而言,自然不是纯粹的物质,而是充满着上帝的存在。自然是超灵的外衣,因此自然能够影响人类心灵的健康和恢复。超验主义认为:"回到自然,感受它对你的影响,灵魂会再度完整。"这句话的寓意当然是指自然的物体是有象征意义的,物质世界只是精神世界的象征而已,因此这也促进了美国文学象征主义的发展(赵红英,2006)。

新英格兰超验主义是国外因素和美国清教共同影响的产物。超验主义宣扬的浪漫理想主义源自德法的理想主义哲学观。值得一提的是,以爱默生和梭罗为代表的超验主义者从印度作品《奥义书》和《薄伽梵歌》以及中国的孔孟之道中受益良多。

超验主义继承了美国清教主义的文化,爱德华兹时代关于神的内心交流和神圣的自然象征主义都能在爱默生的超验主义里找到充分的表现。爱默生等超验主义者都是受过教育、气质温和的宗教信仰者,他们竭尽全力要做的实际上是重申旧时清教的宗教理想主义观点,并借用德国理想主义等学派中的术语来表述自己的思想。另外,我们还注意到超验主义对个人的重视在清教关于自我修养、自我完善的原则里其实有迹可寻。

新英格兰超验主义对美国文学有着十分重要的影响,它孕育了一代文学巨匠的崛起,包括爱默生、梭罗、霍桑、麦尔维尔、惠特曼和狄金森等。美国此后进入了文学史上最多产的时期之一。

二、爱默生的《论自然》

爱默生的《论自然》共有八个章节,这里我们介绍一下每个章节的主要内容,以便了解爱默生的哲学思想。

在第一章《自然》中,爱默生认为自然的面貌不是贫乏单一的,而是丰富多彩的,如果人类的心灵可以与大自然息息相通,保持协调一致,那么人就会一直处于青春状态,并且人类"可以在丛林中重新找到理智与信仰"(爱默生,2015)。人是自然、上帝的一部分。自然并非永远是阳光灿烂,美妙动人的,有时也会阴云密布,死气沉沉。人在不同心境下看自然会有所不同。"大自然是一台背景,它既可做喜庆场合的陪衬,也同样能衬托悲哀的事件"(爱默生,2015)。

在第二章《商品》中,爱默生认为自然为人类的发展提供了丰富的资源,比如"田野既是他的地板,又是他的工作场地,游乐场所,花园和床第"(爱默生,2015)。同时"大自然在它对人类的服务中不仅仅是提供物质,它也是服务的过程与结果"(爱默生,2015)。爱默生想告诉我们,自然界是循环往复的,各种因素相互影响,冰山带来降雨,降雨灌溉农作物,农作物养育动物,所以自然不是静态地提供物质资源,而是在循环运动中为人类服务。但是如果人类认为自然资源是为了人的生存和幸福专设的,人可以尽情地、随意地开采自然资源,那么这种想法是荒谬可笑的。另外在这一章中,爱默生认为艺术也是自然的一部分,因为艺术是利用自然再造或重新组合的,不过之后爱默生举的例子是科技产品,如蒸汽机、火车等。看来爱默生这里提到的艺术是一个广义的概念。

在第三章《美》中,爱默生开篇就告诉我们"大自然满足了人类的一个崇高需求,即爱美之心"(爱默生,2015)。在这一章中爱默生总结了三点:(1)"首先,人对自然形式的简单感觉是愉悦"(爱默生,2015)。当人痛苦、疲惫的时候,来到自然中,这里的美好与宁静对人有治愈作用。人们只有在不经意间才能与最美的景色相遇,如果刻意寻找反而看不到最美好的景色。(2)"对于自然美来说,它的完满充分取决于一种更高级的精神因素。那种能够让人不带任何矫揉造作去真心热爱的美,正是一种美与人类意志的混合物"(爱默生,2015)。人和自然不是完全区分开来的,人的伟大壮举会使山河变色、日月生光,品行高尚的人与周围的环境默契和谐,会成为风景中的主角。在这里爱默生以哈利·韦恩爵士、罗素、荷马、苏格拉底等人为例证明了自己的观点。(3)"自然美除了它们与美德联系之外,它们也同思想有关"(爱默生,2015)。当人们不再满足只是欣赏自然美,想要用新的形式去表现美,这种创造就是艺术。

在第四章《语言》中,爱默生提出了三点:"(1)词语是自然事物的象征。(2)具体的自然事物又是具体精神事物的象征。(3)大自然又是精神的象征"(爱默生,2015)。人类所用的语言就是象征,整个自然是人心灵的象征,物理学的定律可以解释伦理学的法则,比如"整体大于局部""作用与反作用相等",民间谚语也与某种自然事实相关联,"天晴晒干草,打铁要趁热""长命树,先扎根"等。

在第五章《纪律》中,爱默生提出了两点:(1)"大自然是一种理解的纪律,它帮助人认识真理。我们同可感知事物打交道,这就是一种不间断的练习过程,它交给我们有关差异、相似、秩序、本质与表象、循序渐进、触类旁通、统一运筹等必要的知识"(爱默生,2015)。(2)"可感知事物往往与理性的预兆相吻合,并且反映人的良知。一切事物都是道德的,它们千变万化,却总是与精神本质维持着一种不间断的联系"(爱默生,2015)。自然界的各种运行规律暗示了人类世界的道德规则。

在第六章《唯心主义》中,爱默生讲了五点:(1)唯心主义哲学的最初论据来自对大自然本身规律的研究。(2)诗人对大自然的感受是一种更高级的形式。诗歌在论述自然间的规律时,有时会更见洞察力,其形式更为自由,诗人们坚持心灵至上的原则。(3)诗人和哲学家本质上是相通的,区别在于诗人追求的是大自然的美,哲学家想从自然中寻找真理。(4)各种科学思想的发展都源于对于物质存在的疑问。(5)"宗教与伦理,它们可以恰当地被称为思想的操练,或思想在生活中的引申"(爱默生,2015)。

在第七章《精神》中,爱默生认为大自然向人提出了三个问题:物质是什么?它们从何而来?又将向何处变化?唯心理论认为物质是现象并非本质,精神即上帝之存在,它不曾在人的周围特意建造出自然,只是通过人推出了世上万物。

在第八章《远景》中,爱默生认为人之所以与众不同,是因为人是这个自然界中具有头脑和良心的存在,能在自然中寻找到和自己相关联的东西,并能将自己融进自然中。人可以按照自己心中的想法去改变生活,生活也因此会展现出伟大壮丽的前景。物质的变革会影响精神的变革。

三、爱默生思想中的中国元素

在爱默生的思想中有不少中国元素,他的一些哲学思想与中国的哲学思想不谋而合。接下来我们简单探讨下爱默生的思想与道家思想的相通之处。

我们看下爱默生的"超灵"与老子的"道"。爱默生认为人起源于更为高尚的东西,人的背后有一种神秘的力量。所有人都受这种神秘力量的支配,它使个性融于共性中,个人的行为是它部分、连续的存在。爱默生把这种神秘的力量称为"一"(Unity),或"超灵"。爱默生在他的著作中对这种力量的描述时常变换说法,有时又称作"至上存在"(Supreme Being)、精神(spirit)。在《论自然》中爱默生这样描述道:"我们知道最高的,即宇宙精髓,通过人的'灵'呈现。这种精髓不是智慧、或爱、或美、或力量,而是全部合一,'一'为全部的存在,万物为此而生存。精神成就万物,在自然的背后,通过自然,精神乃存。精神为'一'而非混成。精神并非从外在,即时间与空间,而是从内在影响我们。因此,'精神',即至上存在,并非在我们周围建立自然,而是让自然穿过我们的身心,正如生命从旧的毛孔中伸展出新的枝叶一样"(Brooks Atkinson,2000)。老子的《道德经》有许多对"道"的描述,比如开篇中这样写道:"道可道,非常道;名可名,非常名。无名,天地之始;有名,万物之母。故常无欲,以观其妙;常有欲,以观其微。此两者,同出而异名,同谓之玄。玄之又玄,众妙之门"(老子,1997)。爱默生的"超灵"和老子的"道"的相通之处有以下几点:(1)他们都认为"超灵"或"道"是至高无上的东西,是自然界和人背后至上的力量,自然界的运行、人的起源都来源于这种力量。(2)他们都认为"超灵"或"道"不是一种具体有形的存在。爱默生说的"精神"不是智慧、不是爱、不是美、不是力量,总之不是任何一种具体可感的事物,老子认为"道"是非有非无、亦有亦无的一种形而上的存在。老子说:"道之物,惟恍惟惚。惚兮恍兮,其中有象;恍兮惚兮,其中有物。窈兮冥兮,其中有精,其精甚真,其中有信"(老子,1997)。(3)他们都认为虽然"超灵"或"道"是无形的但却可以作用于人,可以影响人,人能感受到它的存在。

爱默生的自然观和老子的自然观也有着相通之处,一是他们都认为自然界是纯真的。爱默生说自然的快乐是简单、善良,人若能与自然相通就会永葆青春;道家追求的也是"归真"。二是他们都看到了自然中的静止与运动的辩证关系。爱默生认为我们欣赏的风景每时每刻都在不停变化,就算是同一片田野,人也能每个小时看到一幅前所未见、以后不会重复的图画;老子所讲的万物阴阳论,相生相克,在运动中产生和谐,也是在论述一种动静观。三是他们都认为自然界中蕴藏着人世间的规则。爱默生认为道德法则存在于大自然的核心中,它向外辐射,照耀四周;老子也特别重视从万物中去认识抽象的"道",又从抽象的"道"来反观普世的万物。

爱默生的思想与道家的思想还有很多异曲同工的地方,这里就不一一论述了。东西方思想各有千秋,但并不是泾渭分明的,两个思想体系都在探讨人类的普世话题,在本质上有着很多相通之处。

参考文献

[1] Brooks Atkinson (ed.). *The Essential Writings of Ralph Waldo Emerson*[M]. New York: The Modern Library, 2000.

[2] Ralph Waldo Emerson. *Nature*[M]. London: Penguin Books, 2008.

[3] 爱默生. 论自然[M]. 赵一凡,译. 北京:生活·读书·新知三联书店,2015.

[4] 老子. 道德经[M]. 威利,译. 北京:外语教学与研究出版社,1997.

[5] 赵红英. 美国文学简史学习指南[M]. 北京:中国传媒大学出版社,2006.

◨ 阅读思考 ◧

1. 请阅读《论自然》和《道德经》,比较爱默生的思想和道家的思想还有哪些相通的地方?

2. 爱默生和梭罗都是自然文学的代表作家,请比较爱默生和梭罗的自然观,看看有哪些相同和不同的地方。

3. 请举例说明超验主义是如何影响之后的美国文学?

Chapter Five   Individual and Nation

Only loyalty can serve the country, and there is no paradise for home.
——Dong Biwu

只有精忠能报国，更无乐土可为家。
——董必武《元旦口占用柳亚子怀人韵》

14

Honest Poverty

Fang Zhimin

【作品简介】

《清贫》(*Honest Poverty*)是方志敏烈士 1935 年英勇就义前在江西国民党监狱中写下的不朽散文。文章描写了在方志敏被捕的那一天，两个国民党士兵想从他身上搜罗出财物，可是从上到下在他身上翻找了半天，除了一块表和一支自来水笔外什么也没有找到。两个士兵不甘心，认为方志敏这么大的官怎么可能没有财物，一定是藏了起来，于是威胁要用手榴弹炸死方志敏，可是无论怎样威胁，如何四处寻找，他们都没有任何发现。文章通过这个真实的事情描写了方志敏朴素的生活，舍己为公的高尚品格，以及为了革命能够战胜一切困难的坚强意志。本文选自 1995 年由上海外语教育出版社出版的张培基的《英译中国现代散文选》。

【作者简介】

方志敏(1899 年 8 月 21 日—1935 年 8 月 6 日)，原名远镇，乳名正鹄，号慧生，江西上饶市弋阳九区漆工镇湖塘村人，无产阶级革命家、军事家、杰出的农民运动领袖，土地革命战争时期赣东北和闽浙赣革命根据地的创建人。

方志敏于 1922 年 8 月加入中国社会主义青年团;1923 年加入中国共产党;参与创建了江西的中共党、团组织，曾任江西省农民协会秘书长、主席;1928 年 1 月，参与领导弋横起义，创建赣东北革命根据地;先后任赣东北省、闽浙赣省苏维埃政府主席，红 10 军、红 11 军政治委员，中共闽浙赣省委书记;曾当选为中共第六届中央委员，中华苏维埃共和国中央执行委员、主席团委员，并获中华苏维埃第一次全国代表大会授予的红旗章。1934 年 11 月，方志敏奉命率领抗日先遣队北上，途中遭国民党军重兵围困，在突围时，因叛徒出卖，1935 年 1 月 29 日被捕，8 月 6 日牺牲，时年 36 岁。方志敏结合马克思主义与赣东北的实情，创造了一整套建党、建军和建立红色政权的经验，毛泽东称之为"方志敏式"根据地。

方志敏的主要作品有《我是个共产党员了!》《我不相信基督教!》《同情心》《呕血》《哭声》《可爱的中国》《死——共产主义的殉道者的记述》《清贫》《诗一首》《狱中纪实》《我从事革命斗争的略述》等。

（1）I have been engaged in the revolutionary struggle for more than a decade. During these long militant[1] years, I have lived a plain life with no luxuries to speak of. Millions of dollars passed through my hands, but I always saw to it that every single cent of the money raised for the revolution was spent for no other purposes. This may sound like a miracle or an exaggeration to Kuomintang VIPs[2]. Self-discipline[3] and self-sacrifice[4], however, are the virtue characteristic of a Communist. Therefore, should anyone inquire of me about my personal savings, let him read the following amusing episode[5]:

（2）On the day of my capture — a most inauspicious[6] day it was — two Kuomintang soldiers discovered me in a wood. Sizing me up, they thought they had come upon a windfall[7] and started making a frantic[8] body search, hopefully to find on me hundreds of silver dollars or some jewellery like gold bracelets or rings. They frisked[9] me from top to toe and passed their hands over everything on me from the collar of my jacket to the soles of my socks, but, contrary to their expectation, they found nothing at all, not even a single copper, except a watch and a fountain pen. They were exasperated[10], suspecting that I had my money hidden somewhere and refused to give it up. One of the two men had in his left hand a wooden-handled grenade[11]. He pulled out the cord[12] from inside the wooden handled and moved his legs one step apart as if he was about to throw the grenade. Glowering at me ferociously, he threatened loudly,

（3）"Out with your money quick, or you die[13]!"

（4）"Hey!" I said drily[14] with a faint smile. "Don't you put on such nasty[15] airs! True I haven't got a single copper with me. You're barking up wrong tree to seek a fortune from me.[16]"

（5）"Shit[17]! Nobody can ever believe a big shot like you ain't got no money[18]!" the soldier with the grenade remained wholly incredulous[19].

（6）"No money?" the other soldier joined in. "Impossible! It must be hidden somewhere. No fooling an old hand like me. " Meanwhile, he bent low to pass his hand again meticulously[20] over every nook[21] and corner of my clothes and the crotch[22] of my trousers, still holding out high hopes of making a new discovery.

（7）" You should believe me and stop messing around!" I explained again. " Unlike your Kuomintang officials who're rolling in money, I'm really penniless. We join the revolution not for personal gain. "

（8）Finally, when they knew for certain that there was no money on me, they gave up the body search. Nevertheless, they lowered their heads to scan[23] here and there the place where I had hidden myself, but again in vain. How frustrated they must have felt! The soldier holding the grenade pushed the cord back into its wooden handle, and turned round to scramble for[24] my watch and fountain pen. The two men, however, settled their dispute by agreeing to divide the money equally between them after selling the spoils. They eyed me up and down with suspicion and amazement before barking out in chorus[25], " come along!"

（9）Dear readers, maybe you wish to know if I have any private property at home. Just a minute! Let me see … Ah, here it is, but nothing much though. I have left with my wife for safekeeping a few changes of used underwear and a few pairs of socks with mended soles[26], all of which I used to wear last summer. She has now put them away in a remote mountain valley to prevent them from being stolen in case of Kuomintang attack, so that I may wear them again this summer. These are all the property I have to my name. But wouldn't the declaration of my " family treasures" make myself an object of lively ridicule to the rich?

（10）To remain honest though poor, to live a clean and simple life — that is what we revolutionaries count on to overcome innumerable difficulties!

语,意为"找错地方"或"找错人"。

[17] 中文原文为"你骗谁"是粗鲁话,相当于"胡说",张培基没有直译,而是译成了 shit。

[18] 中文原文是"像你当大官的人会没有钱"张培基译成"a big shot like you ain't got no money",这里的 ain't 等于 hasn't,常见于口语,而且句子中用两个否定(double negative)表达一个否定,为文化低的人所用的不规范英语,译文非常符合人物的身份。

[19] incredulous /ɪnˈkredjələs/ adj. 不肯相信的;不能相信的,表示怀疑的

[20] meticulously /məˈtɪkjələsli/ adv. 极仔细地;一丝不顾地

[21] nook /nʊk/ n. 僻静处

[22] crotch /krɒtʃ/ n. 胯部;裤裆

[23] scan /skæn/ v. 扫描;浏览;审视

[24] scramble for: 争夺

[25] in chorus: 齐声地;一致

[26] soles /səʊlz/ n. 鞋底;袜底

精华赏析

从《清贫》这篇文章中我们可以看到方志敏同志拥有坚定的革命信念,在这种信念的支持下他坚守清贫,他坦然面对死亡,他相信中国的未来一定美好。

一、革命理想高于天

1921 年 7 月,中国共产党第一次代表大会在上海召开,上海的李达、李汉俊,北京的张国焘、刘仁静,武汉的董必武、陈潭秋,长沙的毛泽东、何叔衡,广州的陈公博,济南的王尽美、邓恩铭,旅日的周佛海,以及由陈独秀指定的代表包惠僧出席会议,代表全国 50 多名党员。共产国际代表马林和尼克尔斯基也出席了大会。2021 年中国共产党建党 100 周年,这一百年来,中国共产党从当初的只有 50 多人的政党发展成如今拥有 9500 万党员、领导 14 亿人口大国的世界第一大党;这一百年来中国共产党领导中国人民从积贫积弱、备受压迫的国家成为今天独立自信、富强民主的国家;这一百年来中国共产党领导中国人民取得新民主主义革命的伟大成就、社会主义革命和建设的伟大成就、改革开放和社会主义现代化建设的伟大成就、新时代中国特色社会主义的伟大成就,这一次次胜利、一个个伟大成就将永载史册。

回首历史,胜利和成就的背后有无数共产党员的英勇奋斗,有无数革命先烈曾付出过生命的代价,今天读到他们的故事,我们还会一次次感动得落泪。我们需要思考是什么力量支撑他们愿意付出一切努力,愿意以生命为代价去战斗呢?从方志敏的故事中,我们意识到这应该是理想的力量、信念的力量,他曾经呐喊道:"敌人只能砍下我们的头颅,绝不能动摇我们的信仰"(方志敏,2021)。

"革命理想高于天。中国共产党之所以叫共产党,就是因为从成立之日起我们党就把共产主义确定为远大理想。我们党之所以能够经受一次次挫折而又一次次奋起,归根到底是因为我们党有远大理想和崇高追求"(习近平,2017)。

方志敏是有着坚定理想信念的共产党员。从入党的第一天起,他就把自己的一切交给了党,无论身处顺境还是逆境,无论是生还是死,他的理想和信念从未动摇过。

1935 年 1 月底,陷于绝境的方志敏不幸被捕。为了"以免他们问东问西的讨厌",方志敏坦荡从容,挥笔写下简短的《方志敏自述》:

方志敏,弋阳人,年三十六岁,知识分子,于一九二三年加入中国共产党。参加第一次大革命。一九二六至一九二七年,曾任江西省农民协会秘书长。大革命失败后,潜回弋阳进行土地革命运动,创造苏区和红军,经过八年的艰苦斗争,革命意志益加坚定,这次随红十军团去皖南行动,回苏区时被俘。我对于政治上总的意见,也就是共产党所主张的意见。我已认定苏维埃可以救中国,革命必能得最后的胜利,我愿意牺牲一切,贡献于苏维埃和革命。我这几十年所做的革命工作,都是公开的。差不多谁都知道,详述不必要。仅述如上(方志敏,2021)。

这篇自述虽然只有 245 个字,但我们看到方志敏经历过艰苦卓绝的斗争,面对一次次的考验,其坚定的革命意志从未动摇过,他深爱着自己的祖国,相信苏维埃必然可以救中国。

自被捕之日起,方志敏就没有指望活着出狱。在《我从事革命斗争的略述》一文中,他写道:我们是共产党员,当然都抱着积极奋斗的人生观,绝不是厌世主义者,绝不诅咒人生,憎恶人生,而且愿意得脱牢狱,再为党工作。但是,我们绝不是偷生怕死的人,我们为革命而生,更愿为革命而死!到现在无法得生,只有一死谢党的时候,我们就都下决心就义。只是很短时间的痛苦,碰的一枪,或啪的一刀,就完了,就什么都不知道了!我们常是这样笑说着。我们心体泰然,毫无所惧,我们是视死如归(方志敏,2021)。

和方志敏同时入狱的还有他的三位同伴,国民党用了种种威逼利诱的手段企图让他们投降,如果他们投降就可以活下来,拒绝投降则会被杀害。生命,对于每一个人来说都只有一次。没有什么比生死抉择更为艰难的。方志敏义无反顾地选择了死,因为他宁愿赴死也不抛弃自己的信仰,就像他在《方志敏自述》中写的:"我愿意牺牲一切,贡献于苏维埃和革命。"

今天捧读方志敏的作品,我们意识到方志敏在赴死之前都还在用最后的时间,最后的气力把未竟的革命事业推向永恒。他利用敌人要他"写点东西"的纸和笔,进行废寝忘食的写作。方志敏早年染有肺病,在监狱中又饱受折磨,身体十分虚弱,写作时间稍长,头就发晕,全身无力。疲惫的时候他会拖着沉重的铁镣在室内移动几步,实在支撑不住的时候,就在床上躺一会,稍微调整下再起来写。

方志敏不知道自己何时会被枪毙,明天或后天,上午或下午,死亡随时都可能到来,可他不去理会这些,只想着如何将心中所想尽快写下来。我们跟随方志敏的文字走到他的身边,眼前仿佛看到了这样一幅场景:那个酷热的夏天,在狭窄的牢房里,他紧握着笔,身体贴近桌子,汗水早已浸湿了衣服。他紧皱着眉头,脸上的神情极为严肃,正在认真构思如何将赣东北苏维埃的建设写出一整篇来。他十分着急地奋笔疾书,这样的写作是在和时间赛跑,可他又不能让自己进入完全忘我的写作状态,他需要时不时地抬头看看牢门,以防敌人突然进来。狱中的写作十分艰辛。方志敏写道:"不管怎样,祥松(即方志敏)还是天天在暗中努力着,为着这,用去了许多思想和心血,他头上的白发,差不多增加了一倍了"(方志敏,2021)。

面对死神,方志敏信念如磐,生命不息,奋斗不已,用手中的笔作战斗武器,写下了《我从事革命斗争的略述》《我们临死以前的话》《在狱致全体同志书》《可爱的中国》《狱中纪实》等重要文稿和信件,把对党、对祖国、对人民的爱,化成了血铸的文字,用生命谱写了爱国主义的千古绝唱和革命英雄主义的如虹浩歌。他写下了自己从事革命斗争的总结、对未来革命工作的建议、对祖国的热爱以及对美好未来的企盼。不仅如此,他还殚精竭虑地保存与传递文稿,将文稿一次又一次地从监控严密的国民党监狱送到白色恐怖的上海,交到地下党手中,创造了中共党史上的一个奇迹。

二、可爱的中国

方志敏热爱着自己的祖国,就像热爱自己的母亲一样。他在《可爱的中国》中把祖国比作了母亲,中国国土辽阔,"就好像我们的母亲是一位身体魁梧、胸宽背阔的妇人",中国还有着无数名川大山,江河湖泊,森林草原,处处皆是美景,"这就好像我们的母亲,她是一位天资玉质的美人",中国的大地物产丰富,这就像母亲有着丰富的乳汁可以养育自己的孩子们。方志敏不吝笔墨赞美着祖国母亲,所以当看到祖国母亲受人压迫和剥削时,他痛不欲生,不仅自己在尽最大的努力救母亲于水火中,还大声疾呼道:"朋友们,兄弟们,赶快起来,救救母亲呀!"(方志敏,2021)。

方志敏始终坚信中国革命事业必然成功,自由、民主、富强的新中国一定能够建立,祖国母亲终能摆脱欺负和侮辱,走向幸福和美好。他对于革命成功后的中国充满着憧憬。在《可爱的中国》一文中,他写道:"不错,目前的中国,固然是江山破碎,国弊民穷,但谁能断言,中国没有一个光明的前途呢? 不,决不会的,我们相信,中国一定有个可赞美的光明前途。中国民族在很早以前,就造起了一座万里长城和开凿了几千里的运河,这就证明中国民族伟大无比的创造力。中国在战斗之中一旦斩去了帝国主义的锁链、肃清自己阵线内的汉奸卖国贼、得到了自由与解放,这种创造力,将会无限的发挥出来。到那时,中国的面貌将会被我们改造一新"(方志敏,2021)。

他还写道:"我相信,到那时,到处都是活跃的创造,到处都是日新月异的进步,欢歌将代替了悲叹,笑脸将代替了哭脸,富裕将代替了贫穷,康健将代替了疾苦,智慧将代替了愚昧,友爱将代替了仇杀,生之快乐将代替了死之悲哀,明媚的花园,将代替凄凉的荒地。这时,我们民族就可以无愧色的立在人类的面前,而生育我们的母亲,也会最美丽地装饰起来,与世界上各位母亲平等的携手了。这么光荣的一天,决不在辽远的将来,而在很近的将来,我们可以这样相信的,朋友"(方志敏,2021)。

一代代先烈应该都在心中描画过祖国美好的未来,他们应该都坚定地相信美好的未来终将实现。今天的我们可以告诉方志敏,告诉先烈们,他们心中美好的愿景都已成为现实,我们伟大的祖国正在经历从站起来、富起来到强起来的伟大飞跃。

方志敏的一生虽然短暂,但他不忘初心,始终坚定地践行着自己的誓言。他的狱中文稿中有一首题为《死!——共产主义的殉道者的记述》的短诗,开篇即以诗明志:

敌人只能砍下我们的头颅,
决不能动摇我们的信仰!
因为我们信仰的主义,
乃是宇宙的真理!
为着共产主义牺牲,
为着苏维埃流血,
那是我们十分情愿的啊!(方志敏,2021)

这表明了他心甘情愿地为"信仰的主义"流血牺牲的决心。信仰的旗帜造就了英雄的传奇。在这块土地上理想之光不灭,信念之光不灭。研读、品味方志敏关于信仰的荡气回肠的文字,我们会体验到一种久违的感动。"我们一定要铭记烈士们的遗愿,永志不忘他们为之流血牺牲的伟大理想。理想因其远大而为理想,信念因其执着而为信念"(习近平,2017)。

◼ 参考文献 ◼

[1] 方志敏. 可爱的中国[M]. 北京：人民文学出版社，2021.
[2] 习近平. 习近平谈治国理政[M]. 北京：外文出版社，2017.
[3] 张培基. 英译中国现代散文选[M]. 上海：上海外语教育出版社，1999.

◼ 阅读思考 ◼

1. 请阅读方志敏的其他作品，和大家分享你所知道的关于方志敏的故事。
2. 你还知道哪些优秀共产党员的故事？从他们身上你学到了什么？

15

The Siege of Berlin

Alphonse Daudet

【作品简介】

短篇小说《柏林之围》(*The Siege of Berlin*)讲述了在普法战争背景下,拿破仑帝国时代的老军人儒夫上校的悲剧故事。年过八旬的儒夫上校极具军人的荣誉感和爱国心,在听到法国惨败的消息后,因过度震惊而中风,却又在听到误传的法军大捷消息后,奇迹般地逐渐康复。小说构思新颖,以儒夫上校的悲剧故事为线,侧面反映了巴黎人民受到普鲁士围攻时的悲惨生活,歌颂了普通法国人民的爱国主义情感。本文选自 2014 年清华大学出版社出版的高晨鹏等编译的《都德短篇小说精选——最后一课》。

【作者简介】

阿尔丰斯·都德（Alphonse Daudet,1840—1897）,19 世纪下半叶法国现实主义作家。都德出生于法国一个破落的丝绸商人家庭,15 岁起就独自谋生,曾在小学担任学生自修辅导员;17 岁那年,他带着诗作《女恋人》,开始了文艺创作之旅;1870 年普法战争爆发,他应征入伍,战争生活激起了他的爱国主义热情,给他带来了很多创作的灵感。都德一生共创作了 13 部长篇小说,4 部短篇小说集和 1 个剧本,代表作有长篇小说《小东西》(1868)、《达拉斯贡城的达达兰》(1872)和《小弟费罗蒙和长兄黎斯雷》(1874),以及短篇小说集《磨坊书简》(1866)和《月曜日故事集》(1873)。其中,《月曜日故事集》以普法战争为背景,反映了当时法国人民的爱国主义情绪,收录了《柏林之围》《最后一课》《小间谍》等知名短篇小说。

(1) We were going up the Avenue des Champs-Élysées[1] with Dr. V—, asking the shell-riddled[2] walls, and the sidewalks torn up by grape-shot[3], for the story of the siege of Paris, when, just before we reached the Rond-point de l'Etoile[4], the doctor stopped and, pointing to one of the great corner houses so proudly grouped about the Arc de Triompe[5], said to me:

(2) "Do you see those four closed windows up there on that balcony? In the early days of August, that terrible

[1] the Avenue des Champs-Élysées:(法语)香榭丽舍大道

[2] shell-riddled: 布满(弹孔)的

[3] grape-shot: 榴霰弹

[4] the Rond-point de l'Etoile:(法语)星形广场,1970 年改名戴高乐广场。

[5] the Arc de Triompe:(法语)凯旋门

August of last year, so heavily <u>laden with</u>[6] storms and disasters, I was called there to see a case of <u>apoplexy</u>[7]. It was the apartment of <u>Colonel</u>[8] Jouve, a <u>cuirassier</u>[9] of the <u>First Empire</u>[10], an old enthusiast on the subject of glory and patriotism, who had come to live on the Champs-Élysees, in an apartment with a balcony, at the outbreak of the war. Guess why? In order to witness the triumphant return of our troops. Poor old fellow! The news of <u>Wissembourg</u>[11] reached him just as he was leaving the table. When he read the name of Napoleon at the foot of that <u>bulletin</u>[12] of defeat, he fell like a <u>log</u>[13].

（3）"I found the former cuirassier stretched out at full length on the carpet, his face covered with blood, and as lifeless as if he had received a blow on the head from a <u>poleaxe</u>[14]. He must have been very tall when he was standing; lying there, he looked enormous. Handsome features, magnificent teeth, a <u>fleece</u>[15] of curly white hair, eighty years with the appearance of sixty. Beside him was his granddaughter, on her knees and bathed in tears. She looked like him. One who saw them side by side might have taken them for two beautiful Greek <u>medallions</u>[16], struck from the same die, one of which was old and earth-coloured, a little roughened on the edges, the other <u>resplendent</u>[17] and clean-cut, in all the brilliancy and smoothness of a fresh impression.

（4）"The child's grief touched me. Daughter and granddaughter of soldiers, her father was on <u>MacMahon's</u>[18] staff, and the image of that tall old man stretched out before her <u>evoked</u>[19] in her mind another image no less terrible. I comforted her as best I could, but in reality I had little hope. We had to do with a case of complete <u>paralysis</u>[20] on one side, and at eighty years of age few people recover from it. For three days the patient lay in the same state of <u>inanition</u>[21] and <u>stupor</u>[22]. Then the news of <u>Reichshofen</u>[23] reached Paris. You remember in what a strange way it came. Up to the evening, we all believed in a great victory, twenty thousand <u>Prussians</u>[24] killed and the Prince Royal a prisoner. I know not by what miracle,

[6] laden with：充满的
[7] apoplexy /ˈæpəpleksi/ n. 中风
[8] colonel /ˈkɜːnl/ n. 上校
[9] cuirassier/kwɪərəˈsɪə(r)/ n. 胸甲骑兵
[10] the First Empire：第一帝国（拿破仑帝国）
[11] Wissembourg：维桑堡（法德边境小镇）
[12] bulletin /ˈbʊlətɪn/ n. 公告；布告
[13] log /lɒɡ/ n. 木头
[14] poleaxe /ˈpəʊlæks/ n. 战斧；屠斧
[15] fleece /fliːs/ n. 羊毛
[16] medallion /məˈdæliən/ n. 奖章
[17] resplendent /rɪˈsplendənt/ adj. 华丽的
[18] MacMahon：麦克马洪，法国元帅，在普法战争中和拿破仑三世一起被普军俘虏。
[19] evoke /ɪˈvəʊk/ v. 唤起；引起
[20] paralysis /pəˈræləsɪs/ n. 瘫痪
[21] inanition /ˌɪnəˈnɪʃən/ n. 身体虚弱
[22] stupor /ˈstjuːpə(r)/ n. 昏迷
[23] Reichshofen：雷舍芬（法国西北部的一小镇）
[24] Prussian：普鲁士人

what magnetic[25] current, an echo of that national rejoicing[26] sought out our poor deaf-mute in the depths of his paralysis; but the fact is that on that evening, when I approached his bed, I did not find the same man there. His eye was almost clear, his tongue less heavy. He had the strength to smile at me, and he stammered[27] twice: 'Vic-to-ry!'

(5) "'Yes, colonel, a great victory!'

(6) "And as I gave him details of the grand exploit of MacMahon, I saw that his features relaxed and his face lighted up.

(7) "When I left the room, the girl was waiting for me at the door, pale as death[28]. She was sobbing.

(8) "'But he is saved!' I said, taking her hands.

(9) "The unhappy child hardly had the courage to reply. The true report of Reichshofen had been placarded[29]; MacMahon in retreat, the whole army crushed. We gazed at each other in consternation[30]. She was in despair, thinking of her father. I trembled, thinking of the old man. He certainly could not stand this fresh shock. And yet what were we to do? Leave him his joy, and the illusions[31] which had revived him? But in that case we must lie.

(10) "'Very well, I will lie!' said the heroic girl, quickly wiping away her tears; and with radiant[32] face she entered her grandfather's chamber[33].

(11) "It was a hard task that she had undertaken. The first few days she had no great difficulty. The good man's brain was feeble, and he allowed himself to be deceived like a child. But with returning health his ideas became clearer. We had to keep him posted concerning the movement of the armies, to draw up military bulletins for him. Really, it was pitiful to see that lovely child leaning night and day over her map of Germany, pinning little flags upon it, and struggling to lay out a glorious campaign: Bazaine[34] besieging Berlin, Froissart in Bavaria[35], MacMahon on the Baltic[36]. For all this she asked my advice, and I assisted her as well as I could;

[25] magnetic /mæɡˈnetɪk/ adj. 有磁性的

[26] rejoicing /rɪˈdʒɔɪsɪŋ/ n. 欢庆

[27] stammer /ˈstæmə(r)/ v. 结结巴巴地说

[28] pale as death：面色苍白

[29] placard /ˈplækɑːd/ v. 张贴

[30] consternation /ˌkɒnstəˈneɪʃn/ n. 惊恐

[31] illusion /ɪˈluːʒn/ n. 幻觉；错觉

[32] radiant /ˈreɪdɪənt/ adj. 喜气洋洋的
[33] chamber /ˈtʃeɪmbə(r)/ n. 房间

[34] Bazaine：巴赞元帅

[35] Bavaria：巴伐利亚州（德国南部）

[36] Baltic /ˈbɔːltɪk/ adj. 波罗的海的

but it was the grandfather who was especially useful to us in that imaginary invasion. He had conquered Germany so many times under the First Empire! He knew all the strokes beforehand: ' Now this is where they will go. Now this is what they will do'; and his anticipations were always realised, which did not fail to make him very proud.

(12) "Unlucky it was of no avail[37] for us to take cities and win battles; we never went quickly enough for him. That old man was insatiable[38]! Every day, when I arrived, I learned of some new military exploit.

(13) "'Doctor, we have taken Mayence[39],' the girl would say to me, coming to meet me with a heartbroken smile, and I would hear through the door a joyous voice shouting to me:

(14) "'They are getting on! They are getting on! In a week we shall be in Berlin!'

(15) "At that moment the Prussians were only a week's march from Paris. We asked ourselves at first if it would be better to take him into the provinces; but as soon as we were outside the city, the state of the country would have told him everything, and I considered him still too weak, too much benumbed[40] by his great shock, to let him know the truth. So we decided to remain.

(16) "The first day of the investment of Paris, I went up to their rooms, I remember, deeply moved, with that agony[41] at the heart which the closed gates, the fighting under the walls, and our suburbs turned into frontiers, gave us all. I found the good man seated on his bed, proud and jubilant[42].

(17) "'Well,' he said, ' so the siege has begun!'

(18) "I gazed at him in blank amazement.

(19) "'What, colonel! you know?'

(20) "His granddaughter turned towards me:

(21) "'Why, yes, doctor, that's the great news. The siege of Berlin has begun. '

(22) "As she said this, she plied her needle with such a sedate[43] and placid[44] air! How could he have

[37] avail /əˈveɪl/ n. 效用；帮助

[38] insatiable /ɪnˈseɪʃəbl/ adj. 贪得无厌的

[39] Mayence：美因茨（德国城市）

[40] benumb /bɪˈnʌm/ v. 使麻木

[41] agony /ˈæɡəni/ n. 极大的痛苦

[42] jubilant /ˈdʒuːbɪlənt/ adj. 兴高采烈的

[43] sedate /sɪˈdeɪt/ adj. 镇定的

suspected anything? He could not hear the guns of the forts. He could not see our unfortunate Paris, all in confusion and dreadful to behold[45]. What he saw from his bed was a section of the Arc de Triomphe, and in his room, about him, a collection of bric-a-brac[46] of the First Empire, well adapted to maintain his illusion. Portraits of marshals[47], engravings[48] of battles, the King of Rome in a baby's dress, tall consoles adorned with copper trophies[49], laden with imperial relics[50], medals, bronzes, a miniature of St. Helena, under a globe, pictures representing the same lady all be curled, in a ball-dress of yellow, with leg-of-mutton sleeves and bright eyes;—and all these things: consoles, King of Rome, marshals, yellow ladies, with the high-necked, short-waisted dresses, the-best-arched stiffness, which was the charm of 1806. Gallant[51] colonel! It was that atmosphere of victories and conquests, even more than anything we could say to him, that made him believe so innocently in the siege of Berlin.

(23) "From that day our military operations were much simplified. To take Berlin was only a matter of patience. From time to time, when the old man was too much bored, we would read him a letter from his son—an imaginary letter, of course, for nothing was allowed to enter Paris, and since Sedan, MacMahon's aide-de-camp[52] had been sent to a German fortress[53]. You can imagine the despair of that poor child, without news from her father, knowing that he was a prisoner, in need of everything, perhaps sick, and she obliged[54] to represent him as writing joyful letters, a little short, perhaps, but such as a soldier on the field might be expected to write, always marching forward through a conquered country. Sometimes her strength gave way; then they were without news for weeks. But the old man became anxious, could not sleep. Thereupon a letter from Germany would speedily arrive, which she would bring to his bedside and read joyously, forcing back her tears. The colonel would listen religiously[55], smile with a knowing air, approve, criticise,

44 placid /ˈplæsɪd/ adj. 平静的

45 behold /bɪˈhəʊld/ v. 看；看见

46 bric-a-brac: 小饰物；小摆设

47 marshal /ˈmɑːʃl/ n. 元帅

48 engraving /ɪnˈɡreɪvɪŋ/ n. 雕刻

49 trophy /ˈtrəʊfi/ n. 奖品；纪念杯

50 relic /ˈrelɪk/ n. 遗物

51 gallant /ˈɡælənt/ adj. 英勇的

52 aide-de-camp: 副官

53 fortress /ˈfɔːtrəs/ n. 堡垒；城堡

54 oblige /əˈblaɪdʒ/ v. 帮忙；效劳

55 religiously /rɪˈlɪdʒəsli/ adv. 十分认

and explain to us the passages that seemed a little confused. But where he was especially grand was in the replies that he sent to his son. 'Never forget that you are a Frenchman,' he would say to him. 'Be generous to those poor people. Don't make the invasion too hard for them.' And there were recommendations without end, admirable preachments upon respect for the proprieties, the courtesy which should be shown to the ladies, a complete code of military honour for the use of conquerors. He interspersed also some general considerations upon politics, the conditions of peace to be imposed upon the vanquished[56]. Thereupon I must say that he was not exacting[57].

(24) "'A war indemnity[58], and nothing more. What is the use of taking their provinces? Is it possible to turn Germany into France?'

(25) "He dictated this in a firm voice; and one was conscious of such candour[59] in his words, of such a noble, patriotic faith, that it was impossible not to be moved while listening to him.

(26) "Meanwhile the siege went on—not the siege of Berlin, alas! It was the time of intense cold, of the bombardment[60], of epidemics and of famine. But, thanks to our care, to our efforts, to the unwearying affection which multiplied itself about him, the old man's serenity[61] was not disturbed for an instant. To the very end I was able to obtain white bread and fresh meat for him. There was none for anybody but him, to be sure; and you can imagine nothing more touching than those breakfasts of the grandfather, so innocently selfish—the old man seated on his bed, fresh and smiling, with a napkin at his chin, and his granddaughter beside him, a little pale because of privations[62], guiding his hand, helping him to drink, and to eat all those forbidden good things. Then, enlivened[63] by the repast, in the comfort of his warm room, the winter wind whistling outside and the snow eddying[64] about his windows, the ex-cuirassier would recall his campaigns in the north and would describe to us

真地

56 vanquish /ˈvæŋkwɪʃ/ v. 征服;战胜
57 exacting /ɪɡˈzæktɪŋ/ adj. 苛刻的
58 indemnity /ɪnˈdemnəti/ n. 赔款

59 candour /ˈkændə(r)/ n. 坦率

60 bombardment /bɒmˈbɑːdmənt/ n. 轰炸
61 serenity /səˈrenəti/ n. 平静;宁静

62 privation /praɪˈveɪʃn/ n. 贫困;匮乏
63 enliven /ɪnˈlaɪvn/ v. 活跃;使更有活力
64 eddy /ˈedi/ v. 起旋涡;旋转

for the hundredth time that terrible retreat from Russia, when they had nothing to eat but frozen biscuit and horseflesh⁶⁵.

（27）"'Do you understand that, my love? We had horseflesh!'

（28）"I rather think that she did understand it. For two months she has had nothing else. From that day, however, as the period of his convalescence⁶⁶ drew near, our task about the patient become more difficult. That numbness of all his senses, of all his members, which had served us so well hitherto⁶⁷, began to disappear. Two or three times, the terrible volleys⁶⁸ from Porte Maillot⁶⁹ had made him jump, with his ears pricked up like a hunting-dog: we were obliged to invent a final victory of Bazaine under the walls of Berlin, and guns fired in his honour at the Invalides⁷⁰. Another day when his bed had been moved to the window—it was, I believe, the Thursday of Buzenval—he saw large numbers of National Guards⁷¹ collected on Avenue de la Grande Armée.

（29）"What are all those troops?' asked the good man; and we heard him mutter⁷² between his teeth:

（30）"'Poorly set up! Poorly set up!'

（31）"That was all, but we understood that we must take great precautions⁷³ thenceforth⁷⁴. Unluckily we did not take enough.

（32）"One evening when I arrived, the girl came to me in great trouble.

（33）"'They are to march into the city tomorrow,' she said.

（34）"Was the grandfather's door open? In truth, on thinking it over afterwards. I remembered that his face wore an extraordinary expression that night. It is probable that he had overheard us. But we were talking of the Prussians; and the good man was thinking of the French, of that triumphal entry which he had been awaiting so long—MacMahon marching down the avenue amid flowers and flourishes of trumpets, his son beside him, and he, the old colonel, on his balcony, in full uniform as at

⁶⁵ horseflesh /ˈhɔː(r)sfleʃ/ n. 马肉

⁶⁶ convalescence /ˌkɒnvəˈlesns/ n. 康复期;恢复期

⁶⁷ hitherto /ˌhɪðəˈtuː/ adv. 迄今为止
⁶⁸ volley /ˈvɒli/ n. (子弹的)群射,齐发
⁶⁹ Porte Maillot: 马约门

⁷⁰ Invalides: 荣军院,又名"巴黎伤残老军人院"。

⁷¹ National Guards: 国民自卫队

⁷² mutter /ˈmʌtə(r)/ v. 咕哝;嘀咕

⁷³ precaution /prɪˈkɔːʃn/ n. 预防措施
⁷⁴ thenceforth /ˌðensˈfɔːθ/ adv. 此后;从那时起

Lutzen, saluting[75] the torn flags and the eagles[76] blackened by powder.

（35）"Poor Father Jouve! He had imagined doubtless that we intended to prevent him from witnessing that parade of our troops, in order to avoid too great excitement. So he was very careful not to mention it to any one; but the next day, at the very hour when the Prussian battalions[77] entered hesitatingly upon the long road which leads from Porte Maillot to the Tuileries[78], the window up there opened softly, and the colonel appeared on the balcony, with his helmet, his long sword, all the glorious old array of one of Milhaud's cuirassiers. I wonder still what effort of the will, what sudden outburst of life had placed him thus upon his feet and in his harness[79]. This much is sure, that he was there, standing behind the rail, amazed to find the broad avenues so silent, the blinds of the houses closed, Paris as gloomy as a huge lazaretto[80], flags everywhere, but such strange flags, white with little crosses, and no one to go to meet our soldiers.

（36）"For a moment he might have thought that he was mistaken.

（37）"But no! Yonder[81], behind the Arc de Triomphe, there was a confused rumbling[82], a black line approaching in the rising sunlight. Then, little by little, the points of the helmets gleamed, the little drums of Jena[83] began to beat, and beneath the Arc de Triomphe, while the heavy tramp of the regiments[84] and the clashing of the sabres[85] beat time, Schubert's Triumphal March[86] burst forth!

（38）"Thereupon in the deathlike silence of the square, a cry rang out, a terrible cry: 'To arms! To arms! The Prussians!' and the four uhlans[87] of the vanguard[88] saw up yonder, on the balcony, a tall old man wave his arms, stagger[89], and fall. That time, Colonel Jouve was really dead."

75 salute /sə'lu:t/ *n.* 致敬；致意

76 the eagles：鹰旗，拿破仑时期军旗。

77 battalion /bə'tæliən/ *n.* 军队

78 the Tuileries：杜伊勒里宫

79 harness /'hɑ:nɪs/ *n.* 马具

80 lazaretto /ˌlæzə'retəʊ/ *n.* 传染（隔离）病院

81 yonder /'jɒndə(r)/ *adv.* 那边

82 rumbling /'rʌmblɪŋ/ *n.* 隆隆声

83 Jena /'jeɪnə/ *n.* 耶拿（德国城市名）

84 regiment /'redʒɪmənt/ *n.* （军队）团

85 sabre /'seɪbə(r)/ *n.* 军刀

86 Schubert's Triumphal March：舒伯特的凯旋曲

87 uhlan /'u:lɑ:n/ *n.* 枪骑兵

88 vanguard /'vængɑ:d/ *n.* 先头部队

89 stagger /'stægə(r)/ *v.* 踉跄；蹒跚

◘ 精华赏析 ◘

阿尔丰斯·都德的短篇小说别具特色,他的知名短篇小说集《月曜日故事集》取材于其在普法战争(1870—1871)前后的见闻,反映了当时法国人民的爱国主义情绪。都德的小说构思新颖,情节曲折,语言生动简洁,《柏林之围》便是其中极具代表性的一篇。

这篇小说从一位医生的视角出发,讲述了老军官儒夫上校的悲剧故事。这个故事虽然篇幅很短,但是情节引人入胜,人物形象丰满,结尾耐人寻味。作者如何在有限的篇幅内呈现精彩的故事,从而让读者印象深刻,回味无穷的呢?这是因为他使用了白描手法,在叙述时以极少的信息量刻画生动的人物形象。那什么是白描手法呢?我们先简单了解一下这种文学表现手法。

一、白描手法

在长篇小说中,作者可以采用多种方式尽可能全方面地介绍故事发生的时代背景、人物特征、故事的起因、经过、发展和结局等,但是短篇小说受篇幅限制,必须在有限的长度内呈现精彩的故事。作者在创作短篇小说时,必须构思新颖,文笔生动,尽量"长话短说",吸引读者继续读下去,进而突出小说的主题,达到既定的艺术效果。因此,优秀的短篇小说家们在创作的时候,必须抓住人物形象与环境形象的典型特征,用质朴的语言作简劲勾勒,而不应进行大量铺垫和过多描述,这就是文学创作中的白描手法(高尔纯,1983)。

中国文学的"白描手法"源自中国传统绘画(古代称为"白画"或"线描"),擅长此画法的画家们仅用墨线勾描,而不着颜色,就能创作出传神的画作。比如唐代绘画大师吴道子便善于"白画"之法,其《八十七神仙卷》不着任何颜色,仅用线条就表现出了宏大的场景,而且画中的人物形象细致入微,形神兼备。北宋画家李公麟将"白画"画法发展为"白描"画法,仅在白描的基础上增加些许墨痕,以增强线描的表现力,其代表作《五马图》线条简练,勾勒出的人物和骏马却形象生动。这种绘画手法后来被引入小说批评领域,被视作一种文学表现手法。

文学上的白描手法指的是作者能够抓住事物的主要特征,用简约凝练而不加修饰的语言,勾勒出生动的形象。白描手法被文学家们运用到各种文学形式中,通过描述一些形象来表达自己的思想、情感和观点等。比如马致远的《天净沙·秋思》:"枯藤老树昏鸦,小桥流水人家,古道西风瘦马。夕阳西下,断肠人在天涯。"诗人使用极其简练的白描手法,提炼出"枯藤""老树""昏鸦""小桥""流水""人家""古道""西风""瘦马"九个意象,却勾勒出了一幅苍凉的秋景图,让人感受到了远行游子的哀愁和思乡之情。我国现代知名作家鲁迅则非常善于,也十分提倡用白描手法刻画人物,如《祝福》中的祥林嫂,在人物出场时作者这样描写道:"五年前的花白的头发,即今已经全白,全不像四十上下的人;脸上瘦削不堪,黄中带黑,而且消尽了先前悲哀的神色,仿佛是木刻似的;只有那眼珠间或一轮,还可以表示她是一个活物"(鲁迅,2015:146)。在这一段文字中,作者没有使用任何评论性或感性化的语言,也没有对祥林嫂的形象进行全面的描述,只是用白描法对祥林嫂的头发颜色、面部表情和眼神的变化进行描写,寥寥数句便传神地刻画出一个绝望麻木的乞丐形象。这种写作手法能够抓住祥林嫂的主要特征,让读者看到祥林嫂受到封建礼教迫害的悲惨境遇,进而突出了小说的主题。

从以上两个例子我们可以看出来,白描手法并非简单地进行外在特征的描写,而是需要作者经过仔细观察,精心提炼出人物或环境的最典型特征,这样,有限的文字才能传达无限的内涵,从而达到事半功倍的效果。

二、《柏林之围》中白描手法的运用

在《柏林之围》这篇小说中,80多岁的儒夫上校听到法军在维桑堡战役中失利的消息后中风,瘫痪在床,之后因为听了误传的雷舍芬战役胜利的消息而奇迹般地好转。发现战争胜利的消息对老人有益,为了帮助老人恢复,他的孙女和医生合力隐瞒了普法战争的真实战况,通过各种方法给老人制造法国频频胜利的假象。神奇的事情发生了,儒夫上校竟然逐渐好转,而且在故事的最后,当他以为法军凯旋的时候,凭借突如其来的生命力,竟然自己站了起来,穿戴整齐,走到阳台上去迎接。可惜到了这一刻,事实的真相浮出水面,意识到普鲁士士兵已经攻占巴黎的儒夫上校十分震惊,倒地而死,死前还大声疾呼:"快拿武器!快拿武器!普鲁士人来了!"

都德没有通过描写普法战争这个大环境来渲染故事氛围,没有对主角儒夫上校进行过多的描述,也没有讲述这位80多岁的老先生的爱国故事或宣扬他的爱国热情,而是采用了白描手法对故事的关键人物和情节进行描写。都德抓住了主角的主要特征,那就是老上校很固执,但作为老军人的他极具荣誉感与爱国情怀,进而增加情节的真实性。同时,小说中没有大篇幅的细节介绍,只是沿着儒夫上校中风—好转—逐渐恢复—死亡这条主线,通过选取关键情节,有效地推动了故事的发展,同时也勾勒出了普法战争的基本情况。通过老人和孙女伙食的对比侧面反映出了当时巴黎人民极端艰难的生活。故事的结尾,老人的幻想破灭,他高声疾呼后便倒地身亡,至此一位爱国老军官的高大形象永远地留在了读者心中。

普法战争开始一个月,巴黎就沦陷,在尚有百万兵力,三分之二的国土未被占领的情况下,拿破仑三世没有选择坚持抗战,反而在色当战役中率军投降。在《柏林之围》中,以儒夫为代表的普通法国人民的爱国热情和统治者的卑躬屈膝、腐败无能形成了鲜明的对比,儒夫上校只是普法战争中千千万万法国人民中的一个,他的呐喊反映了法国人民"与其忍辱生,毋宁报国死"的心声。作者用白描手法讲述故事,仅以儒夫上校的病情变化为主线,以小见大,颂扬了普通法国人民的爱国主义激情,突出了个人命运与国家命运息息相关的主题。

个人与国家相互依存,没有哪个人能够脱离自己的国家而独立存在。"家是最小国,国是千万家""天下兴亡,匹夫有责",国家的兴衰和我们每个家庭、每个人密切相关,只有大家齐心协力,共同建设好我们的国家,才能保证我们每一个人都能过上安定和谐的美好生活。

📓 参考文献 📓

［1］高尔纯. 小说的白描手法浅探[J]. 文艺研究, 1983(3):139-144.

［2］鲁迅. 鲁迅小说全集[M]. 北京:人民文学出版社,2015.

📓 阅读思考 📓

1. 鲁迅先生非常善于用白描手法刻画人物,读一读他的作品,看一看他是如何运用这种手法突出人物形象和小说主题的。

2. 读一读都德的另外一篇知名短篇小说《最后一课》,谈一谈你是怎么看待个人和国家之间的关系的。